Praise for Build a Rental Property Empire

I have been following Mark Ferguson for a while now. Reading his information on InvestFourMore, getting his emails, learning about how to run a business in rentals is great. I have a couple properties, but I am still in the brand new phase, so looking at this book and all it has to offer is wonderful.

If you have questions about starting, working in the rental field, working as a real estate agent and all the things in between you should pick up a copy for yourself. Working at a regular job is great, but having something that you are building yourself is even better.

I am retiring from the military soon, and having another career to start is wonderful and one of those careers is running a rental business. I am learning more so I can do well for my family and then being able to pass this on to others is very rewarding. Enjoy! - Mack Shaffer

This is a terrific and practical guide on how to work on your real estate business (not in it). Mark knows exactly what it is like to work in the Real Estate trenches, as an agent, investor, flipper, and owner of rental properties. I have implemented many of Marks concepts in my business and am already seeing a difference (Offers on Bank Owned properties now being accepted!) I appreciated Mark's insights on financing and managing my business. This book is useful for both novices and experts in Real Estate. - Kim Martin

A truly insightful resource for anyone looking to get into purchasing rental properties. The book goes over in-depth all aspects related the topic and even touches on many other aspects of rental properties that you would never think of originally. I highly recommend this well written and easy to read book as a foundation for yourself before going out into the investing world. - Jeremiah Dalton

This book is filled with real life examples and information from someone who's fully engaged in real estate investing. It's not HGTV and it's not a book of theory from a real estate training corporation. A real guy doing "real" real estate.

Mark has great ideas on deciding whether you want rental property or not, how to determine what to buy, how to finance and when to keep or sell. I've been investing for a number of years and Mark's book has given me many ideas on how to deal with the challenges investors face. This is one of the more practical books on real estate investing that I've read, and I read a lot of them. - Eric Snell

I have been following Mark for over a year now online. I have learned many things through his blog, podcast, etc. that have helped me in building my rental portfolio. If you are looking for some straight to the point, no nonsense approach to learning about real estate investing Mark is the guy. He is well versed in many areas of real estate. You should definitely get this book. - Corey Paszkeiwicz

Build a Rental Property Empire

The no-nonsense book on finding deals,
financing the right way, and managing wisely.

From Investment Expert

Mark Ferguson

 INVESTFOURMORE

ISBN-10: 1530663946
ISBN-13: 978-1530663941

Cover Design: Pixel Studio
Interior Design: Justin Gesso
Editing: Jeremiah Dalton, Barb Ferguson
Printed in the USA

Table of Contents

Dedication

Thank you to Jack Canfield Coaching and my personal coach John Beaman, who taught me many of the techniques in this book.

Special Bonus and Investing Tools

I try to include as much information as I possibly can in my books. This is not a tool meant to get you to sign up for a high-dollar coaching program. This is a step-by-step guide on how to invest in rental properties.

Some people want more and would like more information on me and real estate. If you are looking for more, or to just keep up to date on my investing check out Investfourmore.com.

I have many free resources on my website, an awesome podcast, and much more.

I written multiple books, created video coaching programs, and created coaching programs with personal help from me. A couple of my coaching programs include coaching calls and email coaching with me. If you are looking for more check out the link below with a special discount for those who buy my books.

Either way, enjoy the book!

https://investfourmore.com/bonus

How to Use This Book

This book is all about rental properties and what I have learned about them over the years. Not only have I learned about rentals from buying, financing, managing and selling rentals, but I have learned so much from other investors and from research I have done for my blog.

This book is an encyclopedia of sorts, but is built to be read from front to back. I thought I knew everything about real estate investing before I started my blog. Boy was I wrong! There are always new tips, tricks, and techniques that we can learn. I try to include everything I can in this book and the table of contents lists the main topics by chapter so that it is easy to navigate.

I also discuss many different strategies in this book. There is no one size fit all concept for real estate investing. We all have different goals, incomes, live in different areas, and varying amounts of time we can spend on investing. Some strategies may be perfect for you, while others you may not be ready for.

Why should you listen to me? Below are a few highlights of my career (I am 37 now). I am not someone who just writes about hypothetical success, I have experienced it and I am still actively pursuing it. As of the writing of this book in 2016:

- I own 16 rentals that make me about $8,000 a month. I bought each rental with 20 or 25 percent down and at least 25 percent below market value.
- My 16 rentals have over 1.6 million dollars in equity and I invested about $300,000 to buy and renovate them starting in 2010.

- I have been a Realtor for 15 years and run a real estate sales team of 10, which sells from 100 to 200 houses a year
- I flip 10 to 20 houses a year. As of June 2016, I have 10 flips going and average about a $30,000 profit on each flip I complete.
- I started InvestFourMore.com in 2013 and it has since become one of the most popular real estate blogs with over 300,000 views a month.
- I have been featured on the Washington Post, MSN, Yahoo, Zilllow, Realtor.com, The Street, Forbes, The Huffington Post and many other large media outlets.

There is a lot of information in this book. There are many techniques, which can become overwhelming. Do not try to do everything at once! If you only learn one thing the first time reading this book, it will help you. The next time you read it, maybe you implement a few other things and slowly start building a solid foundation for success. If you take your time mastering one thing at a time, you will be much more successful than if you halfway do 10 things at once.

If you like this book, please let me know. Mark@investfourmore.com. I personally respond to all emails I get and love hearing from my readers. I would really appreciate any reviews you can leave me on Amazon as well. If you are looking for a little more help or even more details I have additional resources available on my blog at https://investfourmore.com/resources/

Introduction

I bought my first rental property in December 2010. I wanted to invest in rentals well before 2010, but things took a lot longer than I had hoped they would. Life always seemed to get in the way, whether it was buying a personal house, getting married, trying to have kids, or something else. In 2010, I decided enough was enough; I was going to buy a rental. I would figure out the money situation and the life situation, and I would start creating a better future for my family and me.

Even though my wife was pregnant with twins, I was able to get my first rental under contract in the fall of 2010. I used conventional financing at the time because I did not know any better. The process was a nightmare! It took almost two months to get the loan when my lender said it would take one month. They wanted an incredible number of details regarding my finances. They wanted an explanation for every deposit I made in my bank accounts that were over $1,000 for the last two years. I would get the lender all the information they requested and then they would request more!

I managed to buy that house, and it has been a great investment. I bought my next rental property less than one year later and then I really started to ramp things up. I bought three more the next year. As of September 2015, I own 16 rental properties, and I plan to buy many more.

My goal is to make cash flow with every rental property I purchase. My 16 rentals bring in over $8,000 a month in income. That is not rent, but money in my pocket after accounting for all expenses, including mortgage payments, taxes, insurance, maintenance, and vacancies. Not only do I make $8,000 a month, but I have increased my net worth by over one million dollars with rentals. Through a mix of buying below market value, making repairs to increase value, and appreciation, my properties have done very well. It is not easy to make that kind of money with rentals and it does not happen overnight. However, it is not rocket science and almost anyone can buy rentals. The trick is making sure you buy the right properties, know how to manage them, and develop a strategy that allows you to keep buying rentals until you reach financial freedom.

I wrote this book to show people what I have learned over the years as a real estate agent, real estate investor, and blogger. When I started my blog, *InvestFourMore.com*, in 2013, I thought I knew most everything about real estate, but boy was I wrong! There are so many strategies and techniques out there that it can be very intimidating for beginners. With this book, I discuss the most feasible and achievable techniques to help people realize the awesome power of real estate and how to start investing in real estate the right way.

1. Why will rental properties help you retire sooner?

I received a degree in business finance from the University of Colorado in 2001. While at college and even in high school, I took many financial and business classes. I thought I learned a lot about the finance world, but what I realize now is they taught me almost nothing about real estate or alternative ways to invest or make money.

We were told to go to college, get a good job, invest money in the stock market, and retire at age 65. The stock market is said to be the best way to accumulate enough money to retire, because of its steady returns over time. If you have seen the retirement calculators that tell us how much to save based on how long we want to live, the amount you need to save to retire is staggering! For most of us, in order to make your money last in retirement, you have to be frugal and spend less money than you did before you retired.

I have more than a few issues with this plan and I choose to use a completely different plan for my retirement. It may have been by complete accident or luck, but I managed to get into the real estate industry and find an incredible way to invest money and retire early. The key to early retirement is investing in rental properties that produce cash flow month after month.

When I graduated from college, I could not find a job that I loved in the finance industry. I decided to go home and work part-time for my father who was a real estate agent. He had been an agent since 1978 and loved the business. He had always made decent money, but for some reason I never wanted to be in the industry. Maybe it was because I was constantly around it (I slept under his desk in the office when I was a toddler) or because I wanted to make my own path. I thought my time working with my dad would be very short, until I figured out what I really wanted to do. As time went by, I realized how much I liked real estate and how much my friends did not like their jobs. I ended up getting my real estate license, and learning how to invest in fix and flips.

Who wants to retire at 65?

In the beginning of my real estate career, I made okay money, but nothing spectacular. I was a decent agent, but honestly, my heart was not in it. I never more than $50,000 a year and some years less. My father also flipped houses occasionally and that part of the business I loved. I was trying to save money and I invested in the stock market thinking that was what I was supposed to do. As time went by, I knew I was not living my life to its full potential.

I have loved exotic cars since I was kid. As a young adult, my dream of owning exotic cars had all but vanished thanks to society telling me how to live and me not pushing back and realizing how much more there was. I was fairly happy as an agent and loved to flip houses, but I was not going to afford any exotic cars with the money I was making. I knew I had to change the way I did things to have a better life.

I started to make my own career in real estate, instead of do what my father did (traditional real estate agent). I started to list HUD homes and REO properties and break away from the traditional real estate model. When I started to make more and more money, I realized that investing in the stock market was not making my money grow very fast. I had no control over my investments and the retirement calculators were depressing. I had to wait too long to retire and I would not have that great of a life in retirement either. I seriously started to wonder why everyone was so set on investing in the stock market and waiting 30 to 40 years before they could retire.

I decided retiring at 65 was not going to be the choice I would make. I am not saying I do not like work, but I do not want to <u>have to</u> work that long. If you make a modest salary and invest in the stock market or mutual funds, you may not even be able to retire at 65 unless you make huge sacrifices. Those sacrifices might mean living an extremely frugal life before and after retirement. In order to retire early without living frugally, you need to change the way you invest or get a much higher paying job. I like the idea of having a high paying job and investing wiser, but this book is about investing wiser not more.

There is a better way to retire than investing in the stock market

The biggest problem I have with conventional wisdom regarding retirement plans is we have to guess when we are going to die. We use a retirement calculator to find out how much money we will need in retirement and put an age in the equation to make sure we do not run out of money. If you get lucky and live too long, guess what? You run out of money and have to work at Walmart handing shopping carts to people! How depressing is it to try to guess when you are going to die and then hope you do not live too long and run out of money. This is a horrible thought, feeling, and way to live life. One reason I love investing in rental properties is you do not have to guess when you are going to die!

I did as much research as I could on the best ways to invest money. I read many books and tried to keep an open mind even though I was in the real estate industry. I looked at the stock market, at bonds, at starting a franchise, at REITs, at tax liens. What kept coming up repeatedly as the best investment and retirement vehicle: rental properties. The great thing about real estate is that if you invest for cash flow, you have money coming in every month for as long as you own the properties.

The cash flow on my rental properties comes in without eating away at the principle balance of my investment. If I have $5,000 a month coming in from rental properties, that $5,000 is going to keep coming in every month until I sell or refinance my properties. The cash flow will most likely increase as rents go up, and I pay off my mortgages over time. I do not have to calculate when I am going to die and worry about if I will outlive my savings with rentals. Instead of guessing how long I am going to live and save, I can calculate how much monthly income I need and then buy enough investment properties to meet that need. Once I hit whatever monthly number I need or want, I will be financially free. I can retire, start a new business, or keep going if I really want the finer things in life or want to leave a legacy.

Rental properties do not have to be a ton of work either. You will have income coming in by doing minimal or no work every year for the rest of your life. You can hire a property manager and let someone else worry about the repairs and vacancies. I spend almost no time on my rentals, because someone else manages them.

Many investors even end up quitting their day jobs, and concentrating on investing in rental properties at a very young age. They buy a couple of properties and realize what a great investment they are. I know many real estate investors who quit their day jobs before they were 40 and lived on their rental income for the rest of their lives. How much money would you have to save to do that with the stock market? (I invested about

$300,000 in to my rentals to generate $8,000 a month and I am 37. To create that much cash flow every month with the stock market for the rest of my life I would have had to invest millions by now.)

Rental properties can be the best route to passive income

It takes money and discipline to locate and purchase your first investment property. Once you learn how to invest in the correct properties that will generate passive income, the process becomes much easier. The more properties you buy and the sooner you get started, the easier it gets. In my models, I project a passive income of $250,000 to $350,000 a year if you can buy three rentals a year for 10 years. Not everyone can buy three rental properties a year, but not everyone needs $250,000 a year to live either. It is possible to buy three properties a year for ten years if you are smart with your money, use techniques to buy properties with little money down, and use your cash flow to buy more properties. This can be very difficult to accomplish for many people, but it is possible with hard work, a budget, and being willing to act fast. Even if you can afford only one property a year for ten years, you can bring in $75,000 to $100,000 a year in passive income from those rentals.

These numbers may seem ridiculous to you, but it is entirely possible to make that much money with rentals. Not everyone will do it because it is not easy. It takes work to find the right properties, save money to invest, and find the right lenders. In addition, it takes discipline to stay on track.

My current rentals all make 15 percent or more cash-on-cash returns. Those returns do not include appreciation, equity pay down, or tax savings. I consider those factors bonuses on top of my cash flow. While you may not be able to get quite as high a return as I do, rentals can still be a fantastic investment for almost anyone if you invest the right way.

I am not a frugal type of guy

My blog, InvestFourMore.com, could be considered a financial blog. I talk a lot about investing and retirement. However, my blog is not like most financial sites you come across. Most retirement blogs are based on living frugally and making a little money last a long time. Personally, I want to buy as many rentals as possible to be able to retire as early as possible with as much passive income as possible. I do not want to penny pinch and worry about what I can afford. I want to be happy and be able to afford whatever I want for my family and myself.

If you want to be successful in anything, it takes sacrifice. I saved money for a long time when I was younger. I never had a car payment until I was 28, and I still have never bought a new car. Does that mean I do not enjoy life? Umm, no. I own a 6,600 sq. ft. home and a Lamborghini Diablo. I am a strong believer in investing in what you love. Not only do I invest in rental properties and flips, but I also invest in things that make me happy. I am not talking about buying an SUV every year to keep up with your neighbors. I am talking about figuring out what really makes you happy and investing in those things. Some people may be happy with living abroad for years on a tight budget, others may be happy with a condo on the beach and some people may want more.

When I stopped letting society tell me what I should invest in, how much money I should be happy making, and what things should make me happy, I became a much happier person. I started making incredible goals, pushing myself further, and achieving more. Things I thought I would never get in my entire life came to me before I was 35. I am definitely not done yet at the ripe age of 37.

This book is not about goal setting and self-improvement, although I think those are vitally important to success. My point is you do not have to live frugal and give up the things you love in order to retire early and be financially free.

Why rental properties are a better way to retire than the stock market

59 percent of people in a recent survey said they are afraid they will outlive their retirement. People should worry about outliving their retirement if they use traditional methods to retire, such as the stock market. However, there are many ways to retire, including ways that you do not have to worry about running out of money. Rental properties are already providing me with a great income that will last my entire life. I will never have to worry about outliving my savings.

Rental properties can take a great deal of cash to buy initially, but in the end, you can make much more retirement income with rental properties than with the stock market, from the same investment.

Why do Americans worry so much about outliving their retirement?

With traditional retirement methods, you save as much money as possible over as many years as possible. The longer you save, the faster your money will grow, thanks to compounding interest. Compounding interest is fantastic for growing your money, but compounding interest is not the reason traditional retirement methods are scary. The scary part is that after you retire and stop saving, you start spending your savings.

If you use a retirement calculator found on almost any retirement website, you have to enter how long you will live and what age you want to retire. The retirement calculator assumes you will use the income your savings produces and the principal balance until you run out of money. If you plan to live to 80, but end up living to be 85 you might have to go back to work or cut back on spending in your later years.

What return will you get from the stock market?

Retirement calculators require an average yearly return in order to figure how much someone needs to retire. Retirement calculators will suggest a yearly return from seven to ten percent. The historic average of the stock market is over seven percent, but many retirement calculators still suggest a higher return. Remember a historical average of seven percent does not guarantee a future gain of seven percent. We saw negative returns in the 2000s and huge returns more recently. The longer you invest, the more likely you will see historical averages. The shorter time you invest, the more likely you will see big gains or losses. If you want to retire early in life, hopefully, you see big gains, not big losses.

The uncertainty in the stock market makes it a very scary way to invest. A difference of a few percentage points in the returns can mean running out of money five or ten years sooner than you had planned.

I see 15 percent cash-on-cash returns on my rental properties, although not everyone will see returns that high. People have varying amounts of time to dedicate to investing. I am a real estate agent, which is a huge advantage. The average investor may not see 15 percent returns when they buy rental properties, but they can see ten percent returns or higher if they take the time to learn to invest. The returns on rentals are based on supply and demand of rental properties in local housing markets. In my experience, the rental rates in most areas are much more stable than the stock market has been. Even during the last housing crisis when we saw housing prices plummet, rents did not drop nearly as much.

Another thing to consider is those returns are based solely on the cash flow from rental properties, not any appreciation, tax advantages, or equity pay down. The returns end up being much higher when you consider the tax savings and equity pay down. Appreciation is a nice bonus as well, but you will not actually see that money unless you refinance or sell the property.

Why stock market returns are not as high as they appear

Seven percent is a good return to many people, but I want a better return on my money. I like the 15 to 20 percent cash-on-cash returns I see from my rentals. The seven percent historic return is not really the true return of stocks because it does not consider inflation. If you consider inflation, the return changes to a 4.4 percent historic return. You will also have brokerage fees when you invest in the stock market and many 401 k's have fees in addition to the brokerage fees! Check out Tony Robbin's book: Money Master the Game to get the full picture on the fees they charge you.

Rental properties naturally hedge against inflation. When inflation is increasing, housing prices and rental rates naturally increase as well. My rents will keep increasing over time as inflation increases, and I will not have to deduct the historic inflation rate from my returns. In fact, inflation actually increases my returns. I get loans on my rentals that allow me to put 20 percent down. If I buy a $100,000 rental property, I put $20,000 down and I usually make some repairs. I will assume I have $30,000 cash in the property. If the house increases $35,000 in value over ten years, (this would be the increase with three percent inflation), my increase in equity would be higher than the inflation rate. My increase in equity would actually be eight percent each year, because I did not buy the house with 100 percent down.

Why you can retire earlier with rental properties than you can with the stock market

The hard part about retiring early with the stock market is you have to save enough money to last your entire retirement life. If you want to retire at 65 and assume you will live to 85, you will need enough retirement to cover 20 years. If you want to retire early, at 45, you will have to have enough retirement to last 40 years. Not only will you have to save much more money to last the extra 20 years of retirement, but you will have much less time to invest and save, which means your money will not grow as fast. Compounding interest has a bigger effect on your money the longer you invest it.

If you invest $100,000 and earn a seven percent return on your investment, it will grow to just under $200,000 in ten years. If you invest it for 20 years, it will grow to $386,000. If you invest it for 30 years, it grows to $761,000. The huge advantage to compound interest occurs in the later years of investing. If you can invest that $100,000 for 40 years, it will grow to almost 1.5 million dollars.

When you retire young, you do not have time to see your money grow exponentially and you will have to invest a huge amount of money for it to last 40 years. For me to produce $6,000 a month from the stock market for the next 50 years I would need 2.5 million dollars saved already! The funny thing is most retirement calculators do not even let you enter a retirement age below 50. To produce that same $6,000 a month income from rental properties it took me less than $300,000 in cash invested.

Does the stock market have better returns than real estate?

There have been many discussions about whether the stock market or real estate produces better returns. Many proponents of the stock market simply point to the historic returns of the stock market compared to the historic returns of real estate. It is true that the stock market has out-gained the housing market over the years. The problem with this argument is that you are comparing housing prices to stock market prices. If you are buying a home as an owner-occupant with cash, the historic gain of housing prices may be a good indicator of your return. However, real estate investors do not consider an owner-occupant purchase with cash a true real estate investment. Real estate investing is not about housing prices, it is about cash flow, leverage, and tax advantages, which housing prices do not account for historically.

The historic increase of housing prices since 1900 is only 3.1 percent a year. The stock market return varies based on the source, but I found it to be from seven to ten percent before inflation. Looking at those figures, (which is what many stock market proponents do), makes it seem like the stock market blows real estate out of the water. However, real estate investing is completely different from buying a house and hoping it goes up in value.

What are the advantages of real estate investing?

- Real estate investors should be investing for cash flow, not appreciation. Only counting the housing price increase is like saying stock market investors cannot count any dividends they made on their stocks.
- Real estate investors tend to use leverage or loans to buy rental properties. The overall housing market index does not take into account using any leverage. It assumes an investor buys a house with all cash.
- Even if an investor buys a house with all cash, they will still make money from the rent they receive. The only situation I can think of that would meet these scenarios is an investor who buys land, never rents it to anyone, and holds on to it assuming it will go up in value. However, most investors still make some income from land whether it is a Conservation Reserve Program (CRP), mineral rights, or farming.
- Real estate investments can be depreciated and stock market investments cannot. The tax savings from depreciation can equal thousands of dollars a year, blowing that 3.1 percent out of the water on its own.
- You can buy real estate below market value; you cannot do that with the stock market.

The closest thing to the 3.1 percent return is buying a home as an owner-occupant. However, you would have to pay cash for the property, because as soon as you use leverage you will be putting much less money down and increasing the return on the cash you have invested. There are problems with assuming that an owner-occupant paying cash will only make 3.1 percent on the money they invest as well.

- People have to have a place to live. If they do not buy a house to live in, they will have to pay rent. You cannot take the money you would have used to buy a house and stick it in the stock market. You would have to use it to rent a home, which would give you a guaranteed zero percent return.

- In my market, it is more expensive to rent a home than it is to buy a home. Even when you consider the taxes, insurance and maintenance that homeowners have to pay, it is usually more cost effective to buy a home.

- When you buy a home with a loan, you can deduct the interest from your income taxes. You are also paying money towards your mortgage and you have a house of your own. Life is not all about the exact return you get on your investment. Consider the fun factor. Consider how much the pride of owning your own home is worth.

After looking at real estate investing or buying a personal residence there is almost no situation where you would only make the 3.1 percent increase the housing market has seen since 1900. There are more factors to consider when buying or selling a house. When you sell a house, you have to pay selling costs, which may include paying a real estate agent. You have to pay title insurance and closing costs. However, if you live in a house for two or more years as an owner-occupant you may not have to pay any taxes at all on the profit you make. This goes to show there is much more to real estate returns than the historic housing market average gain, especially if you invest in rentals.

Why does investing in rental properties beat the housing market's historic return?

I did not buy my rental properties for appreciation; I bought them for the cash flow they produce. With a $25,000 to $35,000 investment, each of my rental properties have produced close to $500 a month in cash flow, which produced about 15 to 20 percent cash-on-cash return. That cash flow is completely independent of the increase in the value of the home. The values of my rentals could go up 40 percent or they could go down 40 percent (some of my rentals are worth double what I bought them for after 4 years) and that could have no effect at all on my cash flow. There is a chance that a huge downturn in the housing market could produce lower rents. However, in my market, the last housing crisis did not cause rents to drop significantly.

It is not easy to get 15 percent returns from the cash flow on my rental properties. One of the reasons I get such great returns is I can buy real estate below market value. I can buy a home that has a fair market value of $150,000 for $120,000. That does not make sense to many, but some sellers want to sell quickly, a home may need repairs, or other circumstances create opportunity to buy below market value. You cannot buy stocks below market value. Yes, you can buy stocks that are "undervalued," but that is not the same as below market value. Market value is what someone would pay for something today in an open market. Undervalued means someone thinks the market has not valued something correctly based on the fundamental financials. When buying undervalued assets you are hoping the market changes its mind or the asset performs better causing the value to increase in the future.

Being able to buy rental properties below market value allows me to get better cash flow and gain instant equity. When I make 15 percent on the cash flow from my rental properties, I do not even consider the returns from buying below market value. I bought rental property number 11 for just over $109,000 and made about $12,000 in repairs. I could have sold the house for at least $150,000 after fixing it up. If you take $150,000 minus the repairs and purchase price, I would make $29,000. For those experienced in real estate, you know I do not get to keep that entire $29,000. I would have to pay a real estate commission, title insurance, recording fees, and closing company fees to sell the home. On a $150,000 sale, those costs would equal about $7,000 (I am a Realtor so I would not have to pay a listing agent).

I came away with an instant $22,000 in equity when I bought and repaired this house. I spent about $32,000 on the down payment and repairs, which means I would make about 65 percent on my investment buying below market value if I ever decide to sell the house. People may say I have not realized that return if I do not sell and that is true. However, the same thing can be said for the stock market, except the stock market is not producing 20 percent in cash flow while I hold the asset.

What has the return been on my rental properties?

If you consider the cash flow I make and the instant equity I gain when I buy a home, I make a great return on my rentals. We have not even considered the increase in value every year that comes with average housing prices as well as many other factors.

I put 20 percent down when I buy a rental property, and I pay down my mortgage every month. On rental property number 11, I paid about $1,500 toward the principal the first year. That amount increases over time as the principal goes down and more of my monthly payment goes towards principal and less towards interest.

When you consider the tax advantages of rental properties which I will discuss shortly, I make even more money. I can depreciate rental property number 11 over 27.5 years, which equates to about $1,050 in tax savings every year.

With those two factors, I make another $2,550 a year, which equates to another eight percent in returns on my $32,000 investment. If you total the returns I make from cash flow, buying below market value, tax advantages, and equity pay down, I am up to 93 percent. I have not even taken into account the appreciation or annual housing price increases yet. To be honest, my returns will not be that high every year, because I will only make the 65 percent for buying below market value once when I first buy the house. That still creates a 28 percent overall return every year, even after buying below market value is taken out of the equation.

The returns on real estate are not limited to the annual housing price gain. If someone tries to convince you that the stock market is a better investment than real estate because of the annual housing gains compared to annual stock market gains, you can point out why that is a false comparison. Annual housing market gains are a very small part of the advantages of real estate.

What are the tax advantages of rental properties?

This book is meant to offer a broad overview of the tax advantages of rental properties, not specific advice. I am not an accountant or an attorney. If you are looking for tax advice, please talk to a tax professional. A number of online tax calculators and estimators can assist you as well. This book gets much of its information from the IRS tax code on rental properties.

Not only does a great rental property provide plenty of cash flow, but rental properties have incredible tax advantages as well. The IRS allows most rental property expenses to be deducted or depreciated, and you can depreciate the structure of the property as well. It is very common for a rental property to produce cash in hand, but thanks to depreciation, show a loss on your taxes.

Please consult an accountant for specific tax questions.

Can mortgage interest be tax deductible on rental properties?

The interest you pay on a rental property can be a deduction on your tax return. You cannot deduct the entire payment, because part of your payment is equity pay down, which is not deductible. Paying down equity is not considered a business expense, since the money is used to reduce debt and is not spent on repairs or maintenance.

There is talk of the IRS eliminating the interest on mortgages as a deduction for primary homeowners. However, that probably will not affect rental property owners because the interest is regarded as a business expense, not a special deduction.

How does the IRS treat depreciation on rental properties?

The IRS treats rental property as an asset that can be depreciated. They assume the rental property will degrade over time until it falls down and is worthless. This is very good for the rental property owner, since most properties will not fall into a pile of rubble as long as they are maintained.

The IRS says a house will last 27.5 years, which means an investor can deduct the cost basis of the rental property in equal increments over 27.5 years. To calculate the amount that can be depreciated; divide the cost basis by 27.5 and that is your deduction for the next 27.5 years.

The cost basis is the cost of the rental property and only includes the structure of a rental property, not the land. If you buy a rental property on its own lot for $100,000, the entire $100,000 is not the cost basis. You have to deduct the value of the land from the purchase price and you have the starting point for your cost basis. You can also add many of the closing costs to the cost basis, such as abstract, title fees, recording fees, and other fees. The entire list is on the IRS website.

If I am bringing in $3,000 of rental income on a property after all expenses, I get to use that $3,000 any way I want. However, it most likely will not show up as $3,000 in taxable income because of depreciation. If the cost basis of my rental property were $100,000, then the depreciation would be $3,636 a year for 27.5 years. The $3,636 would counteract all the income I made, and show a loss of $636! Even though I have $3,000 more in my pocket due to the money my rental property made, I pay no taxes on that money and may even be able to counter other income with that loss.

What is the disadvantage of depreciating a rental property?

If you depreciate a rental property over 20 years and sell the home, you will have a large tax bill from the IRS. The depreciation on rental properties can be recaptured, which means you have to pay back all those taxes you saved with the depreciation deduction. The depreciation is only recaptured if you sell the asset for at least the amount of your cost basis minus the depreciation.

Even though you have to pay back those tax savings, it is still better to pay those taxes 20 years down the road instead of now. With inflation, money is worth less in the future and you can invest that money for 20 years until you have to give it back to Uncle Sam. Think of it as a no interest loan from our government! There are also many ways to avoid depreciation recapture.

The easiest way to avoid paying back the tax savings is to never sell the rental property. After 27.5 years you will not be able to use the depreciation tax break anymore, but you also will not have to pay back any of the previous tax savings if you hold the property forever.

Another way to avoid the depreciation recapture is to use a 1031 exchange. If you sell your rental property, the IRS allows you to exchange that property for a similar property without having to recapture any depreciation. There will be much more information on 1031 exchanges later in the book.

If you happen to pass away while you own rental properties, the properties will pass on to your heirs. When your heirs inherit the properties, the cost basis becomes the current value of the properties, not what the original owner's cost basis was. That means there will be no depreciation recapture.

Planning to hold your rental properties until you die is not a bad strategy tax wise. *There are some limits and restrictions based on the estate tax.*

What other rental property expenses can be deducted?

Not every expense on rental properties is tax deductible, but many are. Since rental properties are considered a business, travel expenses, accounting fees, management fees, and many more expenses are deductible.

If you make repairs on your rental properties they are deductible as well, but improvements are not. Repairing a leaky faucet is deductible, but adding on a second story is considered an improvement and is not deductible.

Even though improvements are not deductible, that does not mean you cannot count them on your taxes. Improvements can be depreciated like the rental property itself. There are different amounts of time over which improvements are depreciated, ranging from 3 to 20 years. You do not have to wait 27.5 years to see the full tax benefit of most improvements.

The IRS has different rules for people in the real estate business and those that are not. If you spend more than half your time on rental properties, you are considered to be in the rental property business. There is no limit to the deduction or losses you can take on your rental properties if you are in the business.

If you are not in the rental property business, you can take a maximum $25,000 loss, depending on how much money you make. The more money you make, the less of a loss you can count towards your other income. The deductions and depreciation will still counteract the money you make on the rental properties, but it might not help reduce your regular income taxes.

How much money can you make on rental properties?

When I was younger, I kept telling myself I did not need the finer things in life; I was happy with whatever I had and could afford. I told myself I did not need expensive things, because I did not believe I could ever afford the things I really wanted. A few years ago, as I became more successful, I completely changed my thinking process. I now believe I can achieve and acquire whatever I want and I was doing myself a disservice by masking my true desires. Buying rental properties has been a key component for me to chase my dreams. Because of the steady cash flow rentals provide, I am much more comfortable spending money on myself and not worrying about money.

One of my passions is automobiles. I love classic and exotic cars. I purchased a 1986 Porsche 928 a few years ago, and I absolutely love that car. The 928 was the most expensive car Porsche made in 1986, but I was able to purchase the car for only $6,000. I think the 928 is one of the all-time bargains for classic/exotic cars, unfortunately not all classic/exotic cars are bargains.

My all-time favorite car is a Lamborghini Miura, which was built in the late sixties and early seventies. The Miura was the predecessor to the famous Lamborghini Countach, which is also one of my all-time favorite cars. A Countach runs at least $100,000 in today's market and a Miura is somewhere in the $500,000 range, if not more. Not only are these cars extremely expensive to purchase, but also maintaining them will cost tens of thousands of dollars a year. It is not easy to maintain or find someone who knows how to maintain a Lamborghini.

*I first wrote this part of the book back in late 2013. If you want to know how crazy the car market is, a Miura will now cost about 1.5 million and a Countach about $400,000! At the end of 2013, I made the goal that I would buy a Lamborghini Diablo in 2014. I changed my goal from buying a Countach, because prices increased so much that the Diablo was a better value and really a better car. In May 2014, I bought a Monterey blue 1999 Lamborghini Diablo. It is a gorgeous car and you can read all about it on my blog. Many think buying a car like that is about the stupidest thing you could do. However, it was a passion of mine for many years, and the car has been a great marketing tool and has increased in value about 75 percent since I bought it!

How long-term rentals give me more stability to go after what I want

I knew if I ever wanted to be able to afford a Diablo, Countach, or a Miura, I would have to make a lot more money, or get very high returns on the money I was investing. I have been able to do both in the last few years and a lot of that increase has been from my decision to start investing in long-term rental properties. I have purchased 16 rental properties so far and I am making over 15 percent cash-on-cash returns on all of them. I know rental properties by themselves will probably not make me enough money to afford a Lamborghini, but they provide a financial security that is tough to beat. I know that money will be coming in month after month, which does not happen with traditional jobs or even businesses.

My super aggressive goal is to own 100 rental properties by 2023. I created this goal back in 2013 and I am a couple of years into it. With my 16 rentals to date, I am a little behind on my projections, but I still have confidence I will get there. You will see my plan in all its glory later on in the book. Even though I am a little behind on my goal, I know the goal has gotten me further along than if I did not have a goal. The goal has pushed me to buy more and to work harder than if I didn't have any goals and was just floating along.

In this section, I will not detail my plan to buy 100 properties, because most people will not choose a goal that big. Most people will have a more modest plan, or at least start out with a more modest plan. Once they see how awesome of an investment rentals are, they may increase their goals over time.

What is the cost of a rental property?

I go over the exact costs to buy a rental in a later chapter, but let's assume it costs $30,000 to purchase and repair one rental for now (You can buy your first rental for much less money using strategies I will talk about later). You also do not have to invest $90,000 a year to buy three rentals in that time because you can begin refinancing rental properties after you own them for a year (in some case 6 months) and take the cash out to invest in more rentals. I usually buy my properties for about $100,000 and put 20 percent down. I make repairs on the homes that can range from $5,000 to $15,000. On some houses, I am able to get the seller to pay for some of my closing costs. I am a real estate agent, so I also get to save a commission on many homes that I purchase. For the most part, I am able to get about $500 a month cash flow on my rental properties with financing in place.

Depending on what market you are in, how much rents are, and what property taxes are, you may be able to make more or less money than I do on my rentals. As I mentioned before, it is not easy to make this much money on rental properties. It may take some sacrifice to get to these numbers, such as investing in another market, getting your real estate license, or even living in potential rental properties.

How much money can you make in ten years?

If you were able to buy three rental properties a year for ten years, you would have about $15,000 a month coming in every month at the end of those ten years based on very simple math. If you bought the properties with 20 percent down and made repairs on all of them, you would have about $900,000 invested into those properties to make that $15,000 every month. This sounds like an okay investment, but there are more things to consider.

The exciting thing is that in order to make the math simpler these numbers are not adjusted for inflation, rent increases, or appreciation.

Appreciation I do not count on appreciation, but it is a nice bonus. The median value in my area has gone from $120,000 in 2012 to $260,000 in 2016. I do not count on this appreciation, but it has been a nice bonus.

Inflation Over time, real estate values have always increased. In addition to real estate values increasing, rents have increased as well. The great thing about rental properties is that when rents increase, your mortgage payment stays the same. Rentals are a great hedge against inflation.

While you might not be able to buy three rental properties a year or even one every year, they are still a great investment. If you were able to buy just one rental property a year that cash flowed $500 a month, you would have at a minimum $5,000 a month coming in after ten years. That assumes the rents never increase for that entire ten-year period.

When you get a great deal on rentals, it also gives you more options to buy properties in the future. I have refinanced 7 of my rentals over the last four years. They still cash flow well even after the refinance and I have been able to take out over $250,000 in cash. This has allowed me to buy more houses faster, without having to save all of the down payment funds. Even though I have spent a lot of cash to buy and renovate my houses, I have gotten much of that back through my refinances.

2. What are the risks of investing in real estate?

The truth is that getting started investing in rental properties is hard. It is not a get rich quick scheme; it takes a lot of effort and determination to be a successful investor. However, I think it is great that investing in rental properties is difficult. If it were easy to invest in rentals, everyone would do it and the returns would be much lower.

I would estimate about two percent of those who set out to invest in real estate ever buy a rental property or a flip. I do not want to scare you off, but it takes work and time to become a great investor. Once you have figured out your niche and have some experience in purchasing rental properties, it all gets much easier. But if you do not take the time to learn the fundamentals of buying rental properties, you can make some huge mistakes and lose money.

The biggest mistakes when investing in rental properties is over-estimating the returns you will get and not managing your properties correctly. However, other mistakes can definitely cause rental properties to be a bad investment, also.

Many investors are scared to fail because they hear so many nightmares about bad tenants and investors who lost money. That fear of failure prevents them from ever investing in real estate and seeing the wonderful benefits rental properties can bring.

It is okay to be a little scared when investing large sums of money in a rental property. Being scared is good if you use that emotion to your benefit. Make sure you have researched the market, returns, and the kind of property you want. Once you have educated yourself about what a good deal is, you have to be able to pull the trigger when you find that good deal.

Are you a failure if you do not succeed right away?

I hate the word fail! I do not ever like to use it because to fail means you gave up. Many people have set backs, they lose money, things do not go as planned, or they change course. That does not mean they failed. I have many goals, and I do not reach all of them. In fact, I set my goals so high that it is likely I will not reach many of them. Setting goals high helps me to achieve more and to keep working hard to accomplish them. Do I consider myself a failure because I did not reach those goals? No. I look at how much further I got because I had goals and at how I can improve things to reach those goals in the future. Sometimes I realize a goal was unrealistic or was not worth my time and effort, so I change it.

My point is that you can only fail at investing in real estate if you never try or you give up. Most people do not do things perfectly the first time, and it takes experience and practice to become proficient. Many real estate investors get stuck in the education phase and they never buy a property. You cannot succeed if you never play the game. Other investors end up accidentally owning a rental property or lose money on their first flip and give up. They proclaim real estate a horrible investment and say they will never do it again. If you gave up at everything that you were not successful at right away, you would not be able to walk, talk, read, drive, or do anything.

On my podcast show I do every week (InvestFourMore Real Estate Podcast on iTunes or my blog) I interview many successful real estate investors. Many of those investors lost money or had a really rough time on their first deal. However, they did not give up, they used their experience to learn and do better the next time.

Why are there so many stories about people losing money on rental properties?

I think most of us who have ever expressed interest in buying rentals to our friends or family have encountered negativity. Someone always seems to know a cousin, uncle, or long-lost friend that lost their entire life savings in real estate. I am a real estate agent, and when I started in the business I even had other Realtors tell me how bad an investment real estate was.

The number one reason most people tell you real estate investing is a bad idea is they do not understand it. Do not assume real estate agents or your lender know about real estate investing. Most agents never invest in real estate and do not understand what a good investment it is. Before you base major financial decisions on advice you get, make sure the advice you are getting is good. The people telling you how bad real estate is have probably never invested themselves and are retelling stories, which may or may not be accurate.

There are many types of real estate investing. Someone hears a bad story about a flip, a rental, or a partnership and they associate that story with every type of real estate investing even though they are completely unrelated.

If you hear a story directly from someone who lost a large amount of money investing, get the entire story. Most people who lose money in real estate did not know what they were doing or they took on huge risks to try to get rich quick. If you educate yourself about investing in real estate and follow certain guidelines, it is hard to lose money.

You may hear how horrible real estate investing is from people whom are currently investing, but if it is so bad, why are they still doing it? There are a number of people who own rentals who will tell you that rentals are a pain and not worth the trouble. So why do they still own them? Usually they are making money and they don't want to sell because they love the checks coming in, or they do not want more competition and discourage others from buying.

I am not saying that not everyone who loses money in real estate does not know what they is doing or that he or she is trying to discourage the competition. It is entirely possible to lose money investing in real estate, even if you know what you are doing. I have lost money on fix and flips, and I have flipped over 100 houses. If you are going to take the advice of people about your future, at least make sure you get the whole story and that it applies to your situation.

How can you lose money investing in real estate?

There are many ways to lose money when you invest in real estate. The more education you get and the more work you do, the more likely you will be to make money instead of lose it. I have listed the most common reasons investors lose money on real estate below:

- **Investors do not know the numbers**: Real estate is all about the numbers. You have to know what your cash flow will be, how much money you need to invest, and what your returns will be. You need to know how much you can afford and how much to keep in reserves. Most investors who lose money do not look at the numbers close enough. They do not consider all the costs when figuring returns on rentals and they do not figure all the costs on flips. They also underestimate the time it takes to flip a house or to make repairs. My biggest pet peeve is when people ask me: is this is a good deal? But they have not calculated any of the numbers. I had a blueprint student, (a coaching program I offer), who was unhappy with my answers when he asked me if a rental property was a good deal. I asked him what the house would be worth after repairs, what the repairs would cost, and what the rent would be. He did not know any of those numbers and was mad that I could not tell him if the house was a good deal! No one can do the work for you; you have to be able to run the numbers to be a successful real estate investor.

- **Investors try to save money by doing work themselves:** Many investors try to save money by managing properties themselves or repairing houses. They assume they will save money by renting homes, making repairs, or managing the entire process. The biggest problem is most first time investors do not know how to manage a property; they have full-time jobs and are not contractors. Picking good tenants takes time, you also have to stay on them to pay rent and visit the property to make sure they are taking care of it. Most horror stories come from investors who rented to the same tenant for seven years and never drove by the house. If you think you can rehab a house by yourself on the weekends in a couple of weeks, think again. It is possible to save money by doing things yourself, but make sure you have the time and are qualified to do the work.

- **Investors assuming prices will increase**: Most investors who lost money in the last housing crisis were over-leveraged and assumed prices would continue to increase. I think we are seeing that same scenario take form in today's market as well. It is hard to find good deals and houses that will cash flow. It is hard to find flips that will make money. When you start fudging the numbers to buy houses, you are asking for trouble. When I buy rentals I make sure they have plenty of cash flow no matter what the market is doing and when I buy flips I assume I will sell it for what it is worth today, not what it might be worth in six months.

- **Investors start investing by accident**: Many people get their first rental property by turning a house they lived in into a rental. They never intended to rent the house, they did not look at rental numbers before they bought, but circumstances caused them to move and rent the house out. Surprise! The house was not a good rental, because it was not intended to be a rental. You need to make sure any house that you rent out will make money. You cannot rely on appreciation.

There are many more ways to lose money investing in real estate. However, I only consider it a failure if you gave up and did not learn anything from your experience.

Why do people fail to invest in real estate?

Many people will lose money investing in real estate because of the reasons listed above. Many more people will never invest in real estate at all, even though they know it is a great way to build wealth and they had every intention of investing. What are the reasons people never get the ball rolling?

- **No money:** It takes money to invest in real estate, even with no money down loans. If you have no money, it is very hard to invest in real estate or anything (it is possible to get started with nothing, but do not expect it to be easy). If you have no money, that does not mean you cannot invest, that means you need to get money! Either learn to save more money or make more money. I can pretty much guarantee there is someone out there in a worse financial situation than you are and was able to save money and buy a house. It will take sacrifice and hard work, but believe me it is better than having no money the rest of your life.

- **Analysis paralysis:** Many investors educate themselves about everything, yet they never buy a property. Education is important, but after a certain point, you will have enough knowledge and information to invest.

- **Too much work:** Most people are not willing to do the work it takes to invest successfully in real estate. It takes time to learn your market, find deals, get a team of professionals to help you, and save money. Most people simply give up when they realize it will not be easy.

- **They are talked out of it:** We have already discussed this, but many people listen to the naysayers and do not invest because they think it is a bad investment. Do not let someone else tell you the best way to invest your money. Figure it out for yourself.

Most aspiring investors never buy a property. They talk themselves out of it, it is too hard, or they cannot get the money together. There are ways to invest with little money. There are many great people online talking about investing in real estate. If you are not willing to work hard at life, you will not get very far. If you want to invest in real estate, do not let someone else decide that you should not or a allow lack of money to be an excuse. Get out there and do it. While there are ways to lose money investing in rentals, if you do your homework and know how to run the numbers, the chances of losing money decrease greatly.

How risky are investment properties?

With potential for big money when investing in real estate, many people automatically think there must be huge risk involved. There is risk in real estate, just like any other investment or walking down the street. If you have a long-term plan built to withstand market fluctuations, there is very little risk when investing in long-term rental properties.

One key to a low risk rental strategy, or any successful real estate strategy, is to buy a property below market value. Buying below market enables you to create instant equity, increase your net worth, and protect you against a downturn in the market.

Let us look at my fourth rental property as an example. I purchased the home for $109,000 in 2012. I put about $35,000 cash into the property for repairs, down payment, and other costs. My loan on the property was about $88,000. My breakeven was $123,000 to get my full investment back out of the home. That home was worth at least 145k fixed up and probably closer to 150k or more when I bought it. Since I bought the home below market, prices would have to drop 20 percent, before the property would be worth less than what I had into it. Prices would have to drop even further, more than

40 percent, for the value to drop below my loan balance. Even if prices nosedived in the next year, I would still be okay.

Cash flow reduces the risk with rentals

I consider cash flow the most important factor in my long-term rental strategy. I eventually plan to live and get rich off the cash flow from my rental properties. When I buy a property and fix it up, I expect at least $500 a month in cash flow.

My rents range from $1,100 to $1,600 a month on my rentals and I cash flow $500 on almost all of them. For me to see negative cash flow, my rents would have to drop more than 40 percent! It is possible that house prices could fall 20 or even 40 percent. We saw that happen a few years ago in some areas of the country, but rents did not drop 40 percent when the housing prices crashed. In fact, many places saw only minimal drops in rental rates, because rental rates are not based on the price of houses. Rents are based on the supply and demand of rental properties in any given area. If we ever see rental rates drop 50 percent, then either the economy has completely crashed or some life-altering event has changed a country or region forever.

I base my strategy on single-family rental properties that are less than 50 years old. The older a property is, the better the chance it will need a major repair. I have enough cash flow coming in to account for major repairs, but homes over 100 years old can have issues come up that could wipe out all equity. It is rare, but a foundation or structural problem can make a property uninhabitable and cost tens of thousands of dollars to repair. By purchasing newer properties, I lessen the chances of running into repairs that could wipe out my profit for a year or even two.

You must have reserves in the bank

Another reason investors get into trouble is they do not have enough money to buy a rental property. They save up just enough for the down payment and the repairs needed on the home. Then when they cannot rent the home right away or a major repair comes up, they do not have the money to weather the storm. Most banks require six months in reserves for mortgage payments on all properties. I think this is the minimum savings you should have before you invest. If you have plenty of cash flow and reserves, you can weather the storm if prices drop or the rental market declines. With plenty of cash flow and reserves in the bank, you will not have to sell your rentals if values drop. We had a drop in prices during the housing crisis and many investor with rentals went bankrupt. However, many investors with rentals made it through the crisis just fine and are doing very well now that the market recovered. The difference was the investors who weathered the storm had equity, cash flow, and reserves.

Should you invest in rental properties?

Everyone reading this book lives in or on some type of real estate. I would think most of you are interested in real estate because you spend the majority of time in some type of real estate. I personally love houses and architecture and I love fixing up properties (my contractor does the actual work). I think it is important for people to be excited about and interested in what they invest. If you do not care about a stock or a mutual fund, you probably are not going to do much research or spend much time looking into the financial data on that investment. Investing in rental properties requires a good deal of due diligence to insure a good investment. If you do not care about houses and are just in it for the money, you may not do as well as others who love the business.

You can still succeed in real estate even if you do not care about real estate, but you will need to discipline yourself. This is not a get rich quick or easy plan. I think it will get you rich much faster than the stock market, but it may take a little more effort.

Do you have the right attitude?

Many people fear any change or starting a new venture. I think it is perfectly normal to be nervous or apprehensive about beginning something as major as investing in rental properties. If you let fear get the best of you and start thinking there is no way you can succeed, you probably will not be successful. Our minds have a funny way of helping us succeed or fail depending on how we feel. If we are positive about our chances and believe we can accomplish something, we are more likely to succeed.

It is easy to let others convince us that our goals and dreams are not possible or are flawed. We tend to listen to them even though we have more knowledge and experience on the subject. We let our minds convince us that the naysayers must know something we do not, and if we embark on this new adventure, it will lead to ruin. Do not listen to them! Be confident in your ambitions and in your future. They would probably love to be starting something new and exciting, but are too scared to do it themselves.

I am not against gaining knowledge and education from the experts. I can sit and listen to experts talk about real estate all day long. If someone thinks real estate is a bad investment because he or she knew someone who once lost money on a flip, I will politely ignore everything he or she has to say. Have confidence in your decision, and do not doubt that if done right investing in real estate is a fantastic investment.

Are you willing to learn and change?

I have been in real estate my whole life. My dad has been an agent since 1978, and I have been helping him since I was three years old. Yet I still learn new things regarding real estate all the time. I thought I was an expert on investing and knew just about everything there was to know before I started my blog. I was wrong, there is so much to learn and do in so many facets of real estate. I think every real estate investor can continue to learn better techniques and ways to invest as long as they want to. You do not have to know everything to invest, but you do need to know the basics. You do not have to learn everything at once, but you have to be willing to learn new ideas and accept that what you thought about real estate may not be reality. Sometimes the best teacher is experience and getting in the game even when you do not know everything.

Are you disciplined enough?

It takes money, time, and patience to become a great real estate investor. If you are not willing to do what it takes to get funding, find properties, and choose a good team you may not succeed. You will need discipline and perseverance to work through the hard times. I love the book *The Art of War*, because it defines resistance as that thing that keeps you from greatness. Every time you are close to finishing a project or reaching a milestone there is always something that pops up to stop you. It could be an unexpected phone call, work task, or taking a break that turns into a day off. The book goes into detail on how to overcome resistance and push through it. If you can recognize resistance and either ignore it or push through it to complete your tasks, then you will accomplish so much more. Most people stop when they meet resistance and will not give that extra effort. If you think you are close to something great or making a break through, do not give up when you meet resistance. Resistance is a sign that you are close to your goals and close to a breakthrough.

If you do not have a lot of money to invest right away (which most people do not) you may have to make changes to your lifestyle. You may have to start a budget, cut down on expenditures, or find ways to make more money. I personally like finding ways to make money, because I hate budgeting and cutting back! It may take a long time to make your first purchase, but do not get discouraged. If you tend to give up easy, you may not be able to last long enough to make it in real estate. Once you make your first purchase, it all becomes easier and everything starts to fall into place. It took me years to invest in real estate after the idea got into my head. It does not have to take years, but it might and that is okay.

The key to any successful real estate strategy is to purchase properties below market value. It is relatively easy to purchase homes actively for sale on MLS for market value. The difficult part is finding the great deal, acting fast, and getting it under contract. Finding motivated sellers that do not have their homes listed on MLS is a great way to find deals, but takes a lot of work and patience as well. Do not get discouraged if you cannot find the right deals immediately. One of the reasons it takes so long to start investing is that you first have to learn what a good deal is and then be patient for it.

If you give up easily and find yourself moving from opportunity to opportunity quickly when they do not pan out, real estate may not be right for you.

Do you have enough time?

You are going to have to have some spare time to be a real estate investor. You have to research your plan, look at houses, manage repairs, and rent your houses or find a property manager. If you are constantly tied up with work or family and never have enough time, think about whether you have the time to add something more onto your plate. If you do not think you have time in your life for something new, maybe you are too busy or you need to change your life. Investing in real estate may be a great first step to increase the amount of spare time in your life. I am constantly working on gaining more free time and delegating tasks to others. Time is our most valuable commodity because we cannot buy more of it. If you have no time, try creating a time budget for yourself. I take all the hours in the week and allocate time for sleep, work, leisure, family etc. Looking at where you spend your time now is a great way to decide if your priorities are in the right place.

Focus is a great way to increase time instantly. I am horrible at trying to do too many things at once. Ultimately, it takes me longer to complete my tasks; I make more mistakes and forget what I am doing when I try to multi-task. It is hard for me, but I when start a task, I force myself to focus on it until I am done or until I have spent a certain amount of time on it. I do not check email, browse the Internet, or do anything else until I am finished with that task.

Hiring help is a great way to increase time and usually increases your results as well. Whenever I hire a new assistant, I delegate tasks I do not like doing. I am happier and get more done when I am not working on tasks I do not like doing. I also have more time to focus on the tasks I do like doing or the tasks that make me more money. A great piece of advice I recently heard is never to work below your income. If you are worth $100 an hour, do not do tasks you can hire out at $20 an hour. Focus on things that make you that $100 an hour or more and let someone else do the less important work.

Are you a people person?

Being a people person is not a requirement, but it sure helps when investing in real estate. The more people you know in real estate, the better your chances of succeeding. Even other investors will help you out if you are willing to go to local investor meetings. Real Estate Investor Associations (REIAs) are a fantastic place to learn about investing in your market and a great way to network. I do not go to as many REIA meetings as I should, but when I do go, I meet wholesalers, like-minded investors, real estate agents, and lenders. Those people may not be able to help me now, but who knows how they may be able to help me in the future.

If you are going to be a real estate investor, you will have to deal with agents, title companies, inspectors, appraisers, contractors, and other investors. The better you can get along with everyone, the more you will succeed. If you really do not like dealing with people, you can always collaborate with or hire someone who does like to network.

Do not give up!

This section is not meant to discourage you, but to educate you. It takes work to become a successful real estate investor, but it all gets much easier once you get your feet wet and start investing. Real estate is so rewarding; I believe the benefits far exceed the work it takes to get started. Successful investors do not need to work or manage homes and they have the freedom to do anything they want. Many investors continue to invest and manage their properties even when they do not need the money because they love it! I hope you choose to invest in real estate, and are as successful as or even more successful than I have been.

If it was easy, everyone would do it, and there would be much less opportunity for those willing to put the work in.

3. How do you know what a good rental property investment is?

Buying a rental property can be a great investment if it is done right. The big question then becomes how do you know what a good rental property investment is? This is a hard question to answer because every market is different, every investor is different, everyone has different financial situations, and everyone has different goals. What may work for me, may not work for you.

I use many fundamentals to judge rentals that can help you decide what a good investment is. The main things I look at when I judge a rental property are:

- Did I buy it below market value and by how much?
- How much does it cash flow each month?
- What are my cash-on-cash returns?
- What do the future prospects look like for the market in which I am buying?

When coming up with these numbers and projections I have to make sure I am figuring everything correctly. I see people figure cash flow wrong all the time. Cash flow is somewhat of a guessing game, because you cannot predict all the expenses. However, there are methods that allow investors to predict accurately what the actual returns will be.

How do you figure the cash flow on rental properties?

Figuring the cash flow on rental properties seems simple, but many people do not include all the expenses they should.

Each rental property will need maintenance and will be vacant at some time and you must account for these costs. I have to be certain to account for all the expenses so that I make as much as I think I will. An investor must factor vacancies and maintenance into expected returns even if a house is in good repair and your area has low vacancies.

Cash flow is the money you make on rental properties. I have a great cash flow calculator on my website: http://investfourmore.com/rental-property-cash-flow-calculator/. There is a place to enter vacancies and maintenance. When you own rental properties you may not have a lot of vacancies or maintenance every year, but in some years, you may have many vacancies and a lot of maintenance that you will make you wonder why you ever bought rental properties.

If you plan for bad years that may have a lot of vacancy and maintenance cost, it will not hurt as much, and you will still make money on your rental properties.

How do you account for vacancies on rental properties?

Vacancy is the time you own a rental property that it is not rented or you are not collecting rent. Vacancies occur when a tenant moves out or stops paying or you cannot rent a property as soon as you had hoped. You will not be collecting rent during vacant months, but you will have to pay utilities on the home (if the tenant normally pays utilities).

Two of the costliest scenarios when owning rental property are evicting a tenant and having a tenant that stops paying rent. It can take months and thousands of dollars to evict a tenant.

I have had problems with tenants not paying rent on time. One of my tenants in rental property number six had to have heart surgery and could not work. He fell behind in rent and I did not have the heart to evict him. We worked out a deal where he moved out, but he owed me over $3,500 in back rent. If you have a tenant who will not pay rent and will not leave, you could pay much more for an eviction. Each state is different when evicting tenants and what it will cost, and the time it will take.

Why do you have to factor in maintenance on rental properties?

I repair all of my rental properties before I rent them. When I first rent my properties, they most likely will not need very much maintenance because they are in great shape. However, I also buy homes that are 30, 40 or even 50 years old. Although I repair homes before I rent them, I do not rebuild the house and things do break. Tenants also may break things for you and you still have to fix them.

My cash flow calculator figures maintenance costs based on how old a house is and how much rehab has been done. The more work that a house has had done, the less maintenance it will need. The newer a house is the less maintenance it will need because the major systems are of better quality and will last longer. I prefer to buy rental properties that are 50 years old or newer because they have a much smaller chance of needing major work.

The most important factor when keeping up with maintenance on rental properties is the quality of the tenants and oversite by the property owner. The better the tenants take care of a home and the more a property owner monitors the property, the less maintenance there will be. The rental houses I have seen that were in the worst condition had been rented to the same tenants for years and the property owners never checked to see the damage being done.

Even if a house does not need maintenance done for years, a big expense could pop up and wipe out all the savings. A roof could cost $5,000 to $10,000. A tenant could trash the paint and carpet in a house, which could easily cost $5,000 or more. The big repairs are why we account for maintenance in our returns, even if a house may not need any other repairs for years.

How much money should you plan to spend for vacancies?

The tricky part about accounting for vacancies is deciding how much money you need to allocate for future vacancies or evictions. A good rule of thumb is to count on ten percent of the rent for vacancies. Ten percent would be just over one-month's rent and would account for one vacant month, any utilities, and other costs you incur while the home is vacant. On my rental properties, I have been very lucky and proactive to get my houses rented right away after a tenant moves out. In Colorado, we have had very low vacancy rates and I have seen about a five percent historic vacancy cost on my rentals.

Here is the vacancy table I use:

Single Family	5%
College Rental	10%
Multifamily	10%

These rates however can vary greatly based on the location of your rental property. If you are in an area that has very high vacancy rates, the expense might be 10 percent on a single family home or 15 percent on a multifamily. Different neighborhoods and different priced rentals, may also have varying vacancy costs.

How much money should you plan to spend for maintenance?

Planning for maintenance costs is very difficult because you never know what will break or how well a tenant will treat a home. In my cash flow calculator, the maintenance costs on my tiered scale range from 5 to 30 percent of the collected rents. The five percent is for an almost new house with all the systems in great condition. The 30 percent is for a house that is 100 years old, and has not had the systems upgraded or any recent remodel completed. The maintenance costs will vary greatly depending on the type of house you buy, the age and the condition of the house, and how well it has been taken care of.

Here is the table I use for my cash flow calculator:

	Good	Average	Needs Work
0-10 Years	5%	10%	15%
10-50 Years	10%	15%	20%
50 Years+	15%	20%	25%

How do you figure the total cash flow?

Rental property number 1

This rental is paid off and has no mortgage. However, I do have a line of credit against it that I use for fix and flips.

Rent	$1,400 a month
Taxes	$60 a month
Insurance	$50 a month
Maintenance	$140 a month (rent x 10% maintenance)
Vacancies	$70 a month (rent x 5% for vacancies)
HOA Fee	$13 a year
Property Mgmt	$112 a month
Total cash flow	**$967 a month**

If I had a mortgage on this property, which I did when I first bought it, my cash flow would be $967 minus whatever the principal and interest payments would be. It is also important to remember that most lenders will escrow the taxes and insurance. Escrow means they include it in your mortgage payment so make sure you are not counting them twice if the lender is including those costs in your payment.

When I bought this house in 2010, I paid $96,900 for it and my payment at the time was about $350 for principal and interest. That would make my cash flow about $600 a month with that mortgage payment included.

What is the 50 percent rule when used for rental property expenses?

The 50 percent rule states the expenses (not including mortgages expense) on a rental will be 50 percent of the rent.

Many investors use this rule to judge the profitability on a rental and only this rule. However, I think using a blanket rule like this is not the best way to analyze a rental property. Here is an example of what the 50 percent rule would say the expenses are on one of my properties.

Rental property number 4

Rent $1,600 a month
Expenses $800
Mortgage $740 (without taxes and insurance)

According to the 50 percent rule I make about $60 a month on this property. However, if I were to use my cash flow calculator, it shows I am making over $350 a month on this property. What is the difference? On the cash flow calculator it figures all of the expenses, it does not use a blanket rule. Here are the expenses on this property using my calculator:

Property Mgmt	$128
Taxes	$83
Insurance	$50
Maintenance	$160
Vacancies	$80
Total cash flow	**$501 a month**

The difference between my estimates and the 50 percent rule is $300 a month or $3,600 a year. Are my expenses really this low or am I just making stuff up? I did an analysis of my rentals last year and my expenses were almost exactly what I had estimated them to be. I have had rental properties since 2010 and my estimated expenses have been very close to what the actual expenses have been. This was not just a one-year anomaly.

Why would the 50 percent rule show the expenses are so much higher than what they may actually be?

There are a number of factors regarding why I do not like the 50 percent rule, and I think it can overestimate the expenses on rentals. The biggest reason I do not like the rule is it assumes all rentals will have basically the same expenses in every state and on every type of property.

- **Property Taxes:** The property taxes in every state can vary by a huge amount. In Colorado my taxes are less than $1,000 a year on most of my properties. In other states those same properties would have taxes five times that amount. **Difference in expenses on taxes: $80 a month versus $400 a month.**

- **HOA dues:** If you own a condo or town home, the chances are you have HOA dues. Many single family homes have them as well. I have one rental with an HOA and the rest have no HOA fees. Some HOAs can charge hundreds of dollars a month. **The difference in HOA expenses: $0 versus $200 a month**.

- **Vacancies:** Different types of properties have different vacancy rates and so do different towns. In Colorado we have had extremely low vacancy rates. In some cases, and during some years, the vacancies have been under 1 percent. In other parts of the country the vacancy rate is over 10 percent. Single family homes typically have lower vacancies than multifamily homes. College rentals will have much higher vacancies than other types of rentals as well. Some properties may have 5 percent vacancies expenses and others may have 15 percent or higher. **The difference in vacancy expenses: $80 a month versus $240 a month.**

- **Maintenance:** Properties will need work, even if they are brand new. The amount of work will vary on the condition of the property and the type of property as well. Multifamily usually has more wear and tear than single family and college rentals can have much more wear and tear. The older a property is, the more maintenance it will require. The worse shape a property is in, the more maintenance it will require. The maintenance expense can vary from 5 to 20 percent as well. **The difference in maintenance expense: $80 versus $320 a month.**

There are other expenses that will make a huge difference as well like insurance. If the property is in a flood or hurricane zone, it will have much higher insurance. As you can see the expenses on similar priced rentals that may cater to different tenants in different areas of the country can vary from $400 (once you add insurance and property manager) a month to $1,160 a month! If we took the same $1,600 in rent that I am receiving on rental property number 4, my expenses could be anywhere from 25 percent of the rent to over 70 percent of the rent. These are extreme examples of what the expenses may be on rentals, but they show how different properties will have much different costs.

Another problem with the 50 percent rule is it uses the rent to determine the expenses. When I bought my fourth rental property in 2012, it rented for $1,300 a month. The rents have gone up over the last three years to $1,600 a month and it may rent for more than that if I were to get a new tenant. Look how much the expenses changed because my rent increased.

- With $1,300 a month in rent, the 50 percent rule says my expenses are $650 a month
- With $1,600 a month in rent, the 50 percent rule says my expenses are $800 a month.

Did my expenses really go up by $150 a month because the rent is higher? It could be argued that since the rent is higher my vacancy expenses would be higher because when a month's rent is missed I would lose more money. I agree with that but here is how much my vacancy costs would increase using different vacancy rates.

- 5 percent vacancy: Expense would increase from $65 to $80 a month
- 10 percent vacancy: Expense would increase from $130 to $160 a month
- 15 percent vacancy: Expense would increase from $185 to $240 a month

Even with 15 percent of the rents accounting for vacancies the increase would only be $75 a month, not $150 a month. With a 5 percent vacancy allowance, the extra cost is only $15 a month. Maybe the other expenses would be higher with the higher rent? My property taxes have gone up slightly, but less than $10 a month, my insurance has not increased, my maintenance has not increased, but my property management has. If we look at property management the increase is about $22 a month. On certain properties, it possible that the expenses would increase $150 a month when the rent changes if many other things change as well. It is also possible that the expenses would not change much at all, which is the problem with the 50 percent rule. It is a blanket rule that does not account for the different expenses that different properties will have.

The 50 percent rule might be dead on for some properties, but for other properties it could be hundreds of dollars a month off. This is why you cannot rely on a blanket rule to figure the expenses. You need to write everything out or use a cash flow calculator to help you know what all the expenses are. Knowing the exact expenses will make you a better investor and help you figure out what is and is not a good rental property.

Is the 2 percent rule a good way to judge rental properties?

The 2 percent rule is a general guideline many investors use to determine if a rental property is a good deal. The basics of the 2 percent rule say the monthly rent from a rental property should be 2 percent or more of the cost of a rental property. I don't believe the 2 percent rule is a good judge of rental properties. The rule is too vague and does not account for many variables with rentals just like the 50 percent rule. Buying rental properties is all about the numbers in a particular market and the 2 percent rule assumes that all costs are the same with every property in every market.

What exactly is the 2 percent rule?

The 2 percent rule is very simple to calculate. If a home costs $100,000 with no repairs needed, the rent should be $2,000 a month. If the home costs $100,000 and you have to do $20,000 in repairs, then the repairs would make the cost basis $120,000 and you would have to rent the home for $2,400 a month.

If you think those are incredible rent to purchase price ratios you are right. If you think it is also virtually impossible to find properties that meet the 2 percent rule you are also right. I know 2 percent rental properties exist, but they are usually low-priced properties under $50,000. I think you can make money with low priced rentals, but I also know you can make a lot of money on more expensive homes that do not meet the 2 percent rule.

I do not like the 2 percent rule, because it only figures what rent should be based on the cost basis. There are so many other variables that need to be considered when buying rentals. The expenses from rental properties are what most people underestimate, and the 2 percent rule was created to make sure investors don't underestimate the expenses. If you use the 2 percent rule to buy properties, you will make money if you can find properties that meet the guidelines. More likely you will never find a decent rental property that meets those guidelines unless you live in an area with very low prices or you buy a turn-key rental. The problem is the rule is so extreme that it makes it impossible for most people to buy a rental property.

If you live in an area with very low prices then the two percent rule may be a good guideline after you have run the numbers to see what costs are in your market. Taxes are different in every state, each rental property is different and even some homes that meet the two percent rule will have a tough time making money depending in the circumstances. My rentals don't come close to meeting the 2 percent rule, but still make a lot of money. My rentals are much closer to the 1 percent rule, but I would not use any rules when trying to decide if a rental property is a good deal.

Many times, properties that meet the 1 percent rule may be a better investment than properties that meet the 2 percent. Sure the 2 percent properties will make more money on paper, but they are usually lower priced rentals. The lower priced rentals come with more turnover, more maintenance, more vacancies and can be harder to finance.

This shows why it is so important to run the numbers yourself when buying a rental; do not rely on a rule. I never used any rules when I bought my rentals. I figured what my cash on cash returns would be based on all the expenses and expected rents. If you take short cuts when investing in real estate, you may miss out on some awesome deals or invest in some horrible deals.

Why you should not count on appreciation with rentals

I base my strategy for investing in rental properties on cash flow, not on my properties appreciating. Do I want them to appreciate? Yes! It allows me to refinance more easily and possibly pull cash out to buy more properties if I need to. However, I do not need my rental properties to appreciate to make money and get good returns. I buy houses for cash flow and not for appreciation.

One of the biggest mistakes I see investors making is buying rental properties with little or no cash flow, and hoping the homes will appreciate. In my mind this is not investing, this is speculating that the market will increase in value. I never buy a property with my only profit potential being appreciation; I want cash flow.

I always buy houses below market value. In addition to buying homes below market value, I always buy properties with positive cash flow. Positive cash flow allows me to bring in income as soon as I rent the home. Because I am investing for cash flow, I do not worry about home values. If home values go down it does not matter to me, because I am making money from cash flow and I do not need to sell the home. In fact, I do not want to sell because the property is making me money every month.

The biggest problem in buying a rental property with negative cash flow is investors usually underestimate their expenses. The fact they are buying a property with negative cash flow means they are usually stretching their buying criteria to make the deal. Repairs and expenses usually exceed expectations, unless you assume there will be many unknown costs. It is always best to error on the side of caution when calculating expenses, especially if you are new to investing.

Many novice investors do not account for the unknown, because they really want to make a deal work. It is very easy to justify numbers that do not make sense when you are a new investor looking for your first deal. I underestimated expenses all the time when I started investing in rental properties. I used minimum repair and expense numbers hoping that things would work out. When you underestimate expenses, you are letting emotions make the deal, which is a big mistake. If you really want to make a deal work and you fudge the numbers to get everything to line up correctly, you may end up with negative cash flow every month.

Even if you plan for negative cash flow most investors cannot maintain it

Most investors who buy properties with negative cash flow very quickly tire of writing checks. As I just discussed, most investors underestimate their expenses and with negative cash flow that can mean they are paying out hundreds of dollars each month on one property. While those investors are waiting for the home to appreciate, they are losing thousands a year in negative cash flow. The investor realizes very quickly that it does not make sense to hope the housing market will increase while they continue to lose money. The investor's only choice is to continue to dump cash into the property every month or to sell at a loss. Even if the investor can sell the home for as much as they bought it, or slightly more, the cost of selling a home will eat up all the profit and then some.

It usually costs 6 to 10 percent of the value of a home to sell it. Investors got into trouble during the housing crisis, because they were investing based purely on anticipated appreciation without regard to cash flow or long-term scenarios. Currently many people feel we are in a similar bubble, although I am not so sure. If you buy houses for cash flow, not appreciation, a housing bubble will not be of great concern.

The simple way to avoid shelling out cash every month on a rental is to invest in a home that cash flows. If values go down, rents may go down as well, but unless your margins are tight, you will still cash flow and you will not have to sell. The easiest way to lose money in real estate is to have to sell your property quickly in a buyers' market. The only buyer may be an investor like me looking for a great deal!

Predicting the real estate market does not work for me

Houses prices historically appreciate, but that does not mean you can predict when and how much prices will go up. In the last decade, the United States has seen a huge upturn in housing prices, a huge downturn, and then another huge upturn. I like to make money when I buy a house by buying below market value. However, many investors live in an area with extremely high real estate prices and they invest hoping for appreciation. I understand why investors buy for appreciation, because it is very hard to find cash flowing rental properties or houses with enough room to flip in highly competitive markets. Investors justify their decision to invest for appreciation, because they feel they are in a highly desirable economic location. I do not like to invest for appreciation because there are so many factors that affect housing prices beyond our control. I love it when my houses appreciate, but I do not need them to appreciate to make money.

Why do some housing markets appreciate more than others do?

Real estate markets constantly increase and decrease in value, with some markets fluctuating much more than others. California has seen huge increases in real estate prices and huge

decreases as well. Check out this graph of the historic home prices in Southern California from aboutinflation.com.

If you look at the chart, you see some fluctuation over the last 60 years in Southern California. This graph does not show the large increase in home values in the last year and a half, but prices have shot up again. Many investors feel California has many things going for it: great weather, good economy, and an increasing population that will continue to push prices up. However, California had those same things going for it when the market crashed. The markets with the highest population growth and the best economies usually see the highest appreciation. However, the areas with the highest appreciation also see the largest declines in values when they market turns.

If you look at the above graph, you see a much more stable real estate market in Dallas. Companies like Toyota are relocating which is leading to more new home inventory. The prices in Dallas did not appreciate as much as California, but they also did not decrease as much as California either. Even with steadily rising prices for decades, Dallas saw a sharp decrease in prices during the housing crisis. If you buy and hold properties long enough in stable or decreasing markets, your home will most likely appreciate given enough time. When you are investing for appreciation without any cash flow coming in, how long can you hold properties until they pay off?

Dallas TX Real Estate Inflation Adjusted Index Historical chart 1953 - 2013

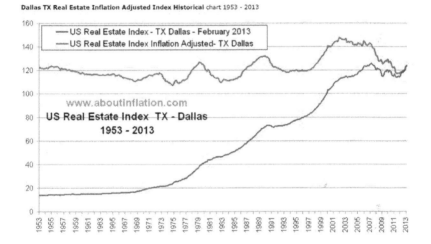

What are the risks of buying for appreciation?

The Dallas and California markets show the differences between highly volatile markets and stable markets. Most people who buy rental properties or flips for appreciation are doing it because they cannot buy for cash flow or a profit in their current market. They are seeing huge value increases and rents do not come close to making up for the prices they have to pay for properties. They hope the appreciation will continue so they will be able to sell for a profit in six months or a year. The problem is that prices do not always continue to rise, even in very stable markets with a great economy and high buyer demand.

If you are counting on appreciation to flip homes, you are running a very risky business. Many investors used this strategy before the housing crisis and went bankrupt when the market turned. If you buy a fix and flip with enough profit to make money using current market prices, you should be okay, even with a market downturn. If you buy rental properties hoping for appreciation and the market turns, you are stuck with a property that makes no money and that you cannot sell. Many investors also did this with rental properties before the housing crisis and went bankrupt when the market turned. When you buy for appreciation, you have to have a lot of appreciation to make up for the cost of selling a house.

There is an easy way to avoid being that person who loses all his rental properties to foreclosure, buy for cash flow, and hope for appreciation.

Is it possible to predict what housing markets will appreciate and when?

Many investors look at every economic indicator and think they can to predict what markets will appreciate. Are their plenty of jobs, local colleges, emerging technologies, etc.? They feel good economic indicators and a strong housing market will promote even higher housing prices. I do not believe this to be the case, because there are so many variables to consider with the housing market. Many investors went bankrupt in the last housing crisis betting on housing appreciation, because all the economic indicators looked strong. What factors will affect housing prices?

Interest rates: If interest rates increase, it could dramatically affect how much house people can afford and could negatively affect housing prices.

National economy: The national economy was a huge part of the last housing crisis; unemployment skyrocketed and people could not afford their houses anymore.

World economy: It does not seem like the economy of China could hurt the U.S. housing market, but it can. The Chinese economy can affect the U.S. stock market, and a decrease in the U.S. stock market could cause concern for the economy, which affects the housing market.

Building supplies: If building supplies continue to increase in cost, new construction prices will continue to increase as well. If there is a shortage of already built homes on the market, people turn to new construction. The cost of new homes can greatly affect the cost of already built homes. An oversupply of new homes can cause local housing markets to decline greatly.

Lending guidelines: The housing crisis was caused in part by loose lending guidelines. People were able to finance over 100 percent of the value of their homes and then when values stopped going up, they were underwater. Lending guidelines changed after the housing crisis making it harder to get a loan for a while. Now lending guidelines are loosening up again, and we may see an increase in foreclosures.

Foreclosures: The more foreclosures there are, the lower prices are because supply increases. I doubt we will see the huge price decreases we saw during the housing crisis, but a large increase in foreclosures could easily cause prices to stop appreciating and decrease. With looser lending guidelines, there is a greater chance of more foreclosures in our future.

Given all the local, national, and international factors that affect housing prices, I think it is difficult for an individual investor to predict what housing prices will do. Prices could continue to rise or they could see a huge decrease if one of these variables changes.

Are you the only one betting on appreciation?

Investors will argue that their local economy is so strong that they can withstand the national variables that may cause prices to decrease. I do not agree with this argument either because there are many other investors with the same idea. In highly competitive markets, there are many investors looking to invest, and they all may be justifying mediocre investments with the same reasons. Those investors are pushing prices up even higher than what the local economy and buyer demand can support. There may even be large hedge funds betting on that same appreciation pushing prices up higher. Just because a market has a great economy and high buyer demand, does not always mean prices will go up.

Can you predict housing prices in stagnant areas with no growth?

I think it is very hard to predict what housing markets will appreciate and when they will appreciate, but it is easier to see what housing markets will not appreciate. If an area has no growth, or negative growth it will be almost impossible for housing prices to increase in value. Housing prices increase because there are too few houses for the number of people looking to buy a home. If there are too many houses for the current population, housing prices will decrease and continue to decrease until the houses are removed or more buyers come to town. Many areas in the Midwest have very stable populations, and they see almost no appreciation because there is always an ample supply of homes for sale. Detroit has started removing houses to decrease the housing supply, because so many people have moved away. It may be possible to predict what housing markets will not go up in value, but I am not sure what good that information is.

Housing prices constantly go up and down. It is very hard for anyone to predict exactly when and how much they will appreciate. Prices may keep going up for one year, two years, or more, but they may also start decreasing in a few months. The United States economy is going pretty well now, but that could change very quickly based on the climate, oil prices, the world economy, and thousands of other things about which I have no idea. The great thing is, you can still make a lot of money in real estate, relatively safely by buying below market value and buying for cash flow.

How much cash flow do you need?

I am a strong advocate that investors should buy rental properties for cash flow and not appreciation. Another question investors must ask themselves is how much cash flow will they need on their rental properties? How much cash flow do you need to be secure? How much cash flow do you need to justify spending money on a rental property? How much cash flow do you need to reach your financial goals?

Positive cash flow is a great thing, but how much is enough? Obviously the more cash flow the better, but awesome cash flowing properties do not exactly grow on trees. It really is a personal decision on how high of a return a person needs to justify spending a specific amount of cash on a rental property. I like to see $500 a month in cash flow on my properties, which I purchased for $80,000 to $140,000. If you are buying less or more expensive properties, your cash flow requirements may be different. Another way to look at the returns is the cash-on-cash return.

I like to see over 15 percent cash-on-cash returns, but I love to see closer to 20 percent. Some people would be happy with 15, 10, or even 5 percent returns on their cash. Remember you will usually have higher returns on rental properties than just the cash-on-cash percentage once you factor in paying down the mortgage, tax advantages, possible appreciation, and buying below market value.

What are cash-on-cash returns and how do you figure them?

People rarely hear the term cash-on-cash return outside of the real estate world. Stocks and most investments are judged by ROI (return on investment), not cash-on-cash. It is very hard to determine the ROI on rental properties, because until you sell a rental property you will not know the actual return on your investment. The cash-on-cash return is a much easier number to calculate because it looks at the cash return from rental properties compared to the cash invested.

The way I calculate cash-on-cash return may not be the exact way an accountant would calculate it, but this technique is the best way for me to judge the returns on a rental property.

Why is it hard to calculate the ROI on rental properties?

ROI stands for return on investment, which is usually a good way to judge investments. With ROI, you calculate all the money you made from your investment and divide it into the cash invested. If you make $50,000 on an investment that cost you $500,000, you have made a 10 percent ROI. With rental properties however, you will not know your true ROI until you sell your rental property.

ROI includes your total investment versus your total returns. Rental properties have many awesome benefits. There are tax benefits thanks to depreciation, leverage, cash flow, appreciation, and ability to refinance a rental property as well to take out cash.

It is simple to calculate the rental income (cash flow) versus the cash invested, but it is harder figuring all the other advantages. My rentals have increased my net worth by well over 1.5 million dollars. However, if I sold my rentals I would have to pay selling costs and high taxes. I would not get all that in cash if I sold and I would have to divide what is left of that money, along with my cash flow and tax benefits over the years I have owned my properties to see what my yearly ROI is. Right now, my estimation of the selling prices and costs are an educated guess and I have not realized any of that gain.

How is the cash-on-cash return calculated on rental properties?

The cash-on-cash return is calculated by determining the cash flow or rental income on a property and dividing it by the initial cash invested into that property. If you spend $25,000 on down payment, closing costs, and repairs on a rental property and get $5,000 in cash flow, your cash-on-cash return would be 20 percent. To make it easy I created a cash-on-cash calculator on my website at http://investfourmore.com/rental-property-cash-cash-return-calculator/

It seems simple to figure the cash-on-cash return on rental properties, but some situations make it difficult. The biggest problem is deciding when to start figuring the cash-on-cash return. If you buy a rental property that needs repairs, it may not be ready to rent for weeks or even months. You will pay the down payment and closing costs when you buy the house, but you will not pay the contractor until he has completed his work. You also will not collect rent until the house has been repaired and rented. I like to start calculating the cash-on-cash return once I have paid all expenses and the home has been rented.

The cash-on-cash return does not tell us everything about rental properties like the ROI will. It does not factor in any appreciation or tax benefits. The cash-on-cash also does not factor in the equity pay down on loans, which can be a significant amount of money. I like to calculate my cash-on-cash return on my rental properties and I consider the other benefits a bonus. If a new rental property provides at least 15 percent cash-on-cash return, I know I will make a lot of money on that property.

How do you determine how much cash flow and what kind of returns you need?

When you are trying to figure out how much return you need on your properties, here are a few things to consider:

- What is your end goal? Do you want to retire in ten years? Do you want to pay for your children's college? Do you want to build an empire? Do you want to be able to make more than you would in the stock market? Your end goal will help you determine how much in cash you need each month.

- Once you know how much money you want every month from your rentals, you have to figure out how soon you need to get there. Is it five years, ten years or longer?

- How much money will you have to invest in rentals? The less money you have and the higher your goals are, the more cash flow you will need.
- After you consider all of these factors, you can start to build your own plan for how many properties you want and how much each property will need to make.

4. How do you know what type of investment property to buy?

Now that you have an idea of how to figure the cash flow on rental properties and what a good rental property investment is, how do you know what type of property to buy? There are condos, single-family homes, college rentals, and multifamily properties. Many investors and gurus say one is better than the other, but which is better depends on you. What is your market like, what are your goals, and what can you get a great deal on? The next few sections will go through the different types of properties you can invest in along with the pros and cons of each.

Are single-family homes or multifamily homes a better choice?

Many investors assume multifamily properties are the better investment, because they are built to produce income for property owners. I invest in single-family homes because they give me great returns, are easy to find, and easy to manage. However, many successful investors also invest in multifamily properties. I believe the better investment depends on what you are looking for and what you can buy in your market.

Can I buy single-family homes below market value?

The main reason I get great returns on single-family rentals is that I only buy properties that are below market value. Good deals are hard to find, but they are out there if you know how to find them. I try to buy properties at 70 to 80 percent of market value. Usually, the properties are cheap because they need work or have very motivated sellers. Not only do I make money as soon as I close because I bought the property below market, but I usually add value through repairs or improvements as well.

I have purchased rental properties that were REOs, short sales, fair market sales, and estate sales. Some of the keys to buying properties below market value are making offers quickly, having cash to purchase properties, strong financing, and having a good reputation for closing on properties. There also has to be an ample supply of homes for sale. In my market, there are many more single-family than multifamily properties. The law of averages states I should be able to find more deals for single-family homes, simply because there are more of them.

I can find much better deals on single-family homes than I can on larger multi-unit projects, simply due to supply and demand. I know in some areas, multifamily properties produce great returns, but in my area, I can actually make better cash-on-cash return by purchasing and renting out single-family homes.

Why can I make more money with single-family homes?

There is no way I could make over 15 percent cash-on-cash returns with multifamily in Colorado; I would have to pay too high of a purchase price. If I were to buy single-family properties at market value, I could not make 15 percent either, but there are so many more single-family properties available it gives me a better chance of getting a great deal on single-family.

The CAP rate on multifamily homes in Colorado is around five percent. The CAP rate on the single-family homes, which I buy below market value is around eight percent, sometimes higher. I do not know for sure why the CAP rate is so high on multifamily in Colorado. I would guess it is because we have a booming economy, great market appreciation, and large institutional investors are buying multifamily properties with cash. Those large investors are not as concerned with getting awesome returns as the small investors are. The large investors are looking for modest returns and a safe place to park their money.

In other areas of the country, I see CAP rates for multifamily at ten percent or higher. This is why it is important to know your market and formulate your own investing strategies. It does not make sense for everyone to do exactly as I do. You need to know your market and what the return will be for different types of assets.

What are the advantages of single-family homes?

I think single-family rentals are easier to manage than larger complexes. With a single-family rental, I do not have to pay any utilities, the tenants pay them all. In multifamily properties, the property owner is usually responsible for the water and sometimes electric and gas as well. Many tenants feel a single-family rental is their own home, not just an apartment or place to live. They usually take good care of the property and even fix and repair items themselves. They also tend to stay longer and renew their leases year after year. My parents have had a single-family house rented to the same family for 14 years!

Single-family homes are usually less expensive to buy than large complexes with multiple units. The large complexes bring in more rent, but because of that, they are much more expensive to buy (at least in my area). The down payment, repairs, and maintenance expenses are usually less with a single-family home than with multifamily properties. Because single family homes are cheaper, it can be easier for investors to buy a single family than a multifamily.

Single-family homes historically appreciate more than multifamily properties. Multifamily properties are valued on the rents coming in and on the condition, while most single-family homes are valued on supply and demand of owner-occupied buyers. If rents go up in an area, multifamily housing prices will rise as well, but only if rents are raised to meet market rental rates.

Single family homes are easier to sell as well. If an investor wants to cash out his investment or needs to sell for another reason, single family homes have a larger buyer pool. Single family homes are typically sold to owner occupied buyers. There is always a market for owner occupied buyers and there are many more of them, than investors. When you own a multifamily complex, the only buyer is another investor. Single family homes are much easier to sell, because the buyer pool is so much larger.

What are the advantages of multifamily homes?

There are also many advantages to multifamily properties. As I mentioned, some areas see higher returns on multifamily properties than single-family properties. Multifamily properties are valued on the income they produce, which can create opportunities. If a multifamily property is under-rented or you can make improvements that greatly increase the income, you can greatly increase the value of the multifamily property.

Many investors buy large multifamily buildings that are run-down or the rents are too low for the market. They slowly repair the property and raise rents, which greatly increases the value. The nice thing about this strategy is you do not have to hope market rents or values increase, you can force the value to increase by increasing the income the property brings in.

If you buy multifamily properties, you will have more units under one roof, which some investors think is an advantage. Usually you will bring in more rent per square foot with multifamily properties, which means the maintenance may be less over time. I think you have to couple this with the fact that rents are usually lower for multifamily and in my experience the tenants do not take as good of care as an apartment as they would a single-family house.

You can buy multifamily properties with conventional or FHA mortgages if there are less than 4 units. You can only have one FHA mortgage in most cases and it is tough to get more than four conventional mortgages and impossible to get more than ten conventional mortgages. Because you are buying more units with one loan, you may be able to buy more total units with FHA and conventional loans purchasing multifamily. There are many other loan options available for single family and multifamily housing.

If you are a beginning investor, looking to buy with little money down, house hacking a multifamily property can be a great way to get started. This is when you live in one unit and rent the other units out to take advantage of owner occupant loans. I talk much more about his in a later chapter.

Are college rentals a good investment?

College rentals can make a lot of money, but are very different from rental properties that are geared towards families. I have 16 rentals as of the writing of this book and all but one of them (a duplex) are single-family rentals. The duplex could be a college rental since t has one college student in the basement and a family in the upper unit. I have been around college rental properties my entire life; my parents and my sister both have college rentals. In fact, my sister used to manage over 100 college rental units when she was a property manager. I used to help her mange those properties when I was in high school.

Many areas see higher rents for college rentals, but college rentals can take a lot more management and maintenance than single-family rental properties.

What qualifies as a college rental property?

A college rental property is any residential rental property that is designed and zoned to be rented to college students. Most college rentals are located close to a college and marketed specifically to college students. College rentals can be multifamily apartment buildings, single-family houses, houses that have been converted to multifamily, or a retail space with an apartment above or below it.

If you are investing in college rentals, it is important to make sure your college rental is zoned correctly. Many cities only allow a certain number of unrelated people to live in a single-family residence, which means that it may be illegal to rent a four-bedroom house to four college students if the house is zoned single-family. If a house is zoned for multifamily, it may be perfectly fine to rent a six-bedroom house to six unrelated people. Always check the zoning before investing in college rental property as it will greatly affect the value. Do not assume a house is zoned for college students because it is close to a college. I have seen properties across the street from large universities that were zoned single-family and not set up for a college rental. If the city finds out you are using the home illegally, it may force you to evict your tenants.

Why do investors want to buy college rentals?

If a property is close to a college, an investor will usually obtain more rent from college students than from a family. Most college students will pay a premium to be close to school and to live with their friends. You could rent a single-family property that is far from the college to students, but you cannot count on that house always being rented and you probably will not get a premium on the rent. Since college rentals demand more rent than a single-family home, many investors feel they can make more money renting to college students. In my experience, the higher rent will not always make up for the increased expenses that come with a college rental.

I was a college student, and I can say from personal experience college students do not always take care of their residences very well. College students may not intentionally destroy a house (although some will), but they are young and inexperienced with taking care of a house. When college students rent a house, it may be their first time on their own. They might not know how to take care of a house even if they have the best intentions. My sister has had students turn off the heat in the middle of winter for Christmas break. The pipes froze and burst causing thousands of dollars in damage. This happened multiple times, not because the students tried to freeze the pipes, but because they were trying to save on heating costs and did not know any better.

College students may not have learned how to clean well or take care of a house. That means the house will see more wear and tear than a single-family rental. Many families take pride in their homes, while college students only need a place to live and party. A family might take care of minor repairs in their home without even telling the property owner. A college student may call the property owner for everything that could and does go wrong.

Unlike single-family residences, most college-rental owners pay some utilities and yard care. Many college rentals are houses that have been divided into multiple units and so do not have separate water meters. The students will expect the property owner to pay water and possibly more utilities if they are not on separate meters.

College rental properties have more turnover than single-family rentals

In one of my single-family rentals, I have had the same tenant for three years. On the other hand, college students are always moving and rarely stay more than a year in one residence. When you have a college rental, you have to expect high turnover and you have to have the properties rented well before the current tenant moves out.

There is a very specific time that college students rent homes for the upcoming school year. Most college rentals are leased in the spring after school is over or in the fall right before school begins. If a home is not rented during these periods, it may not be rented at all or the property owner may have to reduce the rent drastically. The best college renters are usually searching for a place to live months before they have to move in order to make sure they get a good place. That means homes have to be shown while they are being rented. The better your renters are, the better a house will show and the more rent you will get.

Most college rentals are sold to other investors, unlike single-family rentals, which can be sold to either investors or owner-occupants. Because investors buy college rentals, they want to buy a property that is already rented with cash flow. A house that is not rented will be worth much less than one that is.

College rentals may bring in more income than single-family rentals, but they have many more expenses. Depending on your market, a college rental may make more money than a single-family rental, but in my market, I prefer single-family rentals due to fewer expenses and less hassle. Just like multifamily properties, college rentals can also be harder to sell, because investors will be the main buyer pool.

Are condos a good investment?

Finding a great rental property can be tough. In many markets, prices are increasing, and making money on a single-family house or multifamily building is difficult. One option is to buy the cheapest house you can find and make it a rental. You can also buy a townhouse or condo and it turn into a rental property since they are typically less expensive than single-family detached homes.

I think condos or townhouses can be great investments, but you must look at the numbers closely. There are many costs associated with condos that you will not have with single family homes like HOA fees. The appreciation may not be as much on condos and some very scary issues can cause a great condo or townhouse investment to become a nightmare.

What is a condo or townhouse?

A condo is a unit within a large complex of apartments or other condos. There may be units beside, above, or below you.

You rarely have any yard except a shared space with other units.

A townhouse might have a small yard and may have units beside it, but not above or below. Townhomes are typically worth more than condos, because they have less connected neighbors and some land. Both condos and townhomes are worth less than single-family homes that are otherwise similar.

How does an HOA work on a condo or townhouse?

Almost every townhouse and condo has an HOA. The HOA takes care of the shared land in the complex and most take care of the exterior maintenance and landscaping. Many HOAs also pay for the water and may provide common amenities such as a pool, clubhouse, or tennis courts. Some single-family homes are in neighborhoods that have an HOA as well. The HOA fees are usually much higher on a condo or townhouse because the HOA takes care of many more things. Here is a list of many things that an HOA takes care of on single-family detached homes, patio homes, condos, and townhomes.

	Condo or Townhome	Patio Home	Single Family
Common Area	Yes	Yes	Yes
Land-Scaping	Yes	Yes	No
Water Service	Yes	No	No
Exterior Maintenance	Yes	No	No

Exterior Insurance	Yes	No	No
Clubhouse and Pool	Yes	Possibly	Possibly
Trash and Snow Removal	Yes	Possibly	No

A patio home is usually a single-family detached home with an HOA that maintains the lawn. The condo and townhomes have much more involved HOAs, which makes them much more expensive.

In my area, in Northern Colorado, I see HOA fees for most single-family detached homes at around $400 or less a year (if they have an HOA). HOA fees on condos or townhomes are usually at least $100 a month and in some cases $400 a month. HOA fees can be even higher in larger cities with complexes that have security and many more amenities. Only one of my rental properties has an HOA, and it is $300 a year.

Is it bad to have a HOA on a rental property?

I have no problem with having a HOA on one of my rentals. The HOA takes care of the common amenities in the neighborhood and I have never had a problem with them. The only other responsibility of this HOA is to make sure all the homes in the neighborhood comply with the rules and regulations of the HOA. Many HOAs do not allow work trucks to be parked outside or excessive junk to be stored on the yard. For many people this is a good thing and for others it is not. As a property owner, I appreciate having another set of eyes on the property, and I like to know if the tenants have junk everywhere or are not mowing the lawn.

I do not think having a small HOA with few responsibilities is a bad thing. A larger HOA will provide many benefits as well. Even though a larger HOA will be more expensive, it will lower many costs for a property owner. The HOA will pay for exterior insurance and maintenance, which will reduce the property owner's expenses. The HOA will handle yard maintenance and snow removal, which can lower the property owner's expenses as well. In my case, I invest in single-family homes and have the tenants take care of the lawn and pay all utilities, so an HOA does not save me much money.

The drawback with large HOAs is they can charge special assessments if they need extra money for major repairs or if they have financial problems. I know of property owners who had their HOA fees increase greatly in a one year span because the HOA had to repaint the exterior of the entire complex. The HOA fees increased from just over $100 a month to $200 a month for every condo in the complex. Another HOA imposed a $30,000 special assessment on every single condo in a complex to pay for improvements. This particular property owner was planning to flip the condo and all his profit disappeared with this assessment.

An HOA cannot impose a special assessment or raise the HOA fees without agreement from the HOA members, but in many cases the members do not show up to HOA meetings to oppose the changes. Buying a condo or a townhouse with a fixed HOA fee does not mean that the fee cannot be raised or that a special assessment cannot be levied on the property.

Do condos and townhomes appreciate as much as detached homes?

Another factor to consider when buying a condo or townhouse is the value of the property. Condos and townhomes are less expensive than detached homes because they cost less to build and demand is not as great as single-family homes. Single-family homes come with more land and have lower HOA fees. Having an HOA fee reduces the amount a borrower can qualify for when getting a loan. Usually condos and townhomes with the highest HOA fees are worth less than similar condos or townhouses with lower HOA fees because more buyers can afford them. A $100/month HOA fee could reduce the amount a buyer can qualify for by as much as $20,000.

Even though I invest for cash flow when I buy rental properties. That does not mean I do not consider possible appreciation or depreciation on the properties I buy. Some people prefer a condo to a detached home, but most people want a detached home. In my area, condos are the first to start losing value in a down market and the last to increase in value in an appreciating market. While condos and townhouses can appreciate, and often do, single-family detached homes tend to appreciate more.

How can FHA rules affect condo prices?

FHA will loan on condos and townhouses, but they have very strict rules. They will not allow a buyer to use an FHA loan to purchase a condo in a complex if there are too many investors who own properties in that complex. If investors own more than 50 percent of the units in a particular complex, FHA will not loan to anyone in that complex. FHA is a very popular loan and it can greatly decrease values in a complex if the units cannot be sold using FHA. Even though conventional loans do not have to abide by FHA rules.

As you can see, there are many factors you must consider when investing in a condo or a townhouse. The number one factor should be cash flow and how much money you will make. You have to remember to factor in the HOA fees, and the possibility that they may increase in the future. If you buy a condo in an older complex that will need work soon, you may see a huge increase in HOA fees or a special assessment. If many investors decide to buy units in a complex, it could greatly lower the value of every unit due to FHA rules and you will not be able to expect as much appreciation.

I think you can make money with condos, but given similar returns between a condo or townhouse and a single-family detached home, I will take the detached home every time.

Is it wise to buy cheap rental properties?

I prefer single-family rental properties that are slightly below the median sales price in my area. Other investors make money buying multifamily rentals or inexpensive rentals. There is no best way to invest for everyone, but there may be a best way to invest for you based on your market, goals, money available, and many other factors.

In my market in Northern Colorado, the median price is just under $200,000. I have purchased my rental properties from $80,000 to $140,000. I buy my rental properties below market value and make repairs so they are actually worth $150,000 to $200,000 when I rent them out. I would not consider these cheap rentals, because they are not the bottom of my market. In my market, the lowest priced homes are $50,000 to $70,000.

Even though I purchased some of my properties for less than $90,000, it is almost impossible for me to buy properties that fit my criteria for under $110,000 today. When buying my first rental properties, I could have purchased a number of properties for under $50,000, some as low as $30,000. I did not buy these cheap properties for rentals at the time, but looking at prices now, I wish I had! The definition of cheap rental properties varies in every market, but if I had to define it, I would say properties under $50,000 are generally considered cheap rentals.

Why are returns different for different priced rentals?

Rental properties that cost $50,000 or less will have vastly different returns than properties that cost $200,000. Typically, the lower priced rental will have more maintenance and more turnover, as well as lower appreciation over time. There are exceptions to this rule, which can be seen in my market. If I had bought $30,000 rentals in my market a few years ago, I would have made a killing today. Those properties are now worth many times what they were just three or four years ago.

However, since my market had not seen prices as low as they were four years ago since well before 2000. I would not expect every market with $30,000 homes to see the appreciation we did. Many areas that have $30,000 homes for sale have seen low or stagnant prices for years. When buying cheap rental properties, you are usually not betting on appreciation, but investing for cash flow. Many times the rent-to-value ratio on lower priced rental properties is better than on more expensive rental properties. That high rent-to-price ratio is what makes low-priced rental properties attractive to buyers, even with more maintenance and turnover.

Why is the rent-to-value ratio higher on less expensive rentals?

Rental rates are determined by the supply and demand for rentals properties in a given market. Rental rates are not determined by housing prices or the cost to build houses. The lowest rental rates are usually in large apartment buildings. If there is a shortage of apartment buildings in a given market, you will usually see rental rates increase. Eventually when rental rates get high enough, new apartment buildings pop up very quickly to meet the demand, because investors see the need for more units. However, no matter how many apartments are for rent, there will always be people who want to rent single-family homes.

When there is a shortage of single-family homes for rent, builders usually do not build more homes to meet that demand, especially at the low-end of the market. Builders simply cannot build cheap enough in most markets to make new construction rental properties a viable business. Builders target owner-occupant buyers when they build new homes. When there is a shortage of single-family rental properties in an area the rent rates will increase, but unlike apartment buildings, new construction does not ease the supply shortage.

Most markets with low-priced rental properties are found in the Midwest and you may see properties sell for $30,000 that can be rented for $600 to $700 a month. $700 rent on a $30,000 house is a great margin when you consider my properties rent for $1,200 to $1,500 a month.

The rent-to-value ratio may be higher on low-priced rentals, but that does not mean the cash flow is higher. The expenses on a lower priced rental are most likely going to be a higher percentage of the value of the property. Here is an example of how an investor might figure the costs on a higher versus lower priced rental property. These numbers were generated from my cash flow calculator on Investfourmore.com. I am using these numbers based on a higher priced rental property I could buy in my area and a lower priced rental that could be bought in another state.

Higher priced rental bought for $130,000

Rent	$1,500
Maintenance	$225
Vacancies	$150
Taxes	$60
Insurance	$60
Property Management	$120
Total expenses	$615
Cash flow	**$885**

Lower priced rental bought for $35,000

Rent	$700
Maintenance	$140
Vacancies	$70
Taxes	$40
Insurance	$50
Property Management	$56
Total expenses	$356
Cash flow	**$344**

Looking at these numbers, the low-priced rental blows away the high-priced rental when bought for cash. If I were to get a loan on the high-priced rental property, I would have a mortgage payment around $500 a month. That would drop my cash flow to below $400 a month on the high-priced rental property, and if I had to make repairs to this house before I bought it, my cash investment would be similar to the $35,000 the low-priced rental property costs. The returns are not that different between the two properties, but slightly higher with the high-priced rental property. We do need to look at the numbers closer to see why low-priced rentals have different expense ratios than high-priced rentals.

Age: In my cash flow calculator, I devote a higher percentage for maintenance costs on older homes. It is likely the older house will need more maintenance. However, with lower quality tenants you may need to factor in an even higher maintenance allocation.

Lower expenses due to lower rent: The rent is much lower on the cheap property, which makes the expenses much lower for vacancies and maintenance. The entire maintenance allowance for the year on the cheap property is $1,680 and $2,700 on the more expensive property. If the properties were the same size it would not make any sense to have the maintenance that much higher on a more expensive home, but the cheaper rental is much smaller so I think those figures are a decent representation.

Maintenance: I used the same maintenance percentage for the cheap and expensive rental, but this may be misleading. It is true the more expensive rental is rented for more money and lost rent would be higher than the cheap property. However, in my experience the more expensive rentals have more stable tenants. An eviction costs the same no matter what type of rental you have, and the likelihood of an eviction is higher with the less expensive rental. The vacancy cost for the expensive rental comes to $1,800 a year and only $840 a year for the lower priced rental. I think the costs should be similar for both properties.

Insurance: The insurance costs on a house are based on risk and replacement cost. The insurance cost will be less on a smaller home than a larger home, but it will be a higher percentage on the less expensive home. If insurance is $600 a year on a $130,000 house, it will not be $200 a year on the $30,000 house. It may be $400 or $500 a year, which is a higher percentage of the cost compared to the rent.

Property Management: The property management fees should be similar on each property.

When looking at the percentage cost of the expenses on the two properties, the cheap property expenses are over 50 percent of the rent and the expensive properties expenses are just over 40 percent. The expenses may not be high enough for the cheap property, because the vacancies and maintenance may be more than what an investor assumes they will be.

In my experience, expenses have not been as high as this scenario figures, because historically my vacancies and maintenance costs have been lower. While the cheap rental property may look like a slam-dunk on the surface, it does have more expenses and may take more management. That does not mean they cannot make money or that it will not be a good investment.

What are the disadvantages of buying low-priced rentals?

There must be a reason not everyone invests in low-priced rentals with ratios this good. In fact, there are many reasons many investors do not like low-priced rentals.

Higher turnover: When you are renting the lowest priced homes in a market, you tend to get less than ideal tenants. There is a greater chance of evictions, damage, and other problems when renting the lowest priced homes in a market.

More maintenance: Often, the lowest priced rentals in a market are older homes. The older a house, the more maintenance a home will need and lower quality tenants can do more damage to a house.

Less appreciation: I do not like to invest just for appreciation, but it does not hurt to have houses go up in value.

In most cases, the lower the value on a home the less appreciation it will see.

Buy below market value: I buy all my houses below market value and it gives me instant equity. However, 20 percent on a $30,000 house is only $6,000 while 20 percent on a $100,000 house is $20,000. You gain less equity when buying cheaper homes below market value.

Getting a loan: Due to more risk and less profit, most banks do not want to loan on cheap properties. It is very hard to get an investor loan on a $30,000 house.

What are the advantages of buying low-priced rentals?

Buying cheaper properties is not all bad. Lower priced rentals have other advantages in addition to the higher rent-to-value ratio.

Smaller homes: Lower priced rentals are typically older, which means more maintenance. They are also typically smaller which means the maintenance will cost less. Painting a 700 square foot house will be a third the cost of painting 2,000 square foot house. There are fewer windows, smaller furnace, smaller roof, and less floor space. The smaller home may need maintenance more often, but that does not mean the total maintenance costs will be more than on a larger rental.

Can buy with cash: You can spend the same money to buy inexpensive rentals with cash, as you would spend with a loan on a higher priced home. It is difficult for many investors to get loans when they already own multiple rentals, are foreign investors, are investing with an IRA, or show low income on their taxes. Paying with cash is an easy way to buy rentals when you cannot get a loan.

Less chance of loss: With less expensive homes, there is usually less appreciation, but there is also a smaller loss with depreciation as well. Inexpensive homes can go down in value, but if the values drop 30 percent on a $30,000 house versus a $100,000 house, your losses will be much less.

No loan needed: If you are unable to get a loan, you can pay cash for a cheap property. This may be perfect for those looking to invest with their IRA or 401K.

Is it better to buy low-priced or higher priced rentals?

There is no right answer to this question for everyone. You have to figure out for yourself what type of property is right for you. I like higher priced rentals because they are not as old, have less maintenance and less turnover, and sometimes better appreciation. I also have no problem getting loans on my rentals, even with ten mortgages (more on that later).

If you are in a position where it is harder to get a loan, lower priced rentals might be a better option. I prefer to buy rentals locally that I can buy below market value, but if those are not available, I think I would try buying an out-of-state property. If you were having a hard time finding good rentals in your market, buying a cheaper turnkey property could be a good option (we will talk about turnkey properties later on).

I think if you are looking at less expensive versus rentals that are more expensive in your market, you have to look at many factors. Run the numbers on how much money you will make with both properties. Look at historic values on both property types, which property you can get a better deal on and how much management each property will require? If you still cannot decide which type of property to buy, buy one of each and see which one you like better!

Conclusion

Recognizing a great rental property is not easy! It takes hard work to research your market, decide what properties are best, and what properties fit your lifestyle. I have chosen single-family rentals and it has worked great for me, but we are all different.

Can vacation rentals be a good investment?

My wife and I recently went to Turks and Caicos, which is an incredibly beautiful island in the Caribbean. While there, we were tempted to buy a vacation rental. It seems like every time we go on vacation we think about buying a vacation house, but this time we gave it more thought. Turks and Caicos was our favorite place we have ever been and the prices were relatively affordable.

We thought about buying a vacation house, because we love the island and plan to go back repeatedly. At first, buying a vacation rental appears to be a wise decision if you visit the same destination often enough. The plan would be to buy a house or condo on the beach, stay there a few times a year, and rent out the place when we are not staying there. However, when we look at the investing side of a vacation rental, we were reminded why it is not always a wise financial decision.

Before I get started with an analysis of vacation houses, I want to discuss Turks and Caicos. TCI as it is called locally is a chain of islands in the Caribbean between the Bahamas and the Dominican Republic. We choose to vacation there, because the water is crystal clear and has that amazing blue-green color my wife and I love. We have been to Mexico, St Martin, Dominican Republic, and have taken a cruise to a few other destinations in the Caribbean. We enjoyed those destinations, but heard TCI was better, had less people, and was worth the extra money (it is expensive). We were not disappointed in Turks and Caicos; the water was gorgeous, the beaches had soft white sand, and every day we snorkeled at a reef right outside our resort. We saw a giant ray, sea turtles, many tropical fish, a large barracuda, corals, and much more.

The island is not as busy as many other places we have visited and everyone was very friendly. My wife has many food allergies including gluten, soy, dairy, and eggs. The grocery stores were extremely well stocked in allergy friendly and organic food. There are 40 islands in the country, most of them uninhabited, with the same perfect water and beaches. The main island, Providenciales, was expensive, as most are, but was well worth it.

The prices actually seemed somewhat affordable for oceanfront property compared to other places we have been, such as Florida. We stayed at the Coral Gardens, and although there is a rather ugly half-finished resort next to it, it was a lovely resort.

How much money can you make in the Caribbean?

Staying on the island is very expensive. Our one-bedroom condo rented for $400 to $500 a night. It had direct ocean views, a balcony, two baths, and a full kitchen. You can buy similar condos in the same building for under $400,000. On the surface that looks like a great return on your money. Buy a place for $400,000 and rent it for $12,000 a month. That blows the two percent rule out of the water and is a lot higher rent-to-value ratio than I get on my rental properties.

One reason I was intrigued by Turks and Caicos real estate is the rent-to-value ratios. We stayed in Florida on the gulf coast a couple of times in the last few years. On our last trip, we paid $2,400 for a week in a three bedroom, ocean front house. That house was recently for sale for $1.6 million dollars and I guessed it was worth $1.5 million. The rent was less on the beach house in Florida, but the value was over three times as much as the Turks and Caicos condo. This shows how much rents and values can vary in different markets.

The problem with vacation rentals is the cost to manage and maintain them. I pay eight percent of my rents to have my rental properties managed by a property manager. The cost for a property manager on vacation rentals is 20 to 50 percent of the rents! The management fees on the Coral Gardens units that we looked at were 40 percent.

There will be many more vacancies on short-term rentals than on long-term rentals. There are high and low seasons for vacation rentals and you cannot expect to see peak income year round. The total income for 2014 on one unit in TCI was $72,000 and another $62,000. These units were identical and right next to each other, but the income differences show the volatility with vacation rentals. It also shows that you cannot count on $400 a night every night. Weekly rates will be lower, many nights will be vacant, and rates will be much lower in the off-season.

The actual income is not $12,000 a month, but closer to $6,000 a month once you factor in the vacancies and off-season rates.

Why are management fees so high on vacation rentals?

I pay eight percent for someone on my team to manage my rental properties. I used to manage them myself, but once I got to seven rentals I started to run out of time to manage my properties, flip houses, run a real estate team, and write my blog! With a property manager, my properties have become almost completely passive, except when I first buy them.

When you manage a vacation rental, it is an entirely different situation. Vacation rentals take much more marketing, much more active management, have more inquiries from renters, need more cleaning, and are more like a hotel. Managers need to be able to check people in at all times of the day and night and even be a concierge in some cases. More responsibilities and work means you have to pay much higher fees.

Just the property management fees on the Turks and Caicos condos are $20,000 to $30,000 per year! We have not even talked about the other expenses that come with a vacation house.

What expenses would a vacation house have that a regular rental would not?

When you invest in condos you also have to consider HOA or maintenance fees. On beachfront condos, the HOA fees can be very high. There is a pool, maid service, parking lot, and towels. Properties close to the beach have extra expenses. The beach has to be maintained and buildings weather faster due to salt and winds. The occasional hurricane can really cause problems. HOA fees on beachfront condos can easily run $1,000 a month or more.

Vacation rentals must be furnished, have dishes, silverware, linens, televisions, and everything someone would need while staying there. Over time, these items have to be replaced and upgraded to keep the rental unit desirable. If you are charging $400 a night, it had better be very nice.

Vacation rental owners have to pay for all utilities as well. The electric, gas, cable, water, and internet all are added expenses and will most likely cost more in exotic places such as the Caribbean islands. Fresh water comes from rain and desalinization, not wells or rivers. Internet, cable, and electric all cost more.

If you want an oceanfront property, it is almost guaranteed to be in a flood zone. You will have to get flood insurance, which is much more expensive than regular insurance.

Here are the total costs per month of a vacation rental on the beach compared to a regular single-family rental (assuming they rent for the same amount, or you have multiple single-family rentals that rent for the same as one vacation rental):

	Vacation Rental	Single Family
Rent Received	$5,833	$5,833
HOA Fees	$1,000	$0
Property Mgt	$2,333	$467
Utilities	$60	$0
Credit Card Fees	$60	$0
Travel Agent Fees	$300	$0
Maintenance	$600	$600
Taxes	$0	$416
Insurance	$500	$400
Total Costs	**$4,993**	**$1,883**

These are not all the costs, but are meant to show the huge differences between a long-term rental and a short-term vacation rental. I did not include vacancies, because the rents I used for the vacation rental are actual returns. Keep in mind that with a single-family rental property you will have much fewer vacancies than with a vacation rental.

Here are a few more vacation rental costs that I have not discussed.

- If you are renting vacation rentals, most people book with a credit card and you have to pay credit card fees to accept credit cards.
- You pay travel agents a commission to book a vacation rental for you.
- The insurance number could vary greatly. I am assuming five single-family rentals were needed to create that income, but insurance may be more or less, depending on the number of properties. Flood insurance is much higher per property.
- Taxes are very skewed in this scenario on the vacation rental. In TCI, there are no property taxes, but there is a 15 percent tax on all property purchases. You would have to add $60,000 to the purchase price of $400,000 for taxes when you bought the condo. Over five years that would average out to $1,000 a month.
- The utilities on the condos we looked at were not very high, because the HOA took care of the water, electric, and cable. The HOA takes care of the exterior maintenance, but not the interior maintenance. You can see the expenses eat up almost all of the income on the vacation rental. If you consider the huge initial tax bill, all the income is used on the vacation rental and this is if you pay cash!

What about all the money you save when you go on vacation?

The reason most people consider a vacation rental is they think buying a vacation house will save them money. Even though you are actually losing money on this particular vacation condo, maybe it makes sense to buy it if you stay there often enough. You will save thousands on every vacation, right? The problem is, every time you stay at your vacation rental you are taking it off the rental market. You could be renting to someone else and you are losing the rental income.

Is it really an advantage to own a vacation house if you are staying there a week or two every year? Will you also feel obligated to go on vacation every year to the same spot? What if you have to use your vacation time on a wedding, graduation, family reunion, funeral, or another occasion? Most people do not use their vacation properties as much as they thought they would. This is one of the reasons timeshares are such a horrible investment.

All of the numbers I have used so far assume you are paying cash for a vacation rental and you are still losing money! If you get a loan, it will lose even more money. Do you want to tie up $400,000 plus in a vacation rental that you use a couple times a year? That much money would make me over $7,000 a month in rental income, because I can use that money with financing and still make money each month. That $7,000 a month would more than pay for a couple of vacations a year in some nice places! Not to mention, it is not easy to get financing in another country, or even another state.

When would it make sense to buy a vacation rental?

There are some instances when it would make sense to buy a vacation rental, but they can still be very risky.

If you wanted to invest strictly for appreciation, it might make sense to buy a vacation rental. Prices can go down on vacation properties the same as other houses.

If you were going to live in a vacation house for months out of the year, it might make sense.

If you were going to manage the property yourself, you could make money with vacation rentals. However, you have to spend a lot of time on marketing and management.

Even in these scenarios, there are other risks, such as beach erosion, natural disasters, political changes in other countries, insurance changes, and giant half-finished resorts next to your condo!

On the surface, a vacation house may seem like a great investment. They are not making any more oceans and there is only so much beachfront property. If you have to tie up huge sums of cash to buy the property and you lose money every month, is it worth it? For me it is not worth the risk, the money it would take, and the loss of flexibility with my vacation choices. I love Turks and Caicos, but that does not mean I want to spend every vacation there for the rest of my life.

There are many different types of vacation properties and many different locations. Some investors may make a lot of money with their vacation homes, but you have to look at the numbers closely. You also have to remember that the laws and regulations can change. In Florida many areas require at least a one month stay, which hurts ratability of a vacation rental. In Anaheim where we stay at a vacation rental for Disneyland, they passed an ordinance making it illegal to have vacation rentals!

Is it wise to invest in commercial real estate?

Commercial and residential real estate investments are very different and it takes time to learn the ins and outs of each. Commercial real estate may be a great investment for some, but I prefer residential real estate and I think most investors are better off with residential rental properties as well. However, if an investor is well versed in commercial and willing to work hard, you can make a lot of money with commercial real estate as well.

One reason I like residential rental properties is I am a real estate agent who specializes in residential properties. Because I deal with residential properties all day long, I am more familiar with residential rentals than commercial rentals. I know how to buy residential properties below market value and I know my rental market very well. I also invest in residential properties because in my area, residential rental properties tend to give better returns than commercial rental properties.

Are residential rental properties easier to understand than commercial rentals?

Buying a residential rental property is straightforward once you learn your sales and rental markets. You need to know the cost of the house, how much it will cost to repair, how much it will be worth, and for how much it will rent. Even though residential rental properties are not complicated, it still takes time to learn how to invest in them and make money.

Commercial properties on the other hand are much more complicated than residential rental properties. With commercial rental properties, you need to know the same things as you do with residential rental properties, but figuring out those numbers is much more difficult. Factors that affect rent and value are the type of tenant that best suits your building, how long a lease is, how solid your tenant is, and the future desirability of your building. All of this is important with residential, but much more so with commercial. The reason these factors are more important with commercial is that they have a huge impact on the value of the property, whereas single-family residential property is valued from the demand of owner-occupied buyers.

Valuing a residential property is done by determining how much other similar properties are selling for. Many more residential properties sell than commercial properties and it is usually easy to find sold residential properties that are similar to a house you own or are looking to buy. Valuing residential properties based off the sales of other residential properties is called the sales comparison approach.

Commercial properties are rarely valued using the comparison approach, because there are much fewer commercial properties and it is hard to find similar properties that have sold recently. Most commercial properties are valued using the income approach, which is much more complicated than the sales comparison approach.

The income approach uses the income a property generates to value the property. Most commercial properties are valued this way as well as some multifamily residential properties.

The income approach takes the profit a property makes per year and multiplies it by a cap rate to come up with the property's value. The cap rate is not a set figure, but varies in different parts of the country and for different types of properties. When you are buying commercial property, it is very important to know the market cap rates.

What is CAP rate and how do you figure it?

If you have researched investment properties, you have probably heard the terms cap rate and net operating income (NOI). The cap rate on an investment property is a measure of what the returns will be, assuming you pay cash for the property. I do not use cap rate on my investment properties, because it does not factor financing costs. I prefer to use the cash-on-cash return on my properties, but the cap rate can still give you a basic idea of a property's returns.

NOI is the net operating income on a rental property and does not factor in debt service either. The NOI can be another indicator of rental property returns, but can also be easily manipulated.

Cap Rate equals Net Operating Income divided by the price of a property.

For example, if you buy a home for $100,000 and the net income is $10,000 a year, the cap rate is 10 percent. ($10,000/$100,000=10 percent) The cap rate can be figured very easily, but the tricky part is knowing how accurate the income numbers are on a particular property.

Net Operation Income (NOI) is how much the rental property will make after expenses.

Debt service is not included, but property management, taxes, and other expenses should be included. The NOI can easily be manipulated because different investors use different expense numbers. Some investors include allowances for vacancies and maintenance, while others do not. If a property is self-managed, then the property owner many not include any expenses for property management. Make sure you do not blindly trust NOI figures given to you.

Here are expenses that should be included:

- Property taxes
- Property insurance
- Property management fees
- Utilities paid by property owner
- Ongoing maintenance paid by property owner
- Vacancies
- Expected maintenance expenses
- HOA fees
- Any onsite management

How can the cap rate vary greatly on the same property?

If the NOI does not include all expenses on a property, the cap rate is going to be artificially inflated.

If you have $10,000 a year in gross income on a property that does not mean much, because you have not accounted for expenses yet. Accounting for only property taxes and insurance (which I have seen), the NOI might be $8,000 and the cap rate eight percent. However, when you add in the property management, expected maintenance, and vacancies the income may only be $5,000, which would only be a five percent cap rate.

I think the cash flow or cash-on-cash returns are more important, because the cash flow tells you exactly how much money you are going to make, including expenses and debt service. Our cash flow calculator even helps you determine what the maintenance and vacancies may be on a property per month. The cash-on-cash return will tell you what percentage you are making on the money you have invested, which to me is much more important than cap rate.

What can the cap rate tell you about different markets?

The cap rate gives a very basic idea of the return rate on rental properties. If you are looking to invest in long-distance properties, the cap rate can give you an idea of the returns in that area. Average cap rates in the country can range from 5 to 15 percent. There are many other factors to consider when determining where to buy, but cap rate can give you an idea on the returns in different areas.

The cap rates can also give you an idea of the different returns on single-family versus multifamily homes in an area. In Colorado, the cap rate for a multifamily property tends to be around five percent. For a single-family home in my area, you can see cap rates at around eight percent. I buy my properties below market value and see cap rates at ten percent or higher on the purchase of my single-family rentals. In other markets, those percentages may be reversed on single-family and multifamily homes.

The cap rate and NOI can be used to help determine the returns on rental properties, but there are also many other factors to consider such as the cash flow and cash-on-cash returns.

Why does the cap rate on commercial properties change?

If you have a 20,000 square foot warehouse leased for 10 years to a tenant with almost no risk of default, that cap rate will be different from an office building that is half-vacant with mediocre tenants in the other half.

The cap rate will be lower for the property with the stable tenant, because you have a better chance of that tenant paying rent through the end his lease term and the lease is longer. The office building will have a higher cap rate, because there is much more risk involved and it will take work to rent the vacant spaces. Cap rates vary based on the type of tenant, the length of the lease, the credit rating of the tenant, the condition of the property, and market conditions.

As you can see, valuing commercial rental properties can be very complex. You must know the market cap rates for a building, a tenant, and your market. These cap rates are not always easy to figure if you are not very experienced in the commercial real estate market. If you overpay for a commercial building, it could be very hard to ever sell or refinance if needed. Properties that look like an awesome deal may be priced low due to a bad tenant or an uncertain future.

The other problem with valuing properties using the income approach is that you are using information from the current owners for expenses and income. If the owner fudges his numbers or forgets a few expenses, it makes the property look much more valuable than it really is.

Residential properties are usually more stable in a down market

Everybody needs a place to live, but not everyone needs a store or wants to own a commercial investment property. Another reason residential properties are safer than commercial properties is there will be always be a larger buyer pool for residential properties. Even when the market is bad, people will still buy or rent houses, because they need a place to live.

In the commercial market, people may close their shops, work at home, or get another job if the market turns bad. Commercial real estate investors may have trouble getting a commercial loan and will not buy in a down market. This means that it may be incredibly difficult to sell a commercial property in a down market, especially if it is vacant. In a down market, you may have to rent or sell a residential property for less money, but you may not be able to sell or rent a commercial property at all.

Longer leases can be a good thing for investors, but there is a reason commercial leases are longer. Commercial properties typically take longer to rent and are harder to rent than residential properties. Property owners want a longer lease in place on commercial properties, because of the difficulty in leasing them. The cap rate varies so much with commercial properties because when a commercial property goes vacant, it can stay vacant for months or even years. An investor has to consider how long the current lease is and how stable the current tenant is. A ten-year lease is great, but even ten-year tenants can go bankrupt and you are left with a vacant building. Since commercial buildings are usually very specific to the tenant, it could take a long time to lease or a lot of work to retrofit a building for a new tenant.

A commercial lease is very complicated. A commercial tenant has many lease options: a gross lease, triple net, double net, modified gross, etc. The cap rates will change again based on the type of lease and what costs the tenant is paying.

It can be difficult to finance residential properties, but many lenders will loan on them. Typically, you can get 15 or 30-year loan on residential rental properties. With commercial properties, the loan amortization is going to be less than 30 years and most commercial loans will have a balloon payment. A balloon payment means the entire balance of the loan will come due after a certain amount of time, perhaps 5 or 10 years. The investor must pay off the loan when the balloon payment comes due, which is not always easy. Many commercial investors count on being able to refinance their loans when a balloon payment comes due, but that is not always possible. If the lending market becomes tighter, an investor's financials change, or the commercial market changes it may not be possible to refinance.

What opportunities are there in commercial real estate?

Even though commercial real estate can be a very tricky business to be in, there is opportunity to make a lot of money. There are no black and white valuations of commercial properties because there are so many factors to consider with cap rates. That means the people who really know what they are doing can spot good deals or a way to increase the cap rates on properties. If you have a property that is worth $200,000 based on a 10 percent cap rate, that means it is generating $20,000 a year in income. If you can create a more stable lease or rent to more attractive tenants that could lower the cap rate that makes the property more valuable. If the property was generating $20,000 a year income and had an eight percent cap rate, it would be worth $250,000.

An investor could also find a better use for a commercial building, which may increase the income or lower the cap rate. A warehouse may not have a good cap rate in a certain market, because there are vacant warehouses all over. That warehouse could be turned into self-storage units, which are in short supply, increasing the income and lowering the cap rate. Increasing the value of a commercial property could be as simple as taking a vacant building and finding a good tenant on a long-term lease.

For most investors, residential properties are much simpler and easier to understand than commercial properties. A lot of time and experience is required to understand the commercial world and how it functions in the market in which you want to buy. I currently stay away from commercial properties, but I will not rule out investing in them in the future. The most attractive part of commercial investing to me would be increasing the value of properties and quickly turning them like my residential fix and flips. There are so many unknowns with long-term commercial properties because lending can change, financing terms are different, and the vacancies can last a long time.

How do you know what neighborhood to buy rentals in?

When you buy rental properties, the neighborhood the property is located in is extremely important. Landlords who have properties in different neighborhoods can charge different amounts of rent, have houses with different levels of maintenance, and see different turnover rates. Investors can be very successful in every type of neighborhood, but an investor must know what to expect before buying rental property. If an investor is basing their expected returns on a neighborhood with stable tenants and high rents, but end up with high turnover and lower rents, the returns will suffer and the investor could lose money!

If an investor knows they will have to deal with high turnover and maintenance, then they may get great returns in those neighborhoods. The trick is knowing in what type of neighborhood your rental property is. If you have lived in a town your entire life, you may have a good idea about the neighborhoods. Many people are not able to invest in the town they are most familiar with due to relocation or rental property returns. How can investors figure out what neighborhoods they want to invest in when they are unfamiliar with the town?

Why can you not trust a real estate agent to tell you about good neighborhoods?

A real estate agent may seem like the first choice for determining a good neighborhood. However, I am a real estate agent and it is illegal for me to tell my clients or anyone that a neighborhood is good or bad; it is considered steering.

It is illegal for me to recommend neighborhoods because my opinion of what a good neighborhood is may be different from someone else's. If people used my judgement to determine a good neighborhood, they would all buy houses in the same neighborhoods. If everyone bought houses in the same neighborhoods, it would push up values in some neighborhoods and lower values in other neighborhoods.

Not everyone wants to live in the same area. We all have different reasons for living where we do and why we think some neighborhoods are better than others are.

Not only do real estate agents shy away from offering general opinions on neighborhoods, many do not talk about crime rates, school ratings, or demographics such as ethnicity. It is also illegal for agents to talk about many of these characteristics. You may be frustrated that your real estate agent will not give you the neighborhood information you want; it is not because they are a bad agent, it is because they cannot legally do it.

Since a good neighborhood is relative to what buyers are looking for, but it is up to each buyer to figure out what a good neighborhood is to them. A buyer needs to figure out what they want in a neighborhood first. Neighborhood characteristics that a buyer should consider are:

- Crime rates
- School ratings
- Home prices
- Age of homes
- Size of homes
- Size of the town
- Proximity to large population areas
- Local economy
- HOAs
- Type of homes (multifamily or single-family)
- Tax rates

Many more characteristics will affect values and rent rates in a neighborhood. If you want to buy rental properties, the returns you get are going to be determined in large part to how well you research and judge neighborhoods. Remember you are not judging a neighborhood on whether you would live there, but on whether it would be a good investment.

How can investors decide what neighborhood is best to buy rental properties?

Since every market is different, there is no set formula for a great rental property; it boils down to the numbers. You may get higher rent-to-value ratios on low priced homes, but you might have more turnover and maintenance on those homes.

You might have less maintenance and turnover on high priced rentals, but the cash flow may not be as high. I personally like to find a happy medium with good cash flow and low maintenance and turnover.

Once an investor knows what type of neighborhood they want to invest in, here are some tips for determining if a neighborhood meets your expectations.

- Call the local police department. Many times the local police will tell you what the crime rates are and even tell you what neighborhoods have high crime.
- Drive through neighborhoods on the weekends and in the evening. Driving through neighborhoods will give you an idea of the upkeep of houses and traffic.
- Check websites that give neighborhood information statistics such as City Data.
- Ask friends or people you know who live in the town in which you want to invest. If you do not know anyone in that town, try to meet some people! People who are not real estate agents can give you their opinion and much more information on neighborhoods.
- Talk to people in the neighborhoods in which you want to invest. When you are driving around looking at houses and you see someone doing yard work or walking their dog, ask them what they think of the neighborhood.

It is not easy to determine what the best neighborhoods to invest in is. Each investor's idea of the perfect neighborhood will be different based on their expectations on returns, willingness to make repairs, familiarity with a location, and much more. If you do not know a town or neighborhood well, make sure you do your due diligence before you buy.

5. How do you buy real estate below market value?

One of the keys to my investment strategy is to buy houses below market value. This is not easy to do and you cannot just call up a real estate agent and ask them to find you awesome deals from the MLS. It takes patience, hard work, the ability to act fast, and nerves to buy houses below market. If you learn how to buy right, it is a lot of fun and you will make a lot of money.

I have bought every house I have owned, except for the first one, below market value. I bought my first house when I was 22, back in 2002. I bought the house for $188,000 and ended up putting at least $10,000 of materials into the home and a lot of sweat equity over seven years. In 2009, I managed to sell the home for $190,000. Talk about a huge disappointment! I learned that I could not depend on the market to increase to make money in real estate. I had to buy below market value and force equity into the property.

For my next house, I bought a foreclosure from the Public Trustee. We bought this house for $220,000 by borrowing money from my sister and father-in-law (I had to pay cash at the sale). I was able to refinance the property and pay them back in full. My wife and I lived in that house for three years, and thanks to getting an awesome deal and some market appreciation, we sold the house for $350,000. That was a tax-free profit since I lived in the house for at least two years, and I was able to use that money for the down payment on our current house.

The advantages of buying real estate below market value are incredible and definitely worth the effort.

How do you determine market value on real estate?

If you are not a real estate agent it is very difficult to determine fair market value, but still possible. If you are just beginning to invest in real estate, it is wise to use multiple ways to find market value. One of the most important factors in determining what a good investment property is, is the market value.

When you are fix and flipping homes, it is obvious that market value is the most important factor to determine a profit. Actually, ARV (after repaired value) is the most important factor, because you want to know what the home will sell for when it is fixed up. When you are buying long-term rental properties, the market value may not be as important as it is on a fix and flip. However, you still need to know the market value of a long-term rental for many reasons.

- You need to know the market value on a long-term rental because you may have to sell it one day. There are many reasons why you may have to sell, even though you may not plan to when you buy the home. You could have a financial setback, a medical problem, a relationship issue, or some other emergency. You may decide you do not like investing in rentals or you may need the money for an incredible opportunity. I want to buy 100 rental properties, but if a better opportunity comes along and I need to sell some of my rentals, I will have no problem selling them for much more than I bought them.

- A great way to get money to buy more rental properties is to refinance your current properties. Almost every lender will want less than a 75 percent loan-to-value ratio on an investment property refinance. The best way to gain equity is to buy homes below market value. The more equity you have in a property, the more money will be able to take out when refinancing. I have refinanced 7 rental properties over the last four years and taken out over $200,000 in cash. They still have great cash flow even after the refinance because I got great deals on them.

- In order to get loans on multiple rental properties, you have to know a great bank and be able to convince that bank it is a good idea to invest in you. A bank will look at many factors when lending to investors. Most importantly, they want to know that the investor is in a good financial position. If you own eight properties with little or no equity, that is not a good position. Owning eight properties with 50 percent equity is a great financial position to be in and a bank will be more willing to give you a loan.

The easiest way to determine market value is to hire a professional. I am a Realtor and I provide comparative market evaluations for sellers all the time. I also provide values for investors and buyers as well. The trick for the new investor is convincing a Realtor that you are a serious investor and they are not wasting their time. The easiest way to overcome this problem is to buy a house, but that is not realistic for a beginning investor trying to figure values.

My advice is to be perfectly honest with agents. Tell them you are new and you are trying to figure market values. It helps if you have done some work first and can ask them if the value you came up with seems accurate. Then buy them lunch or give them something in return. Simple gestures like buying lunch can make a huge difference in convincing someone to help you.

Do not ask the agent for ridiculous things or make huge requests. Do not ask for 100 values or sales comps from the last two years for an entire town. I recently had an investor ask me for all the cash sold comps in the last year for metro Denver. Then he wanted me to put them all on an excel sheet and email them to him. I had never talked to this investor prior to this request, and I was just a little put off that he expected me to put in hours and hours of work for him. He gave me no reason to do this work and did not even tell me why he wanted this information. To top it all off, I am not even in the Denver market!

How to come up with a house value on when you are not a Realtor

I mentioned that it would be good to have your own value in mind when talking to an agent, but how do you come up with a value yourself? It is not easy to value a home unless you use a website like Zillow. However, Zillow is not always accurate. Some of the values were as much as 40 percent off when I compared my own properties values to Zillow values! I would not trust Zillow to provide a value on a home, although you can get some great information from Zillow.

I use sales comparables to determine property value. I compare multiple sales in the last six months that are as similar as possible to the home I am valuing. I am a Realtor, so I can easily pull up any sold comps I want from MLS. If you are not a

Realtor, it is not as easy to find sold comparables. You can find sold comps online at Zillow and a few other websites, but you do not get all the information you need with those sold comps.

Zillow uses all the sold comps it can find: foreclosures, short sales, and sometimes trustee sales. The reason this is important is you do not always know if those were market sales or just sales. A trustee sale price could simply be the amount the bank was owed and not a market value. You also do not know what the condition of the sale was, any concessions, or the financing terms. You do not know how long a home was for sale, how many price changes there were, or if it was a short sale or REO. These are vital details necessary to make an accurate valuation.

It is possible for an investor who is not an agent to determine a range of values from online comps, but you still need to talk to an agent to make sure your values are accurate. If you have a great agent, they will probably offer you sold comps in an area and make your life much easier!

It is also possible to use active listings to value properties. It is not easy to use this method, because an active listing does not mean it will sell for the asking price or if it will sell at all. Active comps do give you an idea of what is for sale in a neighborhood and what the competition is. I use active comps to value properties along with sold comps. You can use active comps for a broad value, but not a solid value. The best way to use active comps for values is to track them over time. Keep track of the asking price, when they go under contract, and for how much they sell. When you know the history of a sale on a website like Zillow, then that comp becomes much more valuable.

Adjusting for values on an investment property

When you find sold and active comps that are similar to your subject, your work is not done. You then have to decide if you need to make adjustments for the differences between the comparables and the property you are valuing.

If you are valuing a home with a one-car garage and the sales comps you are comparing have a two-car garage, you have to make an adjustment. If the bedroom, bathroom, or room count is different, if square footage is different, views, location, or anything else is different you need to make adjustments. Coming up with how much to adjust is the tricky part. More expensive homes have different adjustment amounts than less expensive homes. Different areas of the country put more value in certain amenities than other parts of the country. I am not going to tell you how much to make adjustments because I am not in your market.

Again, a real estate agent can help you figure out how different amenities add value. When you look at enough homes and comparables, you should start to get an idea of how much features and size add in value. It will take time to get to know your market and accurately be able to figure values and adjustments.

Here are a few adjustments I would make on my rentals in the $150,000 price range.

- 1 car versus 2 car garage: $4,000 to $7,000 adjustment
- 3 bedroom versus 2 bedroom: $2,000 to $4,000 adjustment
- 1,500 square feet versus 1,200 square feet: $6,000 to $12,000 adjustment

A $2,000 adjustment does not seem like very much, but you have to consider the house also has more square footage that would add value as well. You have to look at the entire picture when making adjustments to make sure they make sense.

What are the different ways to buy houses below market value?

There are many ways to buy real estate below market value including buying REOs, short sales, estate sales, HUD homes, off market properties, and even fair market sales. It can take time, work, and the ability to act quickly to get a great deal. Of course getting a great deal is only part of the equation. I have used the techniques listed below to purchase homes for long-term rentals and fix and flips.

How to buy bank owned properties (REOs) below market value

REO (Real Estate Owned) is a term for properties banks have taken back through foreclosure. REO properties are usually listed in the MLS (Multiple Listing Service) by an REO listing agent. I am a REO listing agent myself, and I can tell you that each bank handles their REOs very differently. Some banks repair homes before they list them and others do not fix anything. Some banks are willing to negotiate quite a bit on their prices and others will hardly budge.

REOs are getting harder and harder to find due to the improving housing market. There are still some great deals on REOs, but usually the deals are on homes that need many repairs.

If you find a great deal on a REO, do not be surprised if you find yourself in a highest and best situation. Many banks ask for highest and best when they receive more than one offer on a property. There is a ton of competition for REO properties right now and multiple offers are not rare. Highest and best gives every buyer who made an offer a chance to raise his or her offer and hope it is good enough to get the property. In many highest and best situations, the winning offer is higher than the actual asking price. I will discuss highest and best in more detail later in this chapter as many sellers now use it.

Many banks prefer a cash offer from an investor and sometimes they actually prefer an owner-occupant buyer. Sellers like Fannie Mae, Freddie Mac, and Wells Fargo only allow offers from owner-occupant buyers at the beginning of the listing period. This can be frustrating for investors looking for a good deal, but there is no way around their owner-occupant restrictions. It is against the law to pretend to be an owner-occupant when you will not be occupying the property.

You need a real estate agent to buy almost any REO property. Buyers see vacant REO properties and think that if they can just talk to the bank, the bank will sell it to them well below market value. The truth is that the banks have strict guidelines for how they sell houses and they almost never sell them without putting them in the MLS system. Trying to contact the bank to get them to sell it to you is almost always a huge waste of time, unless they are a very small local bank.

How can you get a great deal on a HUD home?

HUD homes can be an incredible opportunity for investors to get a great deal on a property. However, some investors are apprehensive about bidding on HUD homes, because purchasing a HUD homes is much different from purchasing a traditional listing or even an REO. HUD also gives priority to owner-occupant buyers over investors. Once you know the HUD system, it becomes very easy to submit bids and buy HUD homes. I happen to be a HUD listing broker and I know the HUD system very well.

HUD homes are homes that have been repossessed by the United States government after going through foreclosure. HUD homes were previously purchased with government insured FHA loans. When HUD becomes the owner, they sell the homes through local listing brokers such as myself and list them on www.hudhomestore.com. Hudhomestore.com lists all HUD homes for sale that are not currently under contract. Once a HUD home has a bid accepted on it, it is taken off Hudhomestore.com and the status in MLS is changed to under contract. HUD homes are sold in an online auction format; all bids must be submitted online by a licensed real estate agent who is registered with HUD.

When can investors bid on HUD homes?

HUD has very strict owner-occupancy restrictions on the houses they sell. HUD has two main classifications for their properties: FHA insurable and uninsurable. On FHA insured HUD homes, only owner-occupants, nonprofits and government agencies can bid the first 15 days that the home is on the market (typically called the owner-occupant only period). For uninsured homes, the owner-occupancy only bid period is the first five days. Investors can bid on HUD homes on the sixteenth day for insured properties and on the sixth day on uninsured HUD homes.

When a HUD homes goes under contract, HUD stops the daily count for a home being on the market. If a HUD home goes under contract on the eleventh day and that contract falls apart, then the home would come back on the market 11 days into the bid period. Therefore, some HUD homes have been for sale for 30 days, but are still in the owner-occupant period. An investor can see whether a HUD home is insured or uninsured on the Hudhomestore website.

- If a home is listed as only available to owner-occupants, an investor can see when they can bid by looking at the period deadline. The period deadline will tell you when the last day of the current bid period is.

HUD typically changes the price on HUD homes every 35 to 50 days a home is actively on the market. HUD does not have a new owner-occupant bid period when they change the price on a home. Investors can bid the first day after a price change.

What are the penalties if investors bid as owner-occupants on HUD homes?

A HUD home is federal property, which means that any crime committed involving a HUD property, is usually considered a felony. HUD is very clear that any investor who bids as an owner-occupant is **subject to two years in federal prison and up to $250,000 in fines**. HUD does prosecute investors who have been caught buying in the owner-occupant period. HUD also may take away the ability for the real estate agent representing the buyer and their office to sell HUD homes. Not only HUD, but also other investors, watch these properties looking for investors who are breaking the rules and report them.

It is also a felony for investors to make repairs to a HUD home before they buy it or to move anything onto the property before closing.

Why are HUD homes a great way for investors to buy houses below market value?

HUD has an appraisal done on each of their homes before they are listed. That appraisal is usually the list price and determines how much HUD will take for the home. For whatever reason, many HUD appraisals come in very low compared to market value. If a HUD home makes it through the owner-occupant bid period, they can be a great opportunity for investors. Uninsured HUD homes, (homes that need more than $5,000 in repairs), do not qualify for FHA loans. The more repairs that a HUD home needs, the better its chance of making it to the investor bid period. Uninsured homes are much more likely to be bought by investors. I have sold many HUD homes to investors who were able to flip the house or get a great deal on a rental property, because they needed a lot of work.

HUD uses different formulas in different areas of the country to determine how much less than list price they will accept. In Colorado, HUD usually does not take less than 90 percent of the list price unless a home becomes an aged asset. HUD considers a home to be an aged asset that has been actively on the market for more than 60 days. In my market, once a HUD home becomes aged, HUD may accept 80 percent of list price. If a HUD home is on the market for an extended period, they may take even less. However, the discounts are figured on a case-by-case basis and there is no across the board rule. In other parts of the country, I have seen investors buy HUD homes for 80 percent of the list price in the first month.

On some aged assets, investors are getting HUD homes at 50 percent or less of list price.

If HUD receives a bid that is close to the price they will take, they may counter a buyer. It never hurts to submit a low offer to HUD, the worst they will do is not accept your bid. HUD does not blackball investors who submit many offers; in fact, HUD encourages all bids to be submitted no matter how low they are. The only exception is when an investor is submitting the same bid every single day. There is no need to resubmit a bid over and over and may annoy HUD. HUD keeps track of the bids and usually notifies buyers of a price change or if they will now consider a bid that was too low in the past. I would still submit new bids if the price changes.

Speed is the key to an investor getting a HUD home. Many investors are waiting for HUD homes to make it to the investor bid period and most good deals will be bid the first day investors are eligible.

Investors can also use a trick on uninsured homes to gain an advantage over other investors. HUD opens bids the next business day after the five-day owner-occupant bid period is over. HUD does not open bids first thing in the morning; they usually open them mid-morning or later depending on how busy they are. At the beginning of the sixth day, an uninsured HUD home will be available for investors to bid on, even though HUD may be accepting an owner-occupant bid later in the day. Investors should always try to get their bid into the system on that sixth day, because HUD homes tend to fall out of contract more than other properties.

If an owner-occupant cancels their contract, HUD moves on to any backup offers in their system that are an acceptable price before they put the home back on the market. If the house comes back on the market, an investor who bid on the sixth day could have their bid accepted before any other investors get a chance to bid on the home.

Investors should always have their real estate agent mark yes to backup position when bidding on a HUD home. There is no penalty to buyers if they mark yes to backup position and later on decide they do not want the home. There is also a chance that HUD will accept an investor's low bid if HUD changes the price on the home and that low bid is now in an acceptable range to HUD.

How does HUD handle inspection periods with investors?

A very important point to remember is HUD does not give earnest money back to investors if they cancel their contract. HUD is very clear that they consider investors "savvy" and if an investor cancels due to inspection items, the earnest money is forfeited to HUD. If an investor is using financing and their loan cannot be completed, they may get half of their earnest money back. I always tell investors to expect to lose their earnest money if they cancel a HUD contract. HUD also does not pay for title insurance or any closing fees that other sellers typically pay.

HUD homes can be a great deal for investors who know how the system works. It can take some time to get used to the system and learn all the HUD dates and procedures. Many investors shy away from HUD, because it is different and can be confusing. This creates more opportunity for the investors who are willing to learn the HUD system. My best advice is to find an agent who knows the HUD system very well.

How can you get a great deal from real estate wholesalers?

Wholesaling real estate involves an investor buying a property or getting a property under contract and selling the house or assigning the contract as quickly as possible. The investor may wholesale the property to another investor who will then fix up the property and rent or flip it.

Finding wholesalers is another way for investors to find great deals, but it can be tricky finding good wholesalers and most deals have to be done with cash.

If you want to wholesale, you have to be very careful when you assign contracts on houses. Some states consider finding a buyer and seller as performing duties of a real estate agent. Even if you have the house under contract, it may be considered acting as a real estate agent to assign that contract. If you are placing signs in the yard, advertising on Craigslist, or marketing with flyers without owning the house, it could also be considered practicing real estate without a license. Check with your state laws before performing any of these activities or dealing with investors who perform these activities.

How do wholesalers find their properties?

The best wholesalers tend to find their deals with off-market properties. Off-market properties are not listed for sale, but the owners want to sell. The owners may be too far away, too busy, or too beat down to list the home with a real estate agent. The owners want to sell the home, they just need the right person to find them and make an offer. Here are a few ways that wholesalers find properties.

- **Attend REIA meetings**: You may find investors or wholesalers with off market properties at REIA meetings.

Meeting other wholesalers at the meetings will not do a wholesaler much good unless it is an incredible deal. Investors looking to get rid of homes at the meetings may be a fantastic opportunity. You can also find buyers at REIA meetings, which is also very important to a wholesaler.

- **Send direct mailings**: I send out direct mailings and I have purchased off-market properties because of my letters. I started my mailings this year and I think it will be a successful tactic given enough time and effort. I send mailings to absentee owners and inherited owners. As a Realtor, I can also list homes that may not work out a purchase, but I also have to disclose that I am a Realtor and I disclose that I may be buying homes below market value. It is a double-edged sword, but is still think it is very advantageous to be an agent. I recently bought my first property through direct marketing and I will be the first to tell you I am not an expert yet at direct marketing.

- **Advertising for off-market properties**: Many investors advertise on billboards, with websites, with bandit signs, and with billboards that they buy houses. I have not tried these tactics yet, but I do want to try a few of them. I do not put any signs in my car; I love my cars too much.

- **Websites**: A few websites market to off-market sellers. When the website gets a lead, they sell it to investors who pay to get those leads. I have never used these websites, but I know investors who have gotten deals from the sites.

- **Drive for dollars**: One of the best ways to find off-market properties is to drive around looking for vacant homes.

Many times sellers are motivated when a house is vacant and they will be willing to sell cheap.

The best way to get the best deals as a wholesaler are not easy to implement. It takes time and a great deal of effort to buy homes off-market. If it were easy, all investors would use these tactics, but it is difficult and very few investors market to off-market sellers. It is possible for investors to use these tactics to get flips and rentals as well.

How do wholesalers get houses under contract?

A wholesaler usually has two options: get a contract on a house or buy the house and sell it right away. Many MLS listings require proof of funds or a pre-qualification letter, which makes it tough for wholesalers to buy off the MLS. Most REOs and HUD listings will not let you assign the contract; you will have to buy the home. It is easier to wholesale off-market properties, because they do not require pre-qualification letters. Once a wholesaler gets a contract on an off-market property, they attempt to assign the contract to another investor for a fee or sell the property to another investor as quickly as possible.

What does it mean to assign a contract?

Assigning a contract is a simple concept. The contract has a clause that allows it to be assigned to another person who can step in and become the buyer without the seller's permission. A wholesaler can actually sell the contract to another investor without buying the home. Anyone else can step in and be the buyer as long as they buy the home according to the terms of the contract.

Wholesalers can buy a home to sell immediately without using their own money. I have never done this, but it is possible for investors to buy a home and then immediately sell it without using their own money. First, you need a great title company that will do a double close. The seller sells the home to the wholesaler, who immediately sells the home to the end buyer. The title company uses the end buyer's money to pay the original seller. Please check your state laws to make sure this strategy is legal in your area.

How does a wholesaler find buyers?

Once a wholesaler finds a house to sell or assign, they need a buyer! Usually the margins are very tight on wholesale deals and there is not room to pay real estate commissions. The wholesaler must find buyers in order to make the most money on wholesale deals. A wholesaler must also close very quickly to be able to assign the contract or complete a double close within the contract periods.

As I mentioned earlier, REIA meetings are a great way to find investor buyers. Check recent sales to find who bought houses for cash, as they are most likely investors. I just received a letter from a wholesaler who found me because I bought a house for cash. Hang out where investors who buy houses hang out; trustee sales, auctions, and tax sales are all great places. Advertise to find buyers on Craigslist or in the newspaper. Look for recent cash sales on the MLS or in public records to see what investors are buying houses for cash in your area. Finding buyers is an extremely important part of wholesaling and often a wholesaler's biggest challenge. In some instances, a wholesaler will use another wholesaler with more buyer contacts to help them sell houses.

How can an investor find a wholesaler?

Now that you know what a wholesaler does, you may want to start looking for a few. I have bought a couple of properties from wholesalers, although they were both flips and not rentals. I did not find the wholesaler who I bought properties from, they found me. I am a real estate agent and this wholesaler sent an email to every agent they could find. They said they have off-market properties for sale and if the agents have buyers, they could add the commission on to the buy price. I immediately contacted the wholesaler and told them I was a cash investor. They added me to their email list and every time they get a new property they send me the information.

There are many other ways to find wholesalers:

- Call bandit sign numbers (the signs on the side of the road that say we buy houses).
- Call billboard numbers for people who advertise they buy houses.
- Go to REIA meetups in your area.
- Search online for wholesalers in your area.
- Search Craigslist for people advertising that they buy homes.
- Ask other investors or real estate agents if they know of any wholesalers or received emails like the one I did.

It can be very frustrating finding good wholesalers. Many real estate gurus teach investors how to wholesale properties and claim it is the easiest way to get into real estate without much money. I would estimate 9 out 0f 10 people who call themselves wholesalers, never do a deal. Do not be surprised id most wholesalers you find, never send you a deal. If you can find a good one, it will be well worth it.

How to buy short sales below market value

Short sales are another great way for investors to find deals. Short sales are owned by private sellers who are selling the home for less than they owe the bank. In order to sell the home, the bank has to agree to take less money than what they are owed.

Historically, short sales could take up to six months or even a year to close, because lenders were so slow to make a decision. In the last couple of years, banks have gotten much quicker at making decisions and some short sales are approved in two weeks or less (some banks still take months). Many times on short sales, the first party to make an offer will get the home. You have to act very quickly when a great short sale deal comes on the market. Remember, even if you get your offer accepted by the seller, there is no guarantee the bank will approve the offer. It is wise to wait to perform an inspection or start the loan process until you have written approval of your offer from the seller's lien holders.

You have to be careful when buying off-market properties as short sales. The banks are very strict about how what offers they accept as short sales. If a buyer and seller are using a short sale to sell a house, but not disclosing all the terms to the bank, it could be fraud. A couple of years ago, short sale fraud was the most investigated crime by the FBI. Most banks require that short sales be listed on the MLS by an agent, that the buyer and seller cannot be related, and the homes sells for close to market value. A good real estate agent can help buyers navigate the short sale process.

How to buy fair market sales below market value

Fair market sale homes are owned by a private seller who has enough equity in the home to sell without having to involve the bank in the decision-making (short Sale). It is harder to find great deals on fair market sales because sellers are usually not in a huge rush to sell their home below market value. There are some cases where you can find a great deal on a fair market sale.

I have purchased properties from estates that were great deals. Many times, estates just want to get rid of the home because they have issues or creditors that need to be paid quickly. I have also purchased a home that the seller had recently bought as foreclosure. The home needed a lot of work. They did not have the money needed to complete the repairs, but the market appreciated enough that they could sell the home.

Another situation where an investor can buy below market value is an investor owned home. The investor owned home is usually rented, and although it may be perfect for a first time homebuyer, the first time homebuyer cannot wait three months for the tenants to move out. The only choice for the investor is to sell the home to another investor for a discount. There are some investors who try to flip homes, but run out of money and have to sell before the home is completed.

I buy many of my flips and rentals as fair market sales. We will talk about strategies to buy these properties in later sections about making offers.

How to buy off-market properties below market value

Many investors buy off-market properties that have not been listed on MLS, and have not been marketed in any way. Basically you are using the same techniques a wholesaler uses to find properties, but instead of selling the houses to another investor, you keep them. It takes money and time to be able to purchase these types of investment properties. Investors send out direct mail or postcards or advertise with signs that let people know that they buy houses. I am sure you have heard of "We Buy Ugly Houses." They use billboards, newspaper ads, and their giant trucks to advertise to potential sellers.

There are some home owners who want to sell their home, but do not want to list it on the MLS. The home could need extensive repairs, the sellers may not want anyone to know they are selling the house, the sellers may need to sell extremely fast or other factors may cause a seller to want to sell off the MLS or off-market. The difficulty in buying off market properties is finding motivated sellers, who do not have their homes up for sale.

- **Drive for dollars**: Driving for dollars is when you look for vacant homes. When you find the vacant home you try to contact the owners of the home to see if they will sell it you.
- **Direct marketing:** Direct marketing involves sending postcards, letters, posting bandit signs, creating websites and trying to get sellers to call you.
- **Networking:** There are many people advertising they have off-market properties directly from banks. Please be careful as banks almost never sell off individual

properties without using MLS. You can use your network of investors, agents and other professionals to find off market properties. Be very careful and do not get your hopes up with unknown internet solicitations.

- **Bandit signs:** The easiest way to start marketing to sellers is to stick out a few bandit signs, which are signs that say you buy houses. Investors like to put these on busy street corners or in neighborhoods they want to buy in. Many cities have made bandit signs illegal and if your signs disappear it could be the city removing them or another investor who wants less competition. I do not use bandit signs, because of the real estate agent disclosure issues.

- **Websites:** If you can create a website to attract sellers in your area, it can be a great source of leads. I am not an internet wizard, even though I created this blog I have had a ton of help. This company specializes in creating websites to attract motivated sellers. If you are reading the paperback version of this book go to https://investfourmore.com/2015/08/24/how-to-buy-off-market-properties-from-motivated-sellers/

How can you start a direct marketing campaign?

The most lucrative way to find great off market deals is to create your own direct marketing campaigns. Creating a direct mail campaign is not easy and there is a reason most investors will never venture into this field or will not stay long enough to be successful. I have my own direct mail campaigns and I have purchased and listed homes from direct mail. Since I am a real estate agent I have a couple of different ways to use direct mail, but I have to disclose I am an agent and be very careful buying homes. I always have a seller sign a disclosure that states I am buying the home below market and I may profit from the purchase. **Check with state laws if you are an agent trying to buy off market properties**.

Direct mailing is one of the best ways, if not the best way to find motivated sellers. Direct mail involves sending letters or postcards to people who may be interested in selling their home. There are many different mailings to use and many different segments to send that list out to.

The first step in creating a direct mailing campaign is coming up with a list to send mail too. I use List Source to come up with absentee owners in my area. I also use a company that gives me a list of inherited properties. We send different postcards out to each list and update the lists a few times a year.

Once you have your lists you have to send out letters or postcards to the list. I have seen many varying opinions on whether postcards or letters is better and it seems to come down to testing. Everyone is in a different market and different lists consists of different owners. With some owners a post card works better and with other owners a letter may work better. Try out different letters and post cards and see which one gets you the most motivated sellers calling. Usually you want to say something about buying houses for cash, with no commissions, repairs needed and fast.

One letter will not get the job done. You have to send out five letters or postcards to the same person before they will respond. You want to make sure you respond right away to any calls. We have a dedicated number set up just for postcard calls so we can call them back whether they leave a message or not.

It is a lot of work to set up a direct mail campaign, and it takes a lot of persistence. This is why most investors will not do it or see a campaign through.

What do you say to motivated sellers?

The scariest part of any direct mail campaign is talking to the sellers. Many people will call you very upset that you are sending them mail asking to buy their house. Usually when you talk to them and explain you are buying houses in the neighborhood and are pleasant, they calm down. You will have to deal with some property owners who have nothing better to do than to yell and complain. I had one lady threaten to call the police if I did not stop sending her letters, but she refused to tell me her name or address so I could take her off my list.

There will also be many property owners hoping to sell their house, but they want full retail value without paying a real estate commission. You will also talk to motivated sellers who want to sell right away and are willing to take a lower price for their home, because of the urgency or the condition. I talk as much as I can to the sellers to see why they are selling, how much they want for their house, and when they want to sell. Many times the sellers are happy just to talk to anyone to tell their story.

Since I am an agent I like to give sellers a couple of options. I am very honest with them and tell them that most of the time they will get more money if they list the home on the MLS. Even knowing they will get more money on the MLS there are some sellers who don't want to list on the MLS or the homes are in such bad shape that it makes more sense for me to buy them. Otherwise, as an agent I can list the home for them and make money that way. If you are not an agent you may be able to sell your leads to a real estate agent, but it is illegal in most states for a real estate agent to pay a referral fee to someone who is not licensed.

When you talk to a seller you want to highlight the advantages of selling to you.

- No repairs needed
- No commissions
- No closing costs
- Fast closing
- Cash closing
- No showings
- No appraisal

These advantages are for an investor who can pay cash for houses and close very quickly. Some wholesalers will use these terms as well assuming they can assign a contract to a cash investor who will buy the property. Don't lie to the seller and claim you can buy with cash if you have to get a loan. Almost all the successful investors I talk to have a couple of things in common. They know their market like no one else, they are honest and follow through on deals if they say they will buy a house.

How to get great deals below market from auctions

Buying a house from a foreclosure auction is another way to get a great deal, but it comes with risk. Auctions tend to have less competition because they have stricter requirements for buyers and many times you cannot inspect the house or even see the inside of it before buying. I have bought many houses from auctions over the years and made money on many, but I have also lost money on a few.

The fewer people you have to compete with when buying a house, the better chance you have of getting a great deal. Many times auction companies have strict criteria for buying their houses.

- **Cash purchases:** Many auctions require the buyer to pay cash for houses on which they bid. Foreclosure auctions may require the buyer to have cash the same day they bid or before they bid on a property.

- **No inspections:** Many auctions do not allow buyers to inspect a house before they bid on it, as most traditional sales do. In some cases, a house may be occupied and the buyer cannot inspect the interior until they buy. I am buying a house now that is occupied and I have never seen the interior. If the house is occupied, you cannot just kick out the occupant. You have to evict them or possibly honor their lease if they have one.

- **Non-refundable earnest money:** When you buy a house, you have to submit earnest money to the seller. If your financing falls through or you find a problem in your inspection, you usually get your earnest money back. With an auction property, if you back out of the contract for any reason you usually do not get your earnest money back.

- **Short notice:** Some state foreclosure sales give buyers very little time to know what houses will be bid on and how much the starting bids will be. Other online auctions give buyers much more notice before an auction. In Colorado, we are given the sale list for properties two days before the sale.

- **Clear title:** Many foreclosure auctions do not guarantee clear title. There is no guarantee you are even bidding on the first loan.

All of these factors make it tough for most buyers to purchase homes from auctions. The majority of homebuyers are owner-occupants who need to get a loan. Most investors also need a loan to buy property and auctions that require cash eliminate those buyers as well. Many buyers are scared of auctions because of the possibility of losing earnest money, no inspections, and other issues. That usually leaves experienced investors to battle over properties at auctions. The experienced investors know how much they can pay for houses, handle the risk, and still make money. Some online auctions are less risky than foreclosure auctions, which can provide opportunities for less experienced buyers.

How does the foreclosure auction work in Colorado?

Different types of real estate auctions come with varying degrees of risk. The riskiest are the local foreclosure sales, because they require the quickest payment with the least amount of due diligence available. Every state has different laws regarding foreclosure auctions, which makes it very tough for inexperienced buyers. Make sure you know your local laws before bidding!

A foreclosure auction gives the public a chance to buy homes that are being foreclosed on by the bank or other lien holder. Before the lien holder can take possession of the house through a foreclosure, they have to offer it up for auction. The bank or lien holder will make a starting bid, which may be what is owed on the loan including late fees and interest. The bank can also start the bidding at less than what is owed.

If no one bids on the home at the foreclosure sale, the house will go back to the bank. However, investors or even owner-occupied bidders can buy houses at the foreclosure sale if they bid more than the banks bid (assuming the bank is not bidding as well, which is possibly). I used to buy most of my fix and flips at the foreclosure sale in Colorado and I even bought a personal residence at the foreclosure sale. We stopped buying at the foreclosure sale last year, because competition has increased, pushing prices too high. In my area, I can get a better deal on the MLS than I can at the foreclosure sale.

How the foreclosure sale works in Colorado:

- The pre-sale list is published every Monday afternoon, which lists the properties going to sale and the starting bid.
- The foreclosure sale is on Wednesday morning at 10 AM. You can call the public trustees office on Wednesday before the sale to see if the properties you are interested in are still going to auction.
- The auction is conducted at 10 AM and all bidders must register in person at the public trustee office before the auction. The auction is live and goes very quickly.
- The winning bidders must sign a form and they have until noon on Wednesday to come back to the office with a cashier's check for the full amount of the bid. If the winning bidder does not show up, the second highest bidder is notified and given a chance to buy the property at their highest bid.
- There is a short redemption period, 8 days, for junior lienholders in Colorado. A junior lienholder can redeem the property by paying off the first bid amount in full plus interest.

In Colorado, there is no guarantee you are bidding on a first loan or that you will get a clear title. The day before the sale, Tuesday, we would get an O & E (Ownership and Encumbrance report) from the title company, check out the house as much as we could, and then decide if it was worth bidding on the home.

What are the foreclosure laws in other states?

The process for buying at the foreclosure sale I outlined is only for Colorado. Other states have much different laws and each state handles their auctions differently. Here are a few differences I have heard of:

- Some states require proof of funds before the auction. This requires bringing cashier's checks for the amount you want to bid.
- Some states give much less notice on which houses will go to the sale and what the starting bids will be. I have heard that in some areas you have only a few hours to research properties before they are sold.
- Some states have an owner redemption period, where the previous owner of the home has a certain amount of time to pay off whoever won the bid and get the house back. Some states have redemption periods as long as six months!

Make sure you know exactly how the foreclosure auctions work in your state before you bid. When I used to go to foreclosure auctions, I saw many new investors check out the auctions for weeks to see how they worked. I have also seen new investors bid on a second loan, not realizing there was a first loan.

How did I lose money on houses I bought at the foreclosure sale?

I have made a lot of money from houses we bought at the foreclosure sale, but I have also lost money because of the nature of the auction.

On one deal, we had the winning bid on a house at the foreclosure auction. We had an O & E that showed we were bidding on a first position note and we viewed the home before the sale. We looked through the windows and the house appeared to be completely vacant. After winning the bid we found out the previous owners had filed a lawsuit against the bank, claiming the bank did not foreclosed correctly. The lawsuit had not been recorded yet and we had no way of knowing about it. In the end, the lawsuit was thrown out, but it took the judge a year to look at the case and we had to hold the property that entire time. After interest and carrying costs, we ended up losing money.

In many instances, I had to buy a house without seeing the interior. There are no open houses or showings when you buy a house at the foreclosure sale. Some investors try to get into homes before the sale, but if caught they can be charged with trespassing or even breaking and entering.

When buying a house that you cannot see inside of, you have to consider how much the repairs could be. I usually bought the houses from the auction for flips so I knew how much my repair budget could be to make money. I would always assume a house would need new flooring, paint, appliances, fixtures, and at least $5,000 in other repairs depending on the age of the home. Sometimes we got lucky and the house needed less work, but sometimes it needed more.

I also tried to talk to the occupants before the sale to get as much information as I could. This is not a fun situation to be in when trying to talk to someone about buying their house they are losing to foreclosure. Most people are actually friendly, and they will at least tell you if they are renting or if they own the house. Many times, they have no idea how the process works and you can build rapport by telling them how it works and what the timelines are.

Foreclosure auctions versus online REO auctions

There are many types of auctions, and some banks use another auction to sell the house once they have completed the foreclosure. HUBZU, Homesearch, Auction.com, and many more sites have auctions for REO properties that the bank already owns. These auctions have much different terms than the foreclosure sales and it is much easier to buy from them. Online auctions for REO properties sometimes:

- allow financing
- allow inspections
- allow appraisals
- give title insurance
- pay a real estate agent commission

The online auctions have different terms for different properties and you must be very careful on what you are bidding.

Buying a house at the foreclosure auction can be scary and very risky. I stopped buying because the prices increased to a point where the risk was no longer worth the reward. The inventory of foreclosures in Colorado has dropped significantly and I think investors who counted on the foreclosure sale for inventory had to increase the prices they pay because they do not know any other way to buy. I would not rule out buying from the foreclosure sale, but I would also make sure you have multiple ways to get great deals as the market changes.

How to get great deals from the MLS

Some investors will tell you that it is impossible to find rentals or flips on the MLS (multiple listing service). I buy almost all of my flips and rentals from the MLS. Even if you are not an agent, you can still get deals from the MLS, but you must have a great agent (more on that later). Short sales, REOs, fair market listings, estate sales can all be bought from the MLS. We have talked about what those properties are, but this section will go into detail on exactly how I buy those houses.

There are many deals on the MLS if you know how to find them and in my opinion, it is easier to buy from the MLS than from other places. I used to buy many of my fix and flips from trustee sales, but there is so much competition that prices are higher at the trustee sale than on the MLS. With the trustee sale, you have to pay cash in two hours and many times cannot see inside the home before you buy it. I would rather buy from the MLS where I can complete an inspection, see the home, and get a loan.

I am still buying REOs and short sales, but more of my purchases have been traditional or estate sales. Prices are rising in many areas of the country and that creates opportunity for investors. With rising prices, more fair market sellers are able to sell their homes.

A fair market sale is a home that is not in a REO or short sale situation. Many homeowners bought foreclosures and homes in disrepair in the last few years while prices were lower. Not all homeowners had the money or time to repair the home once they moved in. Some of those homeowners need to sell a home that is not in very good condition. A house that needs repairs creates opportunities. The more work that is needed, the bigger discount it takes to get a home sold. Rental property number five was a fair market sale. It needed a lot of work and was a great deal. I bought it for $88,000 and two and a half years later, it is worth $170,000. You can find detailed numbers and videos of all my rentals on investfourmore.com.

How can rising home prices create opportunity on the MLS?

With rising prices, real estate agents or sellers underprice some homes. I have bought a couple of houses recently that were underpriced and I either had my offer accepted right away or won in a multiple offer situation. Houses may be underpriced because the real estate agent did not know the true value of the home due to an increasing market or because the seller wanted to sell the home quickly.

Rental properties nine and ten were fair market sales that were underpriced; I was able to purchase them well below market value. I purchased rental property nine for $130,000 and with only $3,000 of work, it was worth $180,000. I purchased rental property ten for $99,000 and with a minimal amount of work, it was worth $150,000. If a real estate agent is not paying attention to market price increases, if a house needs some work, or if the sellers simply want to sell their house quickly, it could mean opportunity for investors.

Some sellers get into trouble and cannot make their payments for various reasons. If the market is stagnant or decreasing, these homes have to be sold as short sales or they become foreclosures. When the market is strong, sellers are able to sell their homes, but if they must do it quickly they may be very motivated.

Being a real estate agent gives me a huge advantage when submitting offers quickly. I check MLS many times a day. As soon as I see a great deal, I look at the house as soon as possible. If I like the house, I have my assistant write up an offer and send it to me with DocuSign, which allows me to sign the contract electronically on my phone and send to the seller almost immediately. By being an agent, having an assistant, and using DocuSign, I can send an offer less than an hour after a home is listed. Acting quickly is one of the most important things you can do when buying from the MLS.

Many REO sellers will not accept an offer right away, but many short sales and fair market sales will. Most banks, when selling their REOs, have a five-day period or longer before they will review offers. HUD and some banks have owner-occupied periods when a home is first listed, where only owner-occupants can make offers. This is why short sales and fair markets sales can sometimes be better deals than REOs.

No matter what you do, it takes longer to submit an offer if you are not an agent. One way to speed things up is to ask your agent to set up property alerts for you. In my MLS, I can set up alerts to send an email as soon as specific properties that meet my given criteria are listed. I set these alerts so I will not miss a great deal on the MLS. I was able to buy my last fix and flip thanks to a property alert that told me a home was back on the market. Investors can use sites such as Zillow and Realtor.com, but their listings are not always updated quickly. Zillow also has many listings on their site that show as being for sale that are actually under contract. The best way to be able to submit offers quickly is to have a great real estate agent or be one.

Offer the most you can in multiple offer situations

If you find a great deal, do not be cheap! Do not try to lowball an already great deal. Offer the most you are able to while still making your desired profit. You do not want to stretch your limits when you make an offer; it does not make sense to buy a home that will not make you money. You also do not want to try to steal a home either, if it will cost you the deal.

I may try to offer a little less than I want to pay if I think I can get my offer in before any others. If the home is an amazing deal, I offer full price or sometimes even above full price in hopes that the seller will sign my offer before any other offers come in.

When some sellers (most REOs) get more than one offer, they will ask for highest and best. They want every buyer who sent in an offer to make their very best offer, and the seller will choose what they fell is the best offer. In a multiple offer situation, I do not pay attention to the list price. I offer the most I can that will still make me my desired profit. Sometimes I offer less than the listing price and sometimes I offer more. Do not be scared off by a multiple offer situation!

I hear buyers tell me all the time that they do not want to get in a bidding war. Why not? A bidding war means that a house is priced great and many people want it. Why would other people being interested in a house make you not want to buy it? I think that too many people let their emotions get in the way and they feel the seller should have just accepted their offer and ignored the other offers for some reason. Do not let your emotions stop you from getting a good deal! It makes no sense to withdraw your offer in a highest and best situation.

Make your offer more appealing to a seller by using cash or few contingencies

I am an experienced investor and I am in a great place to be able to offer cash on a property if necessary. I also have a great portfolio lender that does not require an appraisal on loans under $100,000. Most sellers want quick and easy closings, so a cash offer is usually the most enticing to them. If you have to use financing, use as few contingencies as you can. I am able to remove the appraisal contingency on most of my financed offers and I will even remove my inspection contingency in some cases.

On my last three deals, I removed my inspection contingency and I know that helped get my offer accepted. This is risky for someone who does not know what to look for in a house, but if you are getting a good enough deal and know what to look for, it may be a good strategy to use. A cash offer with no inspection contingency will often get accepted over a higher offer with financing and inspection contingencies. However, some sellers, such as HUD, only care about the net price to them and do not care if you use cash or a loan.

Use real estate agent mistakes to your advantage on the MLS

I have bought many houses from the MLS that were listed incorrectly. I bought a house from HUBZU where the listing said no basement, when in fact the house had a full, finished basement with two bedrooms and a bath. I recently bought a rental listed as a three bedroom, two-bath house that was actually a five bedroom, two-bath house. You have to know your market, pay attention to the listing photos, and confirm the information in the listing. Do not be afraid to look at many houses to find the few that are not listed correctly. The more market knowledge you have and the more experience you gain, the easier it will be to spot the mistakes.

You need to be flexible when buying from the MLS

The buyer cannot occupy some houses until months after the sale because they have tenants. In these situations, it lessens the competition because most owner-occupants will not want to buy a home that they cannot move into right away. Many times the tenants can be difficult when you are trying to show the home or they may not keep the house looking nice, which decreases your chances of getting a good deal.

Many times sellers or their agents will underprice homes in a hot market because the real estate agent is not on top of the current pricing trends. I have bought a few houses that were in decent shape for much less than market value because they were underpriced. When I see a house come on the market at a very low price, I waste no time seeing it. I set up a showing as soon as I possibly can. I view the house and if I like it, I make an offer that same day.

How do you know when one seller is more motivated to negotiate than another is?

When you flip houses or buy rentals, you have to get an awesome deal to make any money. Ninety-seven percent of the houses on the MLS will not work for flipping, because there is not enough profit after all the costs are considered. Some homes listed on the MLS can be awesome deals, but the list price does not indicate how much the seller is willing to take. I do not advocate submitting low offers on every house hoping one seller will accept 50 percent of list price. However, some sellers will take significantly less than asking price if you know what to look for.

- **Aged listings**: Some houses sit on the market for months without selling. Many times the sellers priced the home too high, it was hard to set up a showing on the house, the home needed major repairs, or other factors caused the house not to sell. Not every aged listing can be bought for much less than asking price, but some can. HUD homes that are on the market more than 60 days can sometimes be bought at a significant discount. Some sellers will not lower their price when their house does not sell, but may take less than asking price. It does not hurt to submit low offers on homes that have been on the market a long time, but look for other signs as well.

- **MLS comments**: Some comments in the MLS descriptions shout: *make a low offer!* If you see the words as-is, seller motivated, quick close preferred, cash deal, no financing, will not go FHA, out-of-state owner, needs work, needs TLC, or anything else that indicates the home needs work and the seller wants it gone quickly, they may be more willing to negotiate.

- **Fast price changes**: If a home does not sell right away, the seller will usually lower the price. I see house prices lowered around the 30 to 60-day mark in most cases. However, occasionally I see a home pop up on the market and in only seven or ten days the price is changed. This indicates to me that the seller wants it gone quickly! The bigger the price change, the quicker they want it gone.

- **Back on the market**: Homes go under contract and then come back on the market all the time. However, in some cases, a contract falling apart can indicate a house with major problems or it can also motivate the seller. When I see a house come back on the market at a decent price, I will ask the agent why it came back on the market. Sometimes the agent will indicate it was buyer financing or a problem with the inspection. In some cases, the agent will indicate the seller wants to get rid of the home because they were expecting it to sell and the contract fell apart. A house coming back on the market and the price changing at the same time indicates a very motivated seller! If a home repeatedly goes under contract and then comes back on the market, the seller may be motivated by a cash offer and no inspection to get the deal done.

How low should you offer on a house?

As I mentioned earlier, if the home is already an awesome deal do not be afraid to offer list price or higher if the numbers work. Many of my deals were houses that I bought well below list price, because I saw some of the situations mentioned above and knew that the sellers were motivated.

I rarely if ever, submit an extremely low offer. I have never submitted an offer that was 50 percent or less than list price. When I submit a low offer, it is usually about 70 to 80 percent of list price. Offers lower than 70 percent of list price usually offend the seller and even a 70 percent offer might offend them. I do not submit low offers on every house on the MLS, but I select listings that I think will be more likely to negotiate.

When I make my first offer, I do not offer the most I can pay for the home. I leave some room for negotiation, because the seller is most likely not going to accept my low offer. I recently bought a flip listed for $109,900. This was a good price, although not for a flip because of the work needed. Seven days after the home was listed, the seller lowered the price to $104,900. I noticed in the comments that the home needed TLC, was dirty because previous tenants had just moved out, and would not qualify for financing. This was music to my ears! I knew the seller was motivated, because they would not spend $150 to clean the house. I offered $80,000 with no inspection and cash closing in 20 days. The seller countered at $85,000, which I happily accepted. Many times the seller will want to negotiate at least a little so they feel like they got the most money they could out of the house.

What if the seller will not come down low enough to make a deal?

Not every offer I make is accepted. In fact, most houses I make offers on, I do not end up buying. If you want to be a great real estate investor, you cannot be afraid to have your offer rejected or to see someone else get a deal you were hoping to buy. The fastest ways an investor can get into trouble are paying too much for a home, being caught up in a bidding war, or a seller who will not negotiate enough. If the seller will not come down to a price that makes sense for you, do not force the issue and pay too much! Even if the seller does not accept your offer, you still may get the home later.

If I make a low offer, I can usually tell how motivated the seller is. If the seller rejects my offer or acts offended at my offer, I forget about the house and move on. It is not worth my time to negotiate back and forth if the seller is not coming close to my price. If the seller comes down significantly from their list price, I know I have a chance of getting something together.

Sometimes we cannot get together on the price or they accept another offer. In those cases, I am always polite and ask their agent to let me know if anything happens or if the seller is interested in my offer later. Many times the first offer that was accepted falls apart because it was an owner-occupant who later realized how much work the home needed, or maybe a wholesaler got the home under contract, but could not find a buyer. Do not give up if another offer is accepted and do not pay too much.

Should you try to negotiate with the seller on inspection items?

When I make offers, I do not ask for an inspection period. I have enough experience to know what major issues to look out for and what repairs a home needs. I would not suggest waiving the inspection if you are a new investor. Waiving the inspection period gets me many deals, especially when a home comes back on the market. Many of the houses I am interested in have motivated sellers who want to sell the house fast. It costs them time and money if they have to put the home back on the market because of inspection problems. Every time a house comes back on the market, buyers wonder what is wrong with it and the home will not get as high of a price.

If I make an offer without an inspection or financing contingency, the seller knows they will at least get my earnest money if I do not buy the home. This gives me an advantage and I have bought many houses at a lower price than other investors were offering because I waved my inspection.

Some buyers make an offer for more than they want to pay for the house with an inspection contingency. They assume they will be able to use the inspection to ask for a lower price and get the home cheaper. I do not do this, because I feel it is not operating in good faith. While this tactic may work a couple of times or even more, it will also give the buyer a reputation of always asking for a lower price on inspection. Another reason I get so many deals is that agents know me and know I do not play games. If I write a contract for a certain price, I buy the home at the price I say I will. Building a good reputation will give you a better chance of having your offers accepted and agents may come to you when they have a seller who has to close quickly.

Buying from the MLS is not impossible; it is actually my favorite way to buy homes. I am in Colorado, which has one of the hottest markets in the country. You cannot use the excuse that buying from the MLS does not work in my market. There will always be deals on the MLS if you know how to spot them and can act quickly.

How to find an investor-friendly real estate agent

The most important person on an investor's team is a great real estate agent. Real estate agents can play a huge role in getting a deal, losing a deal, valuing a property, and many other factors that can make or lose you money. It can be difficult to find a real estate agent or Realtor who will return calls and respond quickly enough for an investor.

I am an agent and I think it is a huge advantage for investors to be real estate agents as well. If you do not want to become an agent yourself, it is imperative you find a great agent to help you

There is a lot of information for new investors to process when they first start investing in real estate. A great real estate agent can make the process much less painful and make investing much more enjoyable. Finding a great agent is tricky, but you

What is the first thing you should do to find an agent?

As with almost any professional service, the best way to find someone good is through referrals. The first thing I do when I need help from a professional is ask my friends, family, and co-workers for a recommendation. It is usually best to ask as many people as possible, until you start seeing the same name pop up repeatedly. Even if you get a great referral for an agent, you want to make sure the agent knows what they are doing. I have had referrals for agents that turned out horribly.

People become real estate agents for a variety of reasons. Some want a little extra money, some want free time, some think it is a way to get rich quickly, and others want to make a career out of real estate. You want to find the career agent who cares about their job and business, not the agent looking to get rich quick.

Answering the phone or returning a call quickly is the first sign of a good agent. The phone call from a potential client is one of the best leads for an agent, yet many agents ignore calls or take days to return calls. If you call a potential real estate agent, they should either answer their phone or call you back within a couple of hours. Getting a call back quickly is important because investors need speed to get the good deals. If it takes an agent a day or two to call you back, that could mean the difference between getting an offer accepted and another buyer getting the property.

Sometimes the busiest agents cannot answer their phone all the time or return calls right away. Usually the busiest agents are the best agents, but you have to ask yourself if you want an extremely busy agent working for you? Once again, they may be a great agent, but if they have too many clients to act quickly, they may not be the right agent for you.

When looking for an investor-friendly agent, make sure they are competent

After you find an agent who answers their phone, you still have a lot of work to do. You have to make sure they know what they are doing; test their knowledge by asking simple questions about the types of homes you are looking to buy.

1. Have you sold many REO properties?

2. Have you sold HUD homes? Does your office have an NAID number?

3. How do you suggest buyers handle multiple offer situations?

4. How do short sales work?

5. If I were to sell one of my houses, how would you market it?

You should already know the answers to most of these questions, but you want to know if your agent knows. How confident are they when answering these questions? If they are newer and do not know everything, that is okay. They should tell you that they do not know, but they will find out. Real estate is a serious business and there are severe consequences for fraud or mistakes. You do not want your Realtor pretending to know how to do things and get you in trouble.

Is it smart to work with a new real estate agent?

Some people do not like working with new agents, because they are inexperienced. New real estate agents can make up for that inexperience with ambition. Most new agents are motivated and are excited about starting a new career. When I started out, I was very ambitious to work with buyers and sellers and I worked very hard for the few clients I had. As I obtained more clients and more business, I could not give each client as much attention. I will be honest and say I am a horrible agent for investors now. I do not have time to show houses, write offers, or check up on offers. I hand off leads to other agents on my team who do have time. That is another thing a new agent has going for them, they most likely have plenty of time to work for you.

Many investors are very demanding of their real estate agent. They need to act quickly and may make many offers before getting an offer accepted. If you are an investor who wants to make hundreds of low-ball offers, make sure you motivate your agent. They are only paid when they sell a house; they are not paid to make offers. If they are thinking it is a waste of time to submit low offer after low offer, they are not going to work hard for you. Buy them lunch or dinner and discuss strategies. Show them you care and give them a reason to keep working hard. Even though lunch will not make up for the hours of time they spend, it may be enough to keep them going until you get a deal done and they make some real money.

Is your real estate knowledgeable about rental properties?

If you are planning to buy rental properties, it helps if your Realtor knows the rental market and investment property market. It helps tremendously if they can help you determine rents or at least back up your thinking on potential deals. It gives you that extra push to move forward on deals and they may see potential problems that you do not see. You still need to know your market and be able to make decisions on deals yourself. Do not rely solely on your real estate agent to determine what a good deal is. If they are not familiar with rentals, that is okay, too. Many realtors do not have a clue about real estate investing; acting fast for you is much more important.

Being ethical is a very important issue for investors or anyone using a real estate agent. Many buyers want an agent who stretches the rules to get them deals. If a buyer or seller knows an agent is being unethical or breaking laws, the buyer or seller is also liable and can be held just as responsible as the agent can. Even if the buyer or seller does not know their agent is being unethical, they can still be held responsible.

HUD homes are a great example of how buyers and agents can get in trouble. If an agent helps an investor bid as an owner-occupant, both the agent and investor can face criminal charges. HUD homes are government property, which means any laws broken involving them are felonies. Buyers can face up to five years in prison and a fine of $250,000 for breaking HUD rules. Agents can lose the ability for their entire office to sell any HUD homes.

Does your real estate agent have backup when they are not available

Another very important thing to consider with any agent is whether they have backup. Agents go on vacation, get sick, and have accidents just like everyone else. You want to make sure they have someone who can take over their business if they are unavailable. Many agents work on teams. This is a great way to know you will be taken care of if your agent cannot do it himself or herself. As I have mentioned it many times in my blog, speed can mean the difference between getting and losing a deal. The last thing you want is for your agent to be out of town and unavailable to show you a home or make an offer for three days.

It can take a lot of work to find a great agent. If you are an owner-occupant who only buys one house every five years, an agent may not be that important. If you are investor, looking to buy multiple houses a year, a great agent can mean the difference of thousands and thousands of dollars. If you choose an agent that you do not think is doing a great job, do not be afraid to fire them. I have had to fire agents who were helping me because I misjudged their abilities, work ethic, or character.

I have a network of agents across the country through my REO and investing groups. If you need help finding an agent, email me at info@investfourmore.com and I will do my best to refer you to someone.

Should you use multiple agents to find investment properties?

I am a Realtor so I have a definite bias on whether an investor should work with one dedicated agent or work with multiple agents. I also can give the Realtor's perspective on how we work and how an investor can make a Realtor work best for them.

There are many different scenarios for how agents are paid and there are no standard commissions or structures used. The most common scenario I see in my area for most real estate transactions is two real estate agents, one for the buyer and one for the seller. Usually, the seller pays the commissions for both agents. For this example, I will use the HUD commission structure, which is three percent for the buyer side and three percent for the seller side. That can seem like a lot of money for one deal, but Realtors have many expenses.

Realtors must carry a lot of insurance. I carry Errors and Omissions (E&O), general liability, and umbrella insurance policies. Realtors have to pay for license fees, MLS fees, office expenses, and office space.

Most Realtors do not keep their entire commission; they pay a percentage to their broker. In turn, the broker pays for staff, advertising, and other expenses. Commission splits can range from 50/50 to 90/10 depending on what the office pays for and the number of transactions the Realtor closes. Realtors get no benefits! They pay all their health insurance costs, have no matching 401ks, or any of the other benefits of a corporate job.

After factoring in all of these expenses, agents do not make as much as people think. A Realtor usually only gets paid when they sell a house. Realtors may make $5,000 on one sale, but they may also have spent 20 hours with another client who never bought a house and they earned nothing for their time.

The reason I am outlining the way agents are paid is to show you that agents want to make sure that the investors they work with are serious and that they are not working for free. This can determine whether an agent sends good deals to you or to someone else.

Using multiple agents to buy investment properties

Many investors like to use multiple agents to find properties for them. They feel the more agents looking for properties for them, the better chance they have of getting a good deal. They will talk to many agents all over town telling them that they are a serious investor and looking to make some purchases. This strategy can work in some cases, but it can also backfire.

Most agents can sense when an investor or buyer is working with multiple agents and a good agent will flat out ask any buyer if they are working with another Realtor. Realtors are taught in ethics class not to steal other Realtor's clients. It is drilled into our heads that it is very bad to "step on another agent's toes" by showing houses or writing contracts for a buyer that has already looked at homes with another agent.

Because of this training, most agents will naturally shy away from any buyer that says they have seen houses or are receiving listings from other agents or do not have one agent, but are working with whoever has the best deal, etc. This does not mean agents will not help investors working with multiple agents, but they probably will not put a lot of effort into it.

Realtors are usually able to show a buyer any homes listed in MLS, but if they have no connection to a buyer or feel the buyer is not committed to them, they do not have much motivation. They will usually call up the investor if their own listing might meet the investor's needs, but that is about it.

Some investors also feel they may be able to get a better deal on a property if they work with the listing agent instead of their own agent. They feel if there is no buyer's agent involved the listing agent will take a smaller commission and the seller can net the same amount with a lower sales price.

This strategy can work on some homes, but many times the agents still charge the full commission. The buyer also is risking not having proper representation when taking this route. Most states allow the listing agent to represent both sides or act as a transaction broker. However, if the agent has known the sellers for years and just met you, whose interests will the agent really have in mind?

Using one agent to represent you when buying investment deals

Realtors are taught that the best way to do business is to let a buyer choose an agent and then that agent will work exclusively with the buyer. There are a couple of huge positive motivators for a Realtor to use this technique.

- Realtors know that if the buyer makes a purchase, the buyer will use them and they will be paid.
- Realtors know if the buyer decides to sell a home, the client will use them and they will be paid.

An agent who knows that they have a loyal buyer will work hard to send them new listings, search aged listings, and other possible deals. They know if they find the right house, they will be rewarded with a commission check. They have much more motivation because they do not worry that the investor will use another agent on houses that they send the buyer.

It can work to use multiple agents, but usually the investor making these techniques work is doing the property searches himself. He is not relying on an agent to send him listings or leads. He finds a good deal and then approaches the listing agent to try to make a better deal.

If you are new to real estate investing, I suggest you find a hard-working agent to represent you. In my experience, a young agent can be the best, because they are hungry for deals and willing to work hard. The most experienced and successful agents may not have the time to hunt down properties for a new investor, and they may already have a list of investors ahead of you that they will contact first.

Should you become a real estate agent?

Real estate has provided me with a great income and the opportunity to own a business. When I became a real estate agent in 2001, I did not invest in rental properties; I sold houses. When I started to invest in rentals, I could see immediately how big of an advantage I had by being an agent. I saved thousands of dollars in commissions, could find better deals, and made more money because of my real estate license.

One reason I am get such high returns on my rentals is that I save thousands of dollars on each transaction by being a real estate agent. I also do 10 to 15 fix and flips per year and save thousands of dollars on each of those transactions as well. I figured that being a real estate agent saved me over $70,000 in commissions in 2013 alone (each year since then I have saved just as much or more). That does not include the profit I made on deals that I would not have gotten if I were not an agent.

If you plan to buy more than one or two rental properties per year, you may want to think about getting a real estate license. If you do nothing else with your license except buy your own rental properties, it will save you thousands of dollars in commissions a year. On every rental property I buy I save money, because I earn a commission as the buyer's agent. The commission may be 2, 2.5, or 3 percent per deal, but in the end that adds up to a lot of money. If you buy three houses per year at an average price of $100,000, being a real estate agent can save you $7,500 to $9,000 per year.

If you fix and flip those houses and sell them, you will more than double your savings because you will save a commission when you sell the house as well. On a recent fix and flip I bought for $105,000, I earned a 3 percent commission as the buyer's agent. I fixed up the property and sold it for

$175,000. When I list the home, I will save another 3 percent commission. On this one deal, I will save $8,400, because I am a real estate agent.

If you become a real estate agent, you may not save as much money as I have. I have a large real estate team and pay a flat fee to my broker, which allows me to keep 100 percent of my commissions. If you start as a new agent, you most likely will not keep all of your commissions, but it is still a huge advantage.

Advantages of being an investor with a real estate license

Being an agent saves me commissions and it allows me to get more deals as well. Here are some other ways that having a license is a huge advantage:

- As a real estate agent, you get access to MLS and can do your own searches for properties without relying on an agent to find you the right deal. Having access to MLS gives investors a huge advantage because they do not have to wait for an agent to send them listings. I search for listings at least five times a day and routinely make offers the same day a house is listed. An agent can also easily pull sold comparable information from MLS to calculate values on properties. Calculating accurate values is one of the most important things an investor can do to be successful.

- As a real estate agent, you can fraternize with other agents and people in the real estate world. The more people you know in the business, the more people you can tell that you are looking for property. Sometimes the best deals are those that are brought to you, not the deals you find yourself. Let everyone you know that you are looking for investment properties and you never know what will come up. I have bought a couple of properties that were never listed on the MLS because of my contacts in the business.

- The IRS has limits on how much money you can deduct on rental properties if real estate is not your primary job. If real estate is your primary job, then you may be able to deduct many more expenses.

- If you are a real estate agent that does many deals, most agents will know who you are. If you have a good reputation for getting deals done, sticking to your word, and being dependable, other agents will want to work with you on tough deals. Many properties we buy have major issues and are tough to sell. Other agents know me and know I will do my best to get the deal done.

- I already mentioned the commission savings on investment properties, but there is another advantage besides just the money savings. If I save $8,000 in commissions on a fix and flip, I can buy that property for $8,000 more than an investor who does not have their real estate license. That savings allows me to pay more money and get more deals than other investors while still making the same profit.

How can you make money as a real estate agent?

I am biased, but I think being a real estate agent is one of the best opportunities out there. There are many, many forms of income in the real estate business. If you are motivated and dedicated to making it in the business, then you can make serious money. I will not go into details in this book (I have another book on how to be a successful real estate agent), but here are some of the different areas that can generate income.

Property management: If you want to be a serious investor, you will want a property manager to handle your rental properties at some point. If you start your own property management business, you can manage your properties and other properties as well. Not only are you saving ten percent of your rent by doing your own management, but you can also make extra cash by managing other investor's properties.

Retail Sales: This is the most common way to earn money as an agent. Retail sales involve listing houses for private sellers and selling homes to buyers. If you are dedicated and treat this as a real job, you can make a lot of money. Many agents make over $100,000 a year and the very best make much more than that.

Commercial Sales: Commercial real estate takes a lot more experience and knowledge than residential. It is difficult to break into commercial unless you start with a commercial firm who can mentor you. Experienced and successful commercial agents can easily make hundreds of thousands of dollars per year.

REO sales: REO agents list and manage these homes for the banks. Agents can make a very lucrative living if they work with the right banks. It can take years to build up your business and the supply is determined by how many foreclosed homes there are. It is a conflict of interest for REO agents to buy their own listings. Being a REO agent, is not a huge advantage for your own investing.

Short Sales: Short sales are listed for sale by private sellers who are selling the home for less than they owe the bank. There is a huge market for short sales and many agents make a great living specializing in this field. It takes a lot of patience and diligence to close a short sale since the banks have many requirements and can take months to approve a short sale.

Broker Price Opinions (BPOs): A BPO is a one to three page report used to determine value on properties, but is not an appraisal. Licensed agents can complete BPOs for various clients, including banks. They are usually paid between $30 and $80 per order. Some agents make a living only completing BPOs and for others, it is a great way to supplement their income while learning the business.

How can you become a real estate agent?

You must take pre-licensing classes and pass a test in most states to get your real estate license. My assistant got his license through Real Estate Express, which has a great licensing program in all 50 states. Real Estate Express has some of the cheapest prices I have seen, although I have not researched every real estate school. I have many more articles on InvestFourMore.com about becoming a real estate agent. I also wrote a book on real estate agents, *How to Make it Big in Real Estate, From a Million Dollar Agent.*

There are many ways to make money as a real estate agent. Even if you just want to buy or sell a few of your own listings each year, I believe becoming a real estate agent is well worth it.

Final thoughts on buying below market value

Buying below market value is the key to almost any successful real estate investing strategy. If you want to make money flipping or with rental properties, you will need to buy below market. While it is tough to buy below market when starting out, you can still get a deal without waiving your inspection, without paying cash, and without looking at a house hours after it has been listed. However, it will be tougher to get those deals if you cannot act quickly, waive an inspection, or pay cash.

I would not recommend waiving inspections if you are brand new. It takes a lot of experience to know what repairs are needed and to know how much of a profit margin you need in order to absorb extra costs that may occur. When I buy flips or rentals and waive my inspection, I am assuming that a home will need more work than what can be seen. Houses usually need more repairs than you think they will after you start working on them and uncovering things.

While cash deals are a great enticement to many sellers, some sellers, such as HUD, do not care. HUD does not care if you pay cash or use a loan. All they care about is the net price they are getting on the home. Many times I get a loan on houses, even though I make my offer as cash. I put a clause in the offer that says I have the cash to pay for the home if needed, but may use financing from a portfolio lender.

6. How to finance and pay for rental properties.

We have discussed why rental properties are such a great investment, how to buy them below market value, and what makes a good rental property investment. All of this information will not do you any good though if you do not have money or financing to buy a rental. This chapter covers how much you need to buy a rental, how to buy with financing, and how to buy with less money down.

In the early 2000s, you could get financing on an investment property with as little as five percent down. Those days are gone for the most part and it is much tougher to get financing on investment properties. Having said that, it may not be as difficult to obtain loans on rental properties as some banks make it out to be. When I was buying rentals, many banks told me I could not get more than four mortgages in my name. That is not true. What they meant is that their bank would not give me more than four mortgages in my name. There is no law or government restriction on how many mortgages you can obtain.

One great way to increase your cash flow and wealth is by using leverage or mortgages to buy rentals. You can buy more properties with less cash and if you buy the right properties, you will make more money. This goes against what some people believe that you will make more money by paying cash for a property. However, I can prove with some simple math why leverage will make you more money.

Should you pay cash or get a loan on rental properties?

Paying cash for rental properties may seem like a safe bet, but in reality it can cause you to make less money on rentals. When you get a loan, you can increase your returns substantially.

I am going to use some basic figures to outline the benefits of leveraging your money. If you pay cash for a $100,000 house and after all expenses are left with $500 a month in cash flow, you are making about six percent cash-on-cash returns. If you put 20 percent down on a $100,000 house, you will have a mortgage payment, but the returns on your cash invested increase, because you are using much less cash. If you are paying a four percent interest rate, your principal and interest payment will be about $382. You are only making $118 after subtracting the mortgage payment, but you are making seven percent cash-on-cash return, due to the lower initial investment.

Even though the cash-on-cash return is seven percent, you are actually making much more than a seven percent total return in the above scenario. You are also paying down the principal on the loan by at least $118 each month. That $118 equals another seven percent return on your money that you would not have on a cash purchase. You have more than doubled your return by getting a mortgage instead of paying cash. This doesn't even take into consideration that over the 30-year life of the loan, your principal paydown will increase each month which further improves your return.

The exciting part about using leverage is that when you get higher cash flows, the returns increase even more. If you can make $800 a month cash flow without a mortgage, you will be making 9.6 percent cash-on-cash return on the same $100,000 house. With 20 percent down on the same property, you would cash flow $418 a month after the mortgage payments and make over 25 percent cash-on-cash return.

The way to make big money in rental properties is finding properties that will give you a lot of cash flow and buying as many as possible. The way you buy as many as you can is by getting mortgages. I make over $500 a month cash flow on each of my properties, with loans in place. Yes, I would make more per property if I paid cash, but I would have less properties and less total cash flow.

The best part about leveraging your money is it allows you to buy more properties. You can buy three or four homes with $100,000 instead of just one home with all cash. Using the cash flow figures from above and buying three properties instead of one, you would be making $1,254 a month cash flow instead of $800 a month. Not only does your cash flow increase by purchasing more properties, but the equity pay down increases, the tax benefits increase, and the appreciation increases. If you can purchase homes below market, then every time you buy a home, your net worth increases as well!

What are the other advantages of buying multiple properties?

Rental properties have many tax benefits, including depreciation. The IRS allows you to depreciate a percentage of your rental properties every year and write that off as an expense. If you have three houses instead of just one, you can get triple the tax deductions and if the market appreciates, you have the benefit of triple the appreciation.

It is the same situation if rents go up. The more properties you have the more money you will make. I never count on rents to go up or for the homes to appreciate, but it is a nice bonus. With multiple rental properties, you are also paying down the loans on three properties, which increase your returns as well. When you think of the tax savings, possible appreciation, and equity pay down, the returns shoot through roof.

Downside to buying more rental properties with leverage

There is a downside to more properties. You will have to spend more for repairs and improvements since each property will need repairs, not just one. You will also have three rental properties to manage instead of one. However, if you are able to cash flow $400 or more with a mortgage, you will still be way ahead of the game by leveraging your money. You will also have more total cash flow coming in, which can pay for a property manager. We accounted for the repairs and maintenance when we figured the cash flow so it will not be an added expense with more properties, but it will be more work if you manage the properties yourself.

Some people think it is less risky to buy with cash than with a loan, but I disagree. Here are some reasons why cash may be riskier than getting a loan.

- When you buy with cash, you have fewer properties. The fewer properties you have, the less sources of income you have coming in, and the more a loss of an income will hurt. If you have one property paid for with cash, it really hurts when it goes vacant. That is your only source of income from rentals. However, if you have three rentals that have loans on them, one may go vacant but you have two more that are bringing in money.

- When you have multiple rentals, you have more diversification. If you have one rental, you are more susceptible to neighborhood changes, storm damage etc. With multiple rentals, you have less chance of all your properties being damaged or hurt by other factors.
- You actually lose less money when prices go down with multiples properties. I know that may not make sense at first, but consider this. You buy three houses worth $125,000 below market value for $100,000. If the market goes down 20 percent, your houses will be worth $100,000 so you are not losing any money. If you bought one house with cash below market value, you would be in the same boat. If you are able to get even better deals and bought the houses that were worth $125,000 for $90,000 then you would actually still be in good shape if the market goes down 20 percent. You would have three houses worth $100,000 that you bought for $90,000. You would have $30,000 in equity from buying below market value. If you only bought one house for $90,000 with cash and the market went down 20 percent, you would only have $10,000 in equity from buying below market value. This number can be manipulated to show cash or a loan is better depending on how much the prices decrease, how much of a discount you bought the houses for, along with other factors. However, this shows that cash is not always going to be the safest bet.

In my opinion, it is better to use other people's money and increase your returns versus paying cash. Some people are very averse to any risk and do not want any debt at all. If the idea of debt makes you sick to your stomach, maybe paying cash is the best route for you. I will continue to get as many loans as I can and to buy as many rental properties as I can because of the incredible benefits rental properties offer.

How much money do you need to buy a rental property?

The biggest hurdle for most people when purchasing a real estate investment is the money it takes. It is easy to figure out how much money you will need if you are paying cash for a property. It can be a little tougher to figure out how much money you will need when you are getting a loan. There are different loan programs and many different ways to buy rental properties. It is very expensive to buy an investment property since most banks require at least 20 percent down. There will be additional costs as well, but there are ways to invest in real estate for less than you think.

Most banks will require 25 percent down once you have four mortgages in your name. Some banks will stop lending to you all together once you reach ten financed properties. Later, I will get into ways to finance more than four and more than ten properties.

Depending on house values in your area, 20 percent down is a lot of money. The houses I buy are usually right around $100,000, which equates to about $20,000 needed for the down payment. You also need to pay closing costs when purchasing an investment property, which consist of interest, insurance, recording fees, origination fees, tax certificates, appraisals and more. It is usually safe to assume closing costs will be at least three percent of the purchase price, although you can ask the seller to pay part or all of your closing costs. In some cases, I ask the seller to pay part of the closing costs in order to reduce the amount of cash I have into a property. Remember that asking the seller to pay your closing costs may make your offer less attractive. You also may have to pay for an inspection, which can cost $250 to $500. Some sellers, such as HUD, do not pay for title insurance, which can add another $500 to $1,000 to the purchase costs.

How much money do you need for repair and carrying costs on a rental property?

Repairs can add a huge chunk to the amount required to buy a rental property. You have to wait for the repairs to be completed before it can be rented and while you are waiting, you are paying carrying costs (interest, utilities, taxes and insurance), which also increase the amount needed. In a perfect world, it should only take a week or two to have a professional contractor complete most repairs, but it always takes longer.

Repairs usually cost more than you think as well. On a house with minimal repairs, I still assume I will need at least $5,000 in work done before I can rent it. On a house that needs more repairs and updates I can easily spend $20,000 or more. The little things always take time and add up to big repair costs. As a general rule of thumb, I always add $5,000 for unknown costs on any rental or fix and flip that I buy.

Make sure you get bids if you are not an expert at estimating repairs. Estimating repairs can be very difficult, even for experienced investors. Repairs always seem to cost more than the investor thinks they should, and contractors always seem to find more things that need to be repaired.

How much total money will you need to buy a rental property?

Here is a breakdown of the costs I would normally have on a $100,000 rental property:

Down payment $20,000
Closing costs $3,000
Repair costs $10,000
Carrying costs $1,000
Total investment $34,000

These figures are for a home that needs moderate work. I am a real estate agent, which means if I had bought this house from the MLS, I would get back about $3,000 in real estate commissions. I could also ask the seller to pay $3,000 of my closing costs if I thought it would not jeopardize my chances of getting the deal.

If you have to put 25 percent down on a property that would greatly increase the amount you would need. Repairs costs affect how much you would need as well. A higher or lower purchase price will also affect the down payment.

Another factor to consider is that the bank will want you to have money in reserves when you get an investment property loan.

How much in cash reserves will you need on a rental property?

It takes a lot of money to buy rental properties and you must have money in reserves to handle vacancies and maintenance. I have 16 rental properties and it has taken a great deal of cash to purchase them. They also have maintenance that comes up and they go vacant at times. I have to keep money in reserves for maintenance and vacancies, and the bank requires me to have money in reserves for my rentals as well.

You have to have money set aside to handle vacant months and repairs. Most repairs are minor items that do not cost a lot of money, but some repairs such as replacing a roof can cost $5,000 or more. Many times repairs are done when a house is vacant, which means you will not be receiving rent, and you have to pay for repairs.

How much will a bank require in reserves on rental properties?

The money you need to keep in reserves depends on many factors. Older homes need more maintenance and some homes will have more vacancies than others will. Most lenders require investors to have at least six months in reserves for all mortgages in an investor's name before they will give them a loan. To figure how much cash you would need, add up all your mortgage payments, including your personal residence, and multiply by six.

A bank will require all the minimal costs required on an investors mortgage to be accounted for when calculating reserves. Taxes and insurance will be counted when calculating the reserve requirements as well as the mortgage payment. My mortgage payments, which include taxes and insurance, range from $450 to $650 a month on my rental properties. I also have to account for my personal residence mortgage payment, which is over $2,000 a month. I have 16 rentals, but two of those properties do not have loans against them. In total, I need over $50,000 in cash reserves to show my bank that I am in a good enough financial position to purchase more rental properties.

How much in reserves you need varies with each investor and the properties they own. A huge factor when considering how much you need is how much cash flow your rental properties are producing. If you have minimal or negative cash flow you will need much more in reserves. Having to cover part of a mortgage payment on top of paying for vacancies and maintenance can add up quickly. Most banks will also consider the cash flow an investor has on their rental properties when making loans. If you have little to no cash flow, it will be harder to qualify for more loans. I suggest buying rentals for cash flow and not appreciation, but if you have negative cash flowing properties, you should have more than six months of mortgage payments, taxes, and insurance in reserves.

If you have a lot of cash flow coming in from your rental properties, you should be able to build up reserves quickly. If you find you are short on cash, save the cash flow you have coming in until you have a decent amount of reserves built up. Many of the problems investors run into are easily solved if they invest for cash flow!

If you have one personal residence with a mortgage payment of $700 a month and a rental property with a $500 a month mortgage, you would only need $7,200 in reserves according to bank requirements. However, that is not much money if you have to make major repairs on your rental property. Replacing the roof could wipe out your entire reserve. You had better hope the home stays rented and no other repairs come up while you build the reserve back up again. I think an investor should have at least $10,000 saved up in reserves for their rental properties no matter what the bank says your reserves should be. This assumes your rental properties are basic houses that are in decent condition. If you have old rental properties that are in need of maintenance, you may need to save even more.

When you have a reserve for vacancies and maintenance on your rental properties, that money should not be used for personal items or buying more rental properties. You never know when you might need to evict someone or make major repairs. If you do not have the money to complete an eviction or make repairs, you could have major problems renting the home. If you cannot rent the home, you will not be able to bring in more money to cover the expenses. You may find yourself in a heap of trouble and be forced to sell the property.

While it can take over $30,000 to purchase a rental property, make repairs, and cover carrying costs, you may have to have even more in the bank. You should not spend all the cash you have to buy an investment property, and the bank most likely will not let you spend all of your money either. This seems like a huge amount of money, but there are ways to pay with less money down and ways to recoup that money later on, so do not get discouraged.

How to qualify for a loan on an investment property

Qualifying for a loan on an investment property is not always easy; it is much more difficult than qualifying for a loan on an owner-occupied home and it will cost you more money. Many banks consider investor loans riskier than owner-occupied loans. New lending regulations also make it harder for investors to get a loan on rental properties. If you are an investor and want to get a loan on more than four or more than ten properties it really gets difficult. Investors can do many things to give themselves a better chance at being able to qualify for an investor loan.

One of the biggest issues investors run into is that they have to qualify for two houses when they have a loan on their personal residence and want to finance a rental. Because of this, it is very important not to buy the most expensive house for which you can qualify. You must have a low debt-to-income ratio to qualify for a new loan whether it is as an owner-occupant or as an investor. Maxing out your qualification on your personal residence makes it very difficult to qualify for a loan on an investment property because it raises your debt-to-income ratio.

Banks are much tougher on investors than owner-occupants

Just about every bank will require at least 20 percent down on an investment property loan. In some cases, owner-occupants can put no money down on a loan, but banks want investors to put more skin in the game. The origination fees, appraisal, and other loan costs may be more expensive as well, depending on what type of investment property you are buying.

Investors must also have more money in the bank than an owner-occupant. We saw how much an investor has to save to buy a rental, but an owner-occupant may not need any reserves in the bank to get a loan! The reason owner-occupants are favored over investors is that the government encourages homeownership. The more people who own homes, the better it is for our economy. They give subsidies and special programs to owner-occupant homeowners, which allow them to buy homes more easily than investors.

Most banks require a higher credit score for investors looking to buy rental properties. After you have four mortgages, conventional lenders will require at least a 720 credit score from investors, while some owner-occupied loans may allow a credit score under 600. Do not expect to get a loan on an investment property with a credit score under 620.

A common problem with buying rental properties is having a low enough debt-to-income ratio to qualify for a loan. Many times banks will not count rental income after you buy an investment property, which makes it even tougher. The rules regarding rental income vary by the bank and type of loan. My portfolio lender has less strict guidelines than a bank that is going by Fannie Mae guidelines. Many lenders do not count rental income until it shows up on your tax return. Some lenders will only count 75 percent of rental income and others are even stricter.

Is it hard for an investor to get a loan on a home that needs repairs?

Often, homes that need repairs can be bought below market value. However, many lenders will not loan on a house that needs repairs if the repairs affect the livability of the home. Whether you are an investor or owner-occupied buyer, repairs can cause a deal to fall apart, which is why cash offers are attractive to sellers who have a house that needs work. If you are an investor or owner-occupied buyer, there are ways to get a loan on a property when it needs repairs, even extensive repairs.

Most lenders use FHA guidelines to decide what condition a home needs to be in to get a loan. That means all major systems such as plumbing, electrical, and heating need to be in working order. The roof needs to be in good condition and there cannot be any holes in the walls or floors. FHA previously required flooring to be in good condition, but that is no longer the case. All the carpet can be missing from a home and it will still go FHA. The tricky part is that not all lenders follow FHA requirements precisely.

An FHA loan is federally insured by the government and is a big reason that owner-occupants can buy homes with little money down. Conventional loans are not federally insured or sponsored by any government agency (in most cases). There are many types of conventional loans and many different requirements on conventional loans, depending on who the lender is. Some conventional loans require everything an FHA loan requires, some less and some more. My lender does not require any repairs to be made on homes that are in horrible condition. One conventional lender that will not loan on a home does not mean that another conventional lender will have the same guidelines. If you can find a portfolio lender, they may have even less strict guidelines.

The government sponsors other loans such as VA and USDA as well. Different states also have loan programs that have varying requirements. Most government lending programs have the same or even stricter requirements than FHA.

How do you get a loan on a house that needs repairs?

There are many options for working through lender-required repairs. Your choices will differ depending on if you are an owner-occupant or an investor. The first strategy is to ask the seller to make repairs so that the home is in livable condition. What situations allow the seller to make repairs?

- **Traditional seller**: If a seller is selling a home for retail value, they usually expect to make repairs if required by the lender. To get top dollar for a house, it has to be in livable condition. Those of us that want a great deal are usually dealing with sellers who want to sell quickly without doing any repairs. The better deal you are getting, the lower the chance the seller will make any repairs.

- **REO properties**: Some REO sellers make repairs and some do not. The decision to repair or not is usually made on a case-by-case basis depending on how much work is needed. REO homes listed in as-is condition indicate that the seller will not make repairs. However, some REO sellers will make repairs if required to do so by the buyer's lender.

- **HUD Homes**: HUD does not make any repairs under any circumstance for lender-required items. HUD does have a program to allow FHA buyers to make repairs after closing. If you are an investor, and your lender requires repairs to be made before closing, you will have to cancel the contract or find a new lender.

- **Short sales**: Most short sale sellers do not have a lot of money. If you know a short sale needs work and your lender requires things to be done before closing, there is a good chance the work will not be done. The sellers are not receiving any money in most short sales and they do not want to spend any more money on the house.

- **Auctions sales**: Do not expect to have any repairs done on auction properties. Properties that are sold at auction are usually sold in as-is condition and will not be repaired.

Know who you are dealing with before you write a contract on a house

When shopping for a house, you should have already talked to a lender and you should know in what condition the lender requires a home to be. If you are using a conventional loan on a HUD home and the water cannot be turned on, but your lender requires the water to be turned on, guess what will happen? The contract will fail. If a short sale needs $10,000 in work for you to get a loan, the deal will probably never go through. On REO or traditional sales, repairs may or may not be made by the seller. Do not expect HUD or an REO seller to make repairs just because your lender requires it.

If an owner-occupant wants to get a loan on a house that needs repairs, but the seller will not repair the home; the deal is not always over. HUD offers a program for FHA buyers, which allows them to escrow for repairs and add the cost of the repairs to the loan. HUD's program is the FHA 203b loan, which can only be used on HUD homes with repairs less than $5,000. This escrow cannot be used on any other type of loan such as VA or conventional. For repairs over $5,000, an FHA 203k loan can be used on any house. This loan can have an unlimited amount of repairs, but will take more time to close and have more fees. FHA loans are only available for owner-occupants.

An FHA 203k rehab loan is not available to investors, which makes it harder for an investor to deal with homes that need repairs. That does not mean investors are out of luck when buying homes that need work. I buy homes that need a lot of work all the time, and I get loans on almost all of them.

I use a portfolio lender that does not have any repair requirements for homes that I buy. I can buy houses with bad roofs and bad heating, and my lender does not even require me to turn on the utilities. Not all portfolio lenders have the same requirements with repairs, but many will work with investors much more than the big banks will. My portfolio lender has saved many deals for investors and owner-occupants whose original lenders would not loan on a house because it needed too much work.

It is sometimes possible to escrow repairs. In some cases, an investor can escrow the repairs so that they are done after closing. The terms and chances of this happening all depend on the lender. Usually the lender will escrow for minor repairs, but may be hesitant to escrow for major repairs.

Investors can use a Homestyle Fannie Mae Renovation loan to repair houses after they close. This loan is like the FHA 203k loan, but meant for investors.

If your lender will not loan on a house that needs repairs and the seller will not make repairs, do not give up. Ask them about the Homestyle renovation loan, ask about escrowing repairs, or search for a local portfolio lender who might have different guidelines and will give you a loan.

Another option for investors besides portfolio lenders is hard money lenders. Hard money lenders are much more expensive than conventional lenders and only offer short-term loans. Hard money usually works better for fix and flips, because of the short loan term, but it can be used for rentals as well. Hard money lenders may be a decent short-term solution for rental properties, but you will have to refinance the loan very quickly. I will discuss hard money in more detail shortly.

How to lower debt-to-income ratios

One of the most common problems people have qualifying for a personal house or investment property is a high debt-to-income (DTI) ratio. Most lenders want to see a debt-to-income ratio of 45 percent or lower. If your debt-to-income ratio is higher than this, it will be very hard to qualify for a loan. I have investors emailing me all the time and asking how to get around high DTIs. Even my portfolio lender who is very lenient with lending requirements will not loan to people with high debt-to-income ratios. The two options for reducing your debt-to-income ratio are to make more money or pay off debt.

What is debt-to-income ratio and how is it calculated?

The debt-to-income ratio is calculated by taking your monthly debt payments and dividing them by your gross income. If you have $2,000 of monthly debt and $5,000 of gross income, you would have a debt-to-income ratio of 40 percent ($2,000/$5,000 = 40 percent). It is a very simple equation, but it is not always simple coming up with the monthly debt and income figures, especially if you own rental properties.

You must count the property mortgage payment against your debt-to-income ratio. Even though your debt-to-income ratio may be 35 percent right now, a new mortgage payment may push that number to 45 percent and you may not qualify for the mortgage. The DTI will generally be the deciding factor on how large a loan for which you can qualify. The highest payment you can qualify for on a new mortgage would be the payment that pushes you to the maximum debt-to-income ratio a lender will allow. If a lender will allow a 40 percent debt-to-income ratio and a $1,000 house payment pushes you to 40 percent that would be the highest payment you could qualify for. (Notice I am using different maximum DTIs, because different lenders and programs allow different DTIs)

It is your monthly income and monthly debt payments that the banks pay attention to, not total balances. You may not think that having a $2,000 credit card balance would affect your ability to qualify for a loan. However, $200 a month payments would have a huge impact on how high your mortgage could be. A $200 dollar a month difference in mortgage payments can reduce the amount you qualify for by as much as $40,000!

What expenses and income are included in DTI?

Everyone who will be on the loan you are applying for will have to include these figures for debt:

- Minimum credit card payments
- Auto loans
- Student loans
- Consumer loans
- Other financial obligations, including child support and alimony
- If you are keeping your house, count the housing payments. If you are selling your house before you buy the new one, do not count the housing payments.
- Estimated future housing expenses including principal, interest, taxes, insurance, and HOA fees

To calculate your income, you use:

- Your gross monthly salary before taxes, including overtime and bonuses. Include any alimony or child support received that you choose to have considered for repayment of the loan.
- Any additional income, such as rental property profits. This is tricky because some lenders will not count rental income until it shows up on your taxes. Other lenders

will count 75 percent of your rental income if you are an experienced investor or if the house is leased.

Usually it is a little tricky to calculate the debt-to-income ratio because different banks calculate things differently. It is best to let your lender calculate the DTI for you. If the bank comes up with a DTI that seems very high, double-check how they calculated it to see if they are doing something strange or if they put a wrong number somewhere. Some banks count depreciation of investment properties against you, even though that depreciation is not a monthly expense.

Different banks and loan programs use different DTIs. VA and FHA typically limit borrowers to a 41 percent DTI, but in some circumstances, they may increase that percentage slightly. Fannie Mae allows up to a 45 percent DTI on some loans, but you must have great credit. With credit scores under 700, you typically would have to have your DTI under 36 percent. (These numbers are constantly changing)

As you can see, this can all be very confusing trying to figure out yourself. The best thing to do is to talk to a lender and work on lowering your DTI if it is too high.

How can you lower your debt-to-income ratio?

The best way to lower a debt-to-income ratio is to make more money. The more gross income you have, the higher your DTI will be. Lenders look at other things in addition to DTI. It is not easy to start making more money, but many investors and self-employed individuals or business owners claim very little income on their taxes. Claiming little income is great if you do not want to pay too much in taxes. However, claiming little income can make it nearly impossible to qualify for a loan.

You may think you are making $10,000 a month, but if your taxes show you making $2,000 a month, your DTI could be much higher than you think. Claiming more income on your taxes will mean you have to pay the IRS more, but it may be worth it to be able to buy a house.

- Reducing debt is another way to improve your debt-to-income ratio. Debt-to-income ratios take into consideration all monthly debts that show up on your credit report. Usually the shortest debts hurt you the most, because they have the highest payments. Even though you think you are doing the smart thing by getting a 15 instead of a 30-year loan on your primary house, it actually will hurt your DTI ratios. A three-year loan on a car will make your DTI higher than a six-year loan. I am not saying you should always get the longest term possible on debt, but the lower your minimum payments are, the lower your DTI will be. You can always make extra payments if you want to pay off your loans more quickly.

- Minimum credit card payments: credit cards typically have very high interest and very high monthly payments. If you can pay off the entire balance of your credit cards, it will greatly improve your DTI.

- Auto loans: car loans can destroy a DTI! A $600 car payment is equivalent to a $120,000 mortgage and it will reduce your ability to qualify for a mortgage by $600 a month. Do you need to have a new car every three years if it means you cannot buy a house?

- Student loans: Student loans may have low interest and low payments, but they still hurt DTI.

- Consumer loans: Do you have a loan for a TV, furniture, home equity line of credit, or any other monthly payments that show up on your credit? Even a home equity line of credit that you are not using can count against your DTI.

If you do not have the money to pay off your debt, you may be able to consolidate it with a larger loan against your home that would have a lower interest rate and lower monthly payment.

What is the best way to pay off debt?

If you have a lot of credit card debt, car loans, and consumer debt, it is best to pay off one at a time as quickly as possible. The payments will stop affecting your DTI once they disappear from your credit. Paying off one debt at a time will improve your DTI more quickly, much like the snowball method for rentals.

When you pay off one debt, you can use the money you were spending on those payments to pay off the next debt sooner. Pick the debt with the lowest balance compared to the highest payment to pay off first. If you have a $2,000 debt with $200 payments, I would pay that off before you pay off a $5,000 debt with $300 payments. You will pay off the $2,000 more quickly and be able to use that extra $200 a month to pay off the next debt and so on.

If you have a huge car payment, do not be afraid to sell the car and buy a less expensive one. I own a Lamborghini now, but I have never bought a new car. My daily driver for ten years was a 1991 Mustang that I bought with cash.

If you want to buy rental properties, be careful when you buy a house for yourself. Many lenders will tell you how much you can qualify for; not how much you can afford. Buying the most expensive house you can afford, means you probably cannot buy investment properties. Try not to spend all your money on your personal residence; it makes it very hard to save money as well.

There is no magic way to reduce your DTI; it usually takes making more money or lowering your monthly debt payments. A few lenders do not consider DTI, but they are usually lending high dollar amounts on large investment properties or many investment properties at once. If you find yourself with a high DTI, talk to your lender, make sure they are figuring everything correctly, and concentrate on reducing your monthly debt payments.

Should you get a 15 or 30-year mortgage on rental properties?

15-year loans appear to save money over 30-year loans because they have a lower interest rate. However, I would much rather have the flexibility of a 30-year loan when buying rental properties. I use a 30-year loan to buy rental properties because I get more cash flow, and I have more flexibility with the extra money.

What are the advantages of a 15-year loan versus a 30-year loan?

The biggest advantage of a 15-year mortgage compared to a 30-year mortgage is the interest rate. The difference in rates changes daily and varies with different banks, but 15-year loan is usually about .5 percent less than a 30 year fixed mortgage.

Some people think the biggest advantage of 15-year loans is the term of the loan; 15 years versus 30 years. However, I do not agree because you can pay a 30-year loan off early. You do not have to make the minimum payment on a 30-year loan; you can pay more.

If you get a 15-year, $100,000 loan on a rental property at 4 percent interest rate, the payments will be $740 a month (check out bank rate mortgage calculator for calculating mortgage payments). Over the 15 years of that loan, you will pay $33,143 in interest. With a 30-year loan at 4.5 percent interest, the total amount paid in interest over the life of the loan will be $82,406.

On the surface, it looks like you are saving almost $50,000 by getting a 15-year loan. However, you are paying interest over 30 years on one loan and over 15 years on the other. The payment on a 30-year loan is only $507 a month, which is $233 less a month than the 15-year loan. If you were to take that $233 a month and put it back into the 30-year loan each month, the 30-year loan would cost $39,754 in interest and be paid off in less than 17 years. It definitely costs a little more to have the higher interest rate, but over 15 years that is only $550 each year.

Why would a 30-year loan be better than a 15-year loan?

It is true that you will pay less interest with a 15-year loan than with a 30-year loan. However, you are paying a higher monthly payment on the 15-year loan. If you add up the payment savings with the 30-year loan, you save $2,796 each year and $41,940 over 15 years on your mortgage payment.

That extra money can be used for many things that will make you much more money than the $6,000 you saved over 15 years. You can save up the cash flow to buy more rental properties. You can use the money to build an emergency fund. You could also pay off the mortgage early in the beginning and if you ever need the extra money later, you can stop putting extra money toward the mortgage.

Another huge factor when considering whether to use a 15 or 30-year loan is being able to qualify for more properties. Banks look at debt-to-income ratios when qualifying an investor. A 15-year loan has a higher payment and increases your monthly debt payments. The higher your loan payments, the less cash flow you have, and the harder it will be to qualify for new loans.

Using a 30 year ARM (adjustable rate mortgage) versus a 15 year fixed loan

I use 30-year ARMs to finance my rental properties. An ARM is an adjustable rate mortgage that has a fixed interest rate for a certain amount of time. The interest rate on an ARM can adjust up or down after the fixed period is up. My portfolio lender offers 5 and 7 year ARMs with a 30-year amortization. The rate will stay the same for the five or seven years, but can adjust after that term is up. There are limits to how much the rate can adjust each year and a ceiling that it can never go over. The great thing about ARMs is that the rate is lower than a 30-year fixed rate loan and even a 15-year fixed rate loan.

If you get an ARM for your rental properties, you will have an even lower payment than with the 30-year fixed rate loan and you will save even more in interest over a 15-year fixed rate loan. It is the best of both worlds. More on ARMs soon!

Is an adjustable rate mortgage a good loan?

I use an adjustable rate mortgage (ARM) on my rental properties for a number of reasons. I can get more than four loans on a property with ARMs. The rates are lower and an ARM is one of the only loans I can get because I have so many loans.

Adjustable Rate Mortgages (ARMs) have gotten a bad name the last few years, but they work great for me. An ARM is a loan that starts with a low-interest rate, but the interest rate can increase after a set period. A 5/30-year ARM is a 30-year loan with an initial five-year fixed rate, but can increase on the sixth year. There is a cap for how much an interest rate can increase or decrease after the adjustment period. An ARM can adjust up or down depending on what interest rates do.

ARMs have very low-interest rates locked in for a guaranteed period. ARMs can have rates that are one percent or less than a 30-year fixed rate loan. You may have heard horror stories about ARMs in the past; some people used them carelessly. You used to be able to get six month or one year ARMs with very low rates that would then jump to very high rates. Many times buyers could not qualify for the normal 30-year fixed rate loan, but they could qualify for the lower payment the ARM offered. I would not suggest using an ARM if you cannot qualify for a 30-year fixed rate mortgage. If things are that tight, reconsider your finance plan!

Another reason I use an adjustable rate mortgage is that they are one of the few options available from my local lender. I use a portfolio lender who loans their own money and does not sell their loans to investors. My portfolio lender offers a 5 and 7-year ARM as well as a 15-year fixed loan. The 5/30-year ARM has the lowest payment, lowest interest rate, and works perfect for my cash flow strategy. The reason I use a portfolio lender is that many lenders will not loan to investors when they have more than four mortgages. My portfolio lender will lend on as many loans as I can qualify for, but I have to use their limited loan options. If you can get a 30-year fixed loan with a similar rate to an ARM, I would definitely consider it.

ARMs have gotten a bad name the last decade due to the high number of loans that were foreclosed on during the housing crisis. With rental properties, you need to make sure you can qualify for the loan and that you will still have a cash flowing property if the rate on your loan increases over time.

An adjustable rate mortgage may be cheaper than a fixed rate loan

The interest rate on an ARM is lower in the beginning than a fixed rate loan, but the ARM may be cheaper than a fixed rate loan even if you do not pay it off right away. During the five years that the ARM is at its low rate, you are saving money every month over the fixed rate loan. Even if you do not pay off that ARM and the rate adjusts, it would still take years for the total cost of the ARM to catch up to the fixed rate loan. If you reinvest the money you are saving from the ARM, and make a higher return on that investment than the interest rate on the loans, you will make even more money. In my calculations, it would take until about year eight before you spend more money on interest on a 5-year ARM than a 30-year fixed loan. Another thing to consider is that money will be worth less in the future due to inflation. Saving money now and paying more in the future is usually a good thing.

Some lenders will offer balloon payments on their loans. A balloon payment means the loan has to be paid off in 5 or 10 years. My loans do not have balloon payments, but be careful with loans that do. If you buy houses below market value with a lot of equity, you should be able to refinance or sell the house when a balloon payment comes due.

An adjustable rate mortgage is a great loan, especially when you have few other options. Be smart when deciding to use an ARM; it can be a great tool for any investor. The biggest mistake you can make is not being prepared for a payment increase if you are not able to pay off the loan or refinance. If you are prepared to hold the loan, you should be just fine.

How to finance more than four mortgages

Some banks may tell you that it is impossible to get more than four mortgages in your name, but there are banks who will loan on 10, 20, or even 100 properties. If you know where to look, you can find traditional banks and portfolio lenders that will finance more than four properties.

When I bought my first rental property, I used a mortgage broker to fund my deal. He did a great job of finding the right bank for my needs. However, the lender still required me to jump through multiple hoops, send in every financial detail of my life for five years, and justify any deposit over $1,000 for the last year. As a Realtor, I make many deposits over $1,000 and I spent hours and hours hunting down each deposit and explaining exactly what it was. After bending over backwards for the lender, I still had to put 25 percent down to get a decent interest rate. The sad part was I did not have four mortgaged properties at that time; I only had two.

Technically, Fannie Mae guidelines say investors should be able to get a loan for up to ten properties. Even with these guidelines in place, many lenders still will not finance more than four properties, because it is too risky for their investors. If you are diligent and make enough calls, you should be able to find a lender who will loan on up to ten properties. If you want to try an easier route, call a mortgage broker who can help you find a lender who can get it done. These are the requirements for most conventional lenders who will finance from five to ten properties.

- Own five to ten residential properties with financing attached
- A 25 percent down payment (30 percent for 2-4 unit)
- Minimum credit score of 720
- No late payments on any mortgage within the last twelve months
- No bankruptcies or foreclosures in the last seven years
- Two years of tax returns showing rental income from all rental properties
- Six months of PITI reserves on each of the financed properties

Most banks will only allow a 70 percent loan-to-value ratio if you already have four mortgages and want to refinance any of your properties. They also will not allow you to take out any cash with the refinance. I use cash out refinances all the time to take out money for more rental properties. Lenders say it is too risky to do a cash-out refinance for investors with more than four mortgages. In my opinion, if an investor has the 20 percent down and the cash reserves needed, they are less of a risk than a first time homebuyer putting down 3.5 percent or less.

A portfolio lender will finance more than four mortgages and possibly many more

Local lenders that offer portfolio financing are another (my favorite) option for investors. It can take some research, time, and networking to find a portfolio lender, but they have much looser lending guidelines. Portfolio lenders use their own money to fund deals and do not have to adhere to Fannie Mae guidelines. My portfolio lender has no limits on how many loans they will give to investors as long as they have the cash, reserves, and income to support the mortgages. They allow 20 percent down on those properties and do not require your life history to give you the loan.

There are some drawbacks to using a portfolio lender. My local bank does not offer a 30-year fixed mortgage. They offer 15-year fixed and 5/30 and 7/30 ARMs. The local bank charges slightly higher rates and origination fees, but not by much. My last loan on my tenth mortgage was a 5/30 ARM at 4.5 percent. This interest rate was .5 percent higher than my other loans, because I have more than ten mortgages. The local bank may require you to move all your accounts over to them, but that is a small price to pay for investor loans.

How to find a portfolio lender who will finance more than four properties

A portfolio lender is crucial to many investors' strategies because they often loan on multiple rentals and flips. They often have less strict lending requirements than large national banks, making it easier for investors to get loans.

A portfolio lender is a local bank that loans their own money, so they do not have to meet Fannie Mae lending guidelines. This allows the portfolio lender more flexibility, but they do not offer as great a variety of loan programs as large banks do. Each portfolio lender has different terms and loan programs. I can put 20 percent down on as many properties as I can qualify for with my portfolio lender. Some portfolio lenders have less than 30-year amortizations, balloon payments, and other restrictions on their loans.

A portfolio lender will also prefer you to have all your accounts and money in their bank. This is usually not a big issue for most people since a portfolio lender will have very competitive programs and products. The better relationship you build with a portfolio lender, the better loans you will get.

I found my lender through word of mouth. I had heard from other real estate agents that my portfolio lender was the best bank for investors. After I ran into problems financing my fifth rental property with my previous mortgage broker, I contacted my portfolio lender. They had the perfect loans for my investment properties. It took me about a week to move all of my accounts over to their bank so I could easily finance new rentals.

The first way to find a portfolio lender is to ask everyone you know. Some people may not know what a portfolio lender is; ask them if they know a lender that likes to loan to investors. Whom can you ask?

- Real Estate agents know many lenders and may be your best source to find a portfolio lender.
- Other lenders may be able to refer you to a portfolio lender if they cannot do a loan for you.
- Investors in the area will know portfolio lenders; the trick is meeting them. Real estate investor meetings are a great place to meet investors and get local information.
- Ask your local bank whether they are a portfolio lender and what types of investor lending programs they offer.
- Ask title companies whom local investors use to finance their rental properties.
- Ask your chamber of commerce who the most investor-friendly banks in town are.

Searching the internet is the easiest way to start your search for a portfolio lender. Simply search for a portfolio lender in your state on any web search engine. I have tried this a couple of times for people in different states and I always get results. Once you find a bank that mentions portfolio lending in your state, call them, and ask what type of investor programs they offer.

If none of the options above are working and you cannot find a portfolio lender, you may have to resort to calling local banks in your area that are not national chains and see what type of investor loans they offer. If they do not have what you are looking for, ask them if they know which bank might. Keep trying until you have called all the local banks you can find.

What questions should you ask when calling a bank?

Many banks do not advertise that they are portfolio lenders and many people working at the bank may not even know what a portfolio lender is. If a bank says they are not a portfolio lender, do not give up! Ask to talk to a commercial loan officer or the business-banking department. Ask specific questions about what type of investor programs they offer. Here are some good questions to ask:

- Do you loan to investors who already have four mortgages?
- Do you have a commercial loan or business loan department?
- Do you sell your loans or keep them in-house?
- Do you allow investors with four or more mortgages to do a cash-out refinance?
- What terms and loan programs do you offer investors? ARM, 15 or 30-year fixed, balloon.

- What interest rates do you charge and what are the initial costs for your loans?
- What loan-to-value ratios do you offer investors for new purchases and refinances?
- What are your seasoning requirements for refinances?

Finding a portfolio lender is not easy, but it makes investing a lot easier. My portfolio lender has been awesome financing my rental properties and fix and flips.

How do you find a national portfolio lender?

If you cannot find a local lender who will loan on multiple rental properties, a national portfolio lender might be able to help. A portfolio lender can loan on multiple properties because they are using in-house commercial loans. Commercial loans do not have to be used just for commercial properties as the name states; they can be used for residential investment properties as well. Residential loans typically have much more regulation and stricter guidelines than commercial loans. In the past, investors looking to finance more than ten properties had to rely on local portfolio lenders, but there are now nationwide companies offering commercial products for investors looking to finance many properties. I am in the process myself of deciding if I want to refinance eight of my rentals with one of these lenders. The national companies are primarily funded by hedge funds. They tend to loan based on the properties and not the borrower.

What type of loans do the national portfolio lenders offer?

National lenders offer many types of loans, from 5 and 10-year ARMs to 30-year fixed rate loans. Amortizations, rates, and terms differ based on the company and the properties that are being used as collateral. Many of these funds offer hard money loans for fix and flips as well.

I get commercial loans on my rental properties, but they are very similar to a residential product. The loans are ARMs with 30-year amortization, no prepayment penalty, no balloon payment, and great rates that are less than five percent.

National companies offer ARMs as well as 30-year fixed-rate loans. However, the interest rates are higher (6 to 8 percent) and there may be more fees. National lenders tend to be more willing to loan in larger loan amounts and offer blanket loans that cover more than one property. Some local lenders will be hesitant to loan too much to one investor, where the larger lenders are more flexible.

What is a balloon payment and how does it affect rental properties?

Some national and even some local lenders have balloon payments on their loans, requiring you to repay the loan after 5 or 10 years. If you choose a loan with a balloon payment, you must have an exit strategy. Many lenders say they will work with investors and figure out a way to finance them again in 5 or 10 years, but there is no guarantee. Commercial loans with a balloon payment can be very risky. We also do not know what interest rates will be in five years, and it may not make sense or even be possible to refinance in 5 or 10 years if rates rise significantly.

An investor has to have a backup strategy to pay off these loans when the term is over. Using cash flow to pay down the loan may be an option. Investing cash in other high yield investments may be another option. You could also keep a portion of your property portfolio without loans. In the worst-case scenario, you could sell houses to pay off the loan at the end of the term.

How do the national lenders determine how much someone can borrow?

The national lenders have different guidelines than many lenders. Many of the national rental property lenders will not care about debt to income ratios as much as cash flow. They tend to loan 75 percent of the value of homes, but they must have decent cash flow.

- The loan-to-value ratio is calculated from appraisals on each house, which the investor has to pay for.
- There could be prepayment fees on the loans if you pay them off before the term is over.
- Debt Service Coverage Ratio (DSCR) must be 1.2 times the mortgage payment. The DSCR is figured differently on each property, but cash flow is based on the rent minus taxes, insurance, vacancy, maintenance, HOA fees, and any other costs.
- Recourse and non-recourse loans are available. A recourse loan means the bank can come after your personal assets if you default on a loan. Almost all residential and most small commercial loans are recourse loans. Some large commercial loans are non-recourse, which enables limited partners to invest in a large

property without fear of losing their personal assets as well as their investment.

- There may or may not be seasoning periods for refinancing properties and taking cash out.

A few large companies offer portfolio loans to residential property owners. Please visit my site at https://investfourmore.com/2014/03/06/finance-ten-properties-national-lender/, to see an updated list of national portfolio lenders.

What is the best option for investors looking to finance more than ten rental properties?

I love my local portfolio lender. I think they are the number one option if you can find one in your area. If you cannot find a portfolio lender or you have a large number of properties that you want to refinance, the larger portfolio lenders may be a better option.

Should you put rental properties in an LLC?

This may seem like a weird topic for the financing chapter, but LLCs can have a huge effect on the ability to finance properties. Many conventional lenders will not loan to an LLC, but some portfolio lenders will. Before you put all your properties into a LLC, make sure you have your financing figured out.

LLCs can be a powerful tool to protect investors from liability on rental properties. I have a separate LLC for each of my 16 rental properties, but an LLC is not the right choice for everyone. I put my rentals in an LLC mainly to protect myself from liability. However, there are many things to consider when deciding to use an LLC for your rental properties. LLCs can affect financing, increase costs, and have many negative consequences. I am not a lawyer or providing legal advice. If you have legal questions, please consult an attorney.

I have always put my rental properties into a separate LLC for each property. I do this because of the liability risk that comes with owning rental properties. If you own a rental property in your own name, someone can sue you personally and attack your assets. That lawsuit may not only affect your rental property, but your personal assets as well. If you have your rental property in a LLC with a separate checking account, there is a better chance that only that rental property will be affected by a lawsuit.

In Colorado, it is not very difficult to create an LLC. I have my assistant create the paperwork and submit the documents to the Secretary of State. Each state has different requirements and rules to create an LLC. Some states, such as Colorado, have a very easy process to create an LLC while others are much more difficult. Check out your states requirements before you take this on yourself. I learned how to create and submit the paperwork by looking at documents for other LLCs that were created by a lawyer.

In Colorado, it costs $50 to set up a LLC if you create the documents and file yourself. Every year there is a $10 filing fee to keep the LLC active. Other states may charge more or less in fees for an LLC.

It can cost hundreds and possibly thousands of dollars to hire a lawyer to create an LLC. When I asked a lawyer to create an LLC for me, he wanted $850. You have to consider the cost when deciding whether to use LLCs. If it costs you $1,000 to create and $500 a year to maintain the LLC, it may not be worth it. On the other hand, you may want to use one LLC for all your properties. The fewer LLCs you use the less protection you will have.

Why do you need an LLC for each rental property?

This may seem like a weird place to put this chapter, but putting properties in an LLC can affect the financing. Remember to always talk to your lawyer or accountant for specific legal questions or details.

I put all of my rentals in their own LLC. I do this to protect myself from liability. According to my lawyers, if one rental property is affected by a lawsuit, then all the properties in the same LLC can be affected. Likewise, if you have separate LLCs, but have one bank account for all the properties, it can be argued that the rental properties are not separate entities and they could all be affected by the lawsuit.

You could also use one LLC for two rental properties or three to reduce your costs, but again all the properties in that LLC could be affected by a lawsuit. In Texas, they have a series LLC that can reduce the costs of multiple LLCs.

LLCs can help project your rental properties from liability, but LLCs can also create problems. Many banks will not loan to a LLC, they will only loan to an individual person. It is possible to buy a property in your own name, get a loan, and transfer the property to the LLC. The problem with this strategy is that the bank may have a due on sale clause meaning that if the property is sold, the bank can call the loan due immediately. Transferring a property from an individual person to an LLC is considered a sale, even if the individual selling the home owns the LLC.

Most people will tell you the chances of a bank calling a loan due because you sold the property to your LLC are very small. However, it can happen. If they call the loan due, you will have to pay it off by selling or refinancing in a very short period.

There is the option of putting your rental property in a land trust, which in theory does not allow the lender to call your loan due when you transfer the property to an LLC.

I use a portfolio lender who will loan to an LLC, so I have no problem putting all of my properties into LLCs. My portfolio lender will refinance my properties that are in LLCs and let me buy new homes with an LLC or transfer my properties into an LLC. If your bank does not loan to LLCs, you may not be able to refinance or purchase properties with an LLC.

Additional ways to protect yourself from liability

If you decide not to use an LLC or you want more ways to protect yourself, here are some tips.

- Do not be a lazy property owner! Make sure your houses have working smoke detectors and carbon monoxide detectors and are safe. Most lawsuits come from a tenant getting hurt or worse, because the property was not safe.
- Get liability insurance. Property owners can also get an umbrella policy that will cover all their properties and protect against lawsuits. Take to your insurance agent about your options.

An LLC offers protection in case of a lawsuit against a rental property. However, you will have to decide if that extra protection is worth the cost and the possibility of not being able to refinance homes or your loans being called due. Always talk to your bank before you use LLCs to make sure they are okay with it. Always consult your attorney about using an LLC and make sure it is set up correctly to protect you.

LLCs can be expensive to set up in some states, which is another consideration. It is very cheap to set up LLCs in Colorado (less than $50 if you can do the paperwork yourself), but in other states the costs can be much higher.

Conclusion

Financing rental properties is one of the most important things you can do as an investor. Using leverage will increase your returns and make you more money in the end. Financing properties is not always easy and you should never assume you would be able to get a loan for rentals.

One of the first things any investor should do is talk to a lender. If there is problem with your credit, your debt-to-income ratio, or something else, the sooner you know about it the better. If you can start fixing those problems right away, you can buy rentals properties sooner and make more money in the end. If you wait until you are ready to buy a property to talk to a lender or figure out financing, you may be in for a rude awakening if the lender says, "Sorry, we just cannot loan to you right now." You do not want to miss deals or delay your investing because you assumed everything would be okay. If you know you have bad credit or another issue, a lender can help you get it solved much more quickly than trying to do it on your own.

7. How to invest in rental properties with less cash.

There are about 1,000 strategies advertised for investing in real estate with little or no money down. Some of the strategies are great and some are horrible or even illegal. It is expensive to buy real estate and many people use the allure of using no money to get rich to sell programs or properties.

The truth is that you can buy with less cash and in some cases less money down. However, there is no secret recipe or easy way to do it. It will take sacrifice and hard work to buy rentals, find great deals, have cash flow, and buy with less of your own cash.

It is also important to realize that buying with little or no money down is not always a good thing. There are many deals out there where you can buy with less money down, but the properties will not make you any money. It will not do you any good to buy properties with none of your own money if they never make you any money. When using these strategies to buy with less cash, always be certain you are not sacrificing all your cash flow, or betting on appreciation to make your money.

How to buy with little money down

Many people do not have the 20 percent down payment that most banks require when buying an investment property. The easiest way to buy an investment property with less than 20 percent down is to buy as an owner-occupant and later rent out the house, but there are other options for investors as well.

Using a line of credit, refinancing your home, and even credit cards can provide ways to buy investment properties for less money. Seller financing is a great way to put less money down on a rental property if you can find willing sellers. A more advanced technique is to use hard money financing, and refinance to a conventional loan. However, you choose to buy rental property, always research the method to make sure it is legal in your state, okay with your lender, and that you are not stretching your finances too thin.

How to buy an investment property with little money down as an owner-occupant

The easiest way to buy an investment property with less money down is to buy as an owner-occupant, then rent out and keep the property as an investment after you have satisfied your loan requirements. Most owner-occupant loans require the buyer to occupy the home for at least one year. However, once that year is up, the house can be rented and used as an investment property. The down payments for owner-occupied loans range from no money down to 20 percent or more. USDA and VA have great no money down programs, which I discuss later in this chapter. Those programs also have little to no mortgage insurance, which will save an investor a lot of money each month. Mortgage insurance is typical on most loans that have a loan-to-value ratio of more than 80 percent. Mortgage insurance can add hundreds of dollars to your house payment and eat away at your cash flow. The process for buying as an owner-occupant and then turning the house into an investment property is as follows:

- Buy a house as an owner-occupant that will cash flow when you rent it out.
- Move into the house and live there for at least a year.

- After one year, buy another house as an owner-occupant that will cash flow.
- Move into the new house, rent the first house, and repeat the process every year!

Eventually you will build up equity and extra cash flow that will enable you to buy properties with a 20 percent down payment. If you could repeat this process ten times, that would be an excellent way to get started, but no one wants to move ten times in ten years. It can also be tough to convince your family to live in a home that would also be a great rental. As we talked about earlier, you may run into problems qualifying for new houses if your debt-to-income ratio gets too high.

What type of loan allows for investing with little money down?

How do you get a loan that will allow you to buy properties with a lower down payment? This section is all about the different loan options available for owner-occupants who are looking to live in a house and then turn it into an investment property.

How I would buy an investment property with little money down if I had to start over?

If I were to start over buying rentals, I would drastically change the way I did things. When I bought my first house in 2002, I did a little work to it, lived there seven years, and then sold it. I did not make much money and although it was a great house to live in, it did not provide any financial benefit. With what I know now, I could do so much better! I would buy houses as an owner-occupant, live in them one year, and then rent them out after I had satisfied the owner-occupant requirements. I would make sure I bought below market value, and I would buy homes that would provide plenty of cash flow when I was ready to rent them.

With little money to put down on a property, your options are limited, unless you can buy a house as an owner-occupant. If you buy a home as an owner-occupant, you can put three percent or less down on a home! It takes some sacrifice and flexibility to use this method, but it is not always easy to get ahead in life.

I am not advising that an investor pretend to be an owner-occupant. There are serious penalties for pretending to be an owner-occupant, especially on HUD homes (up to two years in prison and $250,000 fine). However, you can buy the home as an owner-occupant, live in it for one year (or whatever the owner-occupant requirement is), and then rent it out. This process can be repeated as many times as you can stand moving into a new house every year.

What type of loans allow for a smaller down payment?

Many owner-occupant loans allow for a small down payment. Most investor loans require at least 20 or even 25 percent down. An owner-occupant has many more options to buy a home with little money down.

FHA loans

FHA loans are government-insured and can be obtained with as little as 3.5 percent down. You can only have one FHA loan at a time unless you have extenuating circumstances such as job relocation. You do have to pay mortgage insurance on FHA loans, which I will discuss later. There are limits to the amount an FHA mortgage can be and varies by state and even by city.

USDA loans

USDA loans can be used in rural areas and small towns. These loans most likely cannot be used in medium-sized towns or large towns/metro areas. The loan is a fantastic loan for those that qualify and want to buy a home in the designated areas. USDA loans can be obtained with no money down, but have mortgage insurance as well.

VA loans

The United States Veterans Administration administers VA loans. You have to be a veteran, active duty, or certain honorably discharged military to get VA loans, but the loans can be obtained with no money down and no mortgage insurance! VA is a great option for those that qualify because the costs are so much less without mortgage insurance.

Down payment assistance programs

Many states have down payment assistance programs. In Colorado, we have a program called CHFA. The program helps buyers get into owner-occupied homes with very little money down. CHFA actually uses an FHA loan, but allows for less than a 3.5 percent down payment. Check with lenders on your state to see if they have any down payment assistance programs.

Conventional mortgages

Even conventional mortgages have low down payment loans available for owner-occupants, as low as three percent. You will most certainly have to pay mortgage insurance with any conventional loan that has less than 20 percent down. Unlike some of the other loan options available, owner-occupants can have as many conventional mortgages in their name as they want.

FHA 203K Rehab loan

A FHA 203K rehab loan allows the borrower to finance the house they are buying and the repair after closing. This is a great loan if a home needs work, but the buyer has limited funds to repair the house. There are more upfront costs associated with this loan, because two appraisals are needed and lenders have higher fees for 203K loans. The same down payments and mortgage insurance will be needed as with a regular FHA loan. The borrower must be able to qualify for the loan amount after the work is done.

What loan costs does a buyer need to consider besides the down payment?

On almost any loan, you will have more costs than just the down payment. The lender charges an origination fee, appraisal fee, prepaid interest, prepaid insurance, and possibly prepaid mortgage insurance. In addition, you may have more costs that the title company charges such as a closing fee, recording fees, and possibly title insurance. In most cases, the seller pays for title insurance, but with HUD and VA foreclosures, the buyer has to pay for title insurance. These costs can add up to another 3.5 percent of the mortgage amount or sometimes more. A lender can give you an estimate of these costs before you get your loan.

The lender and title company charge more fees than just the down payment, but that does not mean that you have to pay them upfront. You can ask the seller to pay closing costs. You can obtain loans such as VA and USDA with no out-of-pocket cash if you can get the seller to pay closing costs. You may still have to put down an earnest money deposit, but that can be refunded at closing in some cases. When you ask the seller to pay closing costs it reduces the amount of money they are getting from the sale so you might actually pay more for the home than if you did not ask for closing costs. However, in my mind paying a little more for the house and financing those costs to save cash is better than paying more money out-of-pocket for a little cheaper home.

What is mortgage insurance?

Consumers must pay mortgage insurance when they put less than 20 percent down on a home loan. Lenders charge mortgage insurance to help mitigate risk because the less money someone puts down, the riskier the loan is. There are many different types of mortgage insurance and a few loans do not charge mortgage insurance, but they are rare. Some mortgage insurance can be removed after a certain amount of time and some cannot. The cost of mortgage insurance also varies greatly depending on the loan program you use.

During the great depression in 1934, the Federal Housing Authority (FHA) was created to help the economy. Prior to FHA, for the most part everyone had to have 20 percent down to get a loan. Most banks thought 20 percent down payments would show consumers they could afford a house. The practice of putting 20 percent down made the housing market much more stable, but it also meant fewer people could own a home.

Usually the more people who own a home and the more houses that are bought and sold, the better our economy does. That is why there are huge tax incentives when buying a house as an owner-occupant or as an investor. The government encourages homeowners to buy houses with less than 20 percent down by offering FHA insured loans. FHA was not meant to finance homes, but to create insurance for banks who gave consumers loans with less than 20 percent down. Many private mortgage insurance companies work with conventional loans to offer less than 20 percent down.

Once banks started lending with less than 20 percent down, the risk of default increased greatly and it was not worth it. To help mitigate that risk, lenders charge the borrower mortgage insurance, which can be about one percent of the loan per year. The mortgage insurance allows banks to loan to borrowers who cannot put 20 percent down because the insurance will reduce the losses the banks incur in a default.

Although the bank requires mortgage insurance on properties with less than 20 percent down, the bank does not keep the money paid for mortgage insurance. On conventional loans, private mortgage insurance companies take the premiums, and if a property defaults, the mortgage insurance company will either take the property or pay off the bank for the amount insured.

With FHA loans, the mortgage insurance is paid to the federal government who insures the loans for the banks. FHA homes that are foreclosed on and repossessed by the government become HUD homes.

How much is mortgage insurance on residential properties?

FHA has set guidelines for how much mortgage insurance is. The current cost is 1.75 percent upfront and the monthly fee varies based on the amount of the loan. The amount FHA charges changes frequently since FHA must keep two percent of its total liability as cash. Due to the housing crisis, the fund dropped well below two percent, which caused FHA to increase mortgage insurance.

The upfront mortgage insurance is paid when the buyers close on their new home and the monthly payments are made as long as the loan exists. The payment on a $100,000 loan would be $506 (without taxes and insurance) based on a 4.5 percent interest rate. The payment increases to $574 after FHA mortgage insurance is added. The upfront mortgage insurance cost would be about $1,700, which can be financed into the loan.

Private mortgage insurance (PMI) varies with different banks and loan programs. Private mortgage insurance typically costs from 0.5 to one percent of the entire loan amount each year. On a $100,000 loan, the homeowner would pay $83.33 per month or $1,000 a year with a one percent fee.

FHA mortgage insurance must be maintained for the life of the loan. However, some types of Private Mortgage Insurance can be eliminated after a certain amount of time and equity build up. Some private mortgage insurance programs can be removed after two years if the loan is 80 percent or less than the value of the home. If your home goes up in value or you pay off a lot of your loan balance, you may be able to get the PMI removed. The lender may require an appraisal or a simple BPO to determine the value of the property. Not all conventional loans will allow the borrower to remove the PMI, so ask your lender when applying.

Another option to put less money down is to use a 20 percent down first loan and a second loan. The first loan is for 80 percent of the value of the home and the second loan could be 10 or 15 percent of the value of the home. These loans were more common before the housing crisis, and are still available. The second loans that are available now are for owner-occupants only and tend to have much higher interested rates than first loans. The actual savings of getting a first and a second is not minimal over getting a first with mortgage insurance.

How does mortgage insurance affect real estate investors?

Mortgage insurance does not affect most real estate investors, because they do not put less than 20 percent down. However, investors put less money down by buying as an owner-occupant and then renting out the home after they have satisfied the owner-occupant requirement. When an investor buys as an owner-occupant with less than 20 percent down, they most likely will have to factor in the expense of mortgage insurance. If they use PMI, they may be able to get the mortgage insurance removed, but not on an FHA loan. Make sure to account for that extra expense when figuring the cash flow on a property.

There are some 15 percent down options for investors available, but the cost of mortgage insurance usually makes it much more advantageous to put 20 percent down.

How will loans with less money down affect cash flow?

Whenever you get a loan with less than 20 percent down, you are going to raise your monthly payment. Not only does your payment increase because the loan amount increases, but the mortgage insurance will add even more to your mortgage payment. Many times the difference between a 20 percent down loan and a five percent down loan can be hundreds of dollars per month.

It is very important to run the numbers on any house you buy that you eventually plan to rent out to make sure the home cash flows after all expenses, including vacancies and maintenance. It is vitally important you buy these homes below market value to leave yourself enough room to cash flow and sell the home if needed. When you have little money available for down payments and repairs, it usually means you have little money for vacancies and maintenance when the house is rented. In the worst-case scenario, if you bought it below market value and you cannot rent it or if you lose your job, you will be able to sell the home and make a profit.

I believe the sooner you start investing the better. Make sure you have a backup plan for if things do not go as planned when you buy an owner-occupied property that you plan to turn into a rental. Could you sell the home if needed after a year? Are you willing to live in the home longer than a year if things do not go as planned?

How to use house hacking to buy with less money down

House hacking has become common in the real estate investing world. You may not have heard the term house hacking, but you may be familiar with the practice. House hacking is buying a multifamily property, living in one unit, and renting out the other units. House hacking can be a great way to start buying rental properties because you can buy with low-money down owner-occupant loans and still collect rent right away.

When you buy a single-family home as an owner-occupant you cannot rent the home for a year (because you are living in it), which can make it harder to buy multiple properties. When you buy a multifamily property as an owner-occupant (which is legal as long as it is 2-4 units), you can live in one unit and collect rents on the other units right away.

House hacking helps you to build a rental history sooner and to be able to qualify for more rentals sooner than if you bought a single-family home. Most banks will not let you count rents collected as income until they show up on your taxes. This makes it very difficult to qualify for new loans when you already own a rental property, but do not have a long rental history.

What are the disadvantages of house hacking?

House hacking is a great way to start buying rentals, but it takes some sacrifice. When you buy as an owner-occupant, you have to live in the house for at least one year in most cases. If you are buying a multifamily house, you will have to live in one unit of the property for at least one year.

Depending on what stage of your life you are in, living in an apartment can be fine or miserable. If you are a single college student, you are probably used to living in apartments. However, if you have a family and kids, you may be used to living in a nice single-family home. It may be very difficult to live in a multifamily property if you are used to something nicer.

For some people, house hacking is worth it but for others, the sacrifice and family stress it would cause are not worth it.

After that year is up, you can sell or rent the property out. If you live in one unit of a multifamily house, you can rent out that unit. You have to live in the property more than 50 percent of the time to be considered an owner-occupant. You cannot leave one unit vacant and pretend to live there.

After renting out the unit you were living in, you could buy another rental as an owner-occupant and repeat the process. As I have already discussed, it is easier to qualify for more loans when you have a longer rental history. House hacking makes it easier to buy more rental properties than single-family homes, if you need the rent to count as income.

If you buy the right multifamily property, you should be able to live there for free or even make money while you are living in one unit. For example:

- A three-unit property with 3-bedroom, 1-bath units, renting for $800 per unit
- The property cost $150,000. With three percent down, the payments would be $900 a month (including mortgage insurance).
- With taxes, insurance, maintenance, and vacancy costs, the total monthly expenses would be about $1,450 to $1,550 depending on taxes in your area.
- You would bring in $1,600 a month in rent, which is less than your monthly expenses and you get to live in the property for free (excluding utilities). When you move out your cash flow would increase even more.

This kind of deal is not available in all markets, but they are out there. I still prefer single-family rentals, but house hacking is a great option to get started, especially if multifamily homes have good rent to value ratios in your area.

How to buy rental properties with no money down using hard money or private money

Many investors use hard money as a short-term solution to fund real estate deals. Hard money can be used to fund fix and flips or buy rental properties until long-term financing can be put in place. I fix and flip homes as well as investing in long-term rentals, but I do not use hard money. Using hard money is more expensive than traditional financing and I have other short-term financing in place.

Hard money is used to finance properties for six months or a year. Hard money lenders use much different terms than a traditional bank. They charge very high interest rates from 10 to 16 percent plus points. Points are a percentage of the total loan and can add up quickly when a hard money lender is charging 2, 3, or even 4 points on a loan.

The advantage of a hard money lender is that they may loan the entire amount of money you will need to complete a deal. Most hard money lenders base the amount of the loan on the after repaired value (ARV), how much it will be worth once you fix up the home. They will loan 65 or 70 percent of ARV.

Here is an example of how one hard money lender structures a deal. You buy a home for $60,000 with an ARV of $130,000. The hard money lender will loan up to 70 percent ARV, or $91,000. They will need bids or estimates for repairs and will pay for repairs the same way as a construction loan. They will pay for 25 percent of the repairs needed at closing and the other payments will come in 25 percent increments as the repairs are completed. The lender does not charge any interest or points until you sell the home at which point you pay them the loan principal, interest, and points. This particular hard money lender charges 15 percent interest and 4 points, but they will reduce the points paid after you do a few deals with them.

On this deal, if you use the money for six months, the interest will be $6,825 and the points will be $3,640. There are hard money lenders that charge lower interest and points, but will want a split of your profits. I do not use hard money lenders myself, because of how much they charge, but for investors who have no other options it can work out well.

Where can you find hard moneylenders?

There are many hard moneylenders out there, but many only loan in specific states, while some loan nationwide. The best way to find a hard moneylender is to search for one in your state on any search engine. I have listed some hard moneylenders below. I have a list of national hard money lenders here: https://investfourmore.com/2015/08/10/how-to-find-a-nationwide-hard-money-lender/

What is private money?

Private money is money that comes from a private person. The person loaning the money is not a bank, mortgage company, hard money lender, or portfolio lender; they are just a person. Regular people will loan money on real estate because interest rates on other secured investments are low right now. Have you looked at what the rate is on a CD? For a five-year CD the average is less than one percent! You cannot even come close to keeping up with inflation with that rate. Many wealthy people are looking for a higher yield investment that is still secured. Loaning on real estate may be the perfect answer for them to increase returns and create great opportunities for investors.

How do you find private money for investment property?

The biggest problem with private money is finding someone to loan you private money! Many websites claim to have private money lenders that they can connect you with for a small fee. In my experience, those websites take your money and connect you with a hard money lender at best. A real private money lender wants to loan their money to someone they know and trust. They do not want to loan to a complete stranger who may not be trustworthy or have a clue what they are doing. I am still trying to find a source for good private lenders, but I think I am limited to one option; people I know. I use private money from my sister who wants a better return on her son's college money. She trusts me, she knows I know how to make money, and she is willing to loan her money at a very reasonable rate: seven percent with no points. This is a higher rate than she could get with a CD or other secured investment. It is cheaper for me than financing with hard money.

How to buy a rental property with no money down using hard money or private money

According to Fannie guidelines you can refinance a loan with no seasoning period. Fannie guidelines do not allow a cash-out refinance without a seasoning period, but if you finance the repairs and purchase price of a property, you still might get all your cash back out. You can get a long-term loan to replace the hard money loan without waiting a year, as you would with a cash-out refinance.

For example, if you buy a home for $100,000 with hard money lending 100 percent of the purchase price and financing $35,000 in repairs. The total loan is now $135,000. You fix up the home and refinance using a Fannie loan, which will loan up to 75 percent of the new appraised value. If the appraisal comes in at $185,000, you could finance up to $135,000. If the appraisal had come in at $190,000, you could still only refinance $135,000 because you cannot take any cash out. This technique can be rather expensive because you have to pay the higher interest rate on the hard money loan, the initial points, and the refinance costs with Fannie Mae. However, you just bought a long-term rental and fixed it up with almost no out-of-pocket costs!

If you use private money, you would structure the deal the same way, by getting a loan with the private money lender and then refinancing after the home is fixed up.

How to buy a property with little money down using a turnkey rental property provider

A new trend in the U.S. is buying turnkey rental properties that are purchased, repaired, rented, and managed by a turnkey provider. Turnkey properties are a great opportunity for investors to buy rental properties out-of-state when homes are too expensive in their own area. There are turnkey providers who offer as little as five percent down for investors, but they tend to have very high interest rates. With most turnkey properties, you will not have to make any repairs, which reduces the amount of money you need. However, because they are rented, managed, and repaired many turnkey properties are priced at a premium. It is tough to get a great deal on a turnkey rental. There will be much more on turn-key properties later in the book.

How to use seller financing to buy investment property with little money down

Some sellers may be willing to carry the loan on a house or finance a second loan to allow a buyer to put less than 20 percent down. If your bank is willing to offer 80 percent loan-to-value, the seller may loan the other 20 percent, which would equal no money down for the buyer. The seller may also offer a number of other loan-to-value percentages that can help a buyer get into to a home for less than 20 percent down.

Finding seller-financed properties is not easy. Most sellers are not looking to finance a loan when they sell. In order to find seller financed listings, look for homes that have no loans against them and an MLS listing description saying that seller financing is available. The seller's terms can vary greatly depending on how desperate they are to sell and what exactly they want out of the deal. Do not expect to pay four percent interest on a seller-financed loan; they will want a premium on any money they lend. It is also harder to find great deals with seller financing, which is a key to my strategy. There are many new restrictions on financing, including seller financing, thanks to the recent Dodd-Frank Act. Be sure to check with an attorney on the legality of seller financing.

How to partner with another investor to buy investment property with little money down

The biggest problem for most investors is finding the money to flip or the down payment for rentals. In some cases, an investor has a lot of money, but no time to find deals, renovate houses, or perform other tasks. In other cases, an investor may have the knowledge and time to invest, but no money. If done right, a partnership can be a mutually beneficial way to invest in real estate.

I do not have a partner in my business, but I used to partner with my father. It would have been tough for me to flip houses or sell real estate without a partner to help with financing and mentoring. However, in some ways I think having a partner held me back by providing a comfort zone that allowed to me to relax more than I should have. Having a partner for real estate deals can be a great way to get started, but if you do not set things up right, it can be a disaster and destroy relationships.

How does a partnership work with rental properties?

Rental property partnerships can be even riskier than fix and flip partnerships. The tough part is predicting how the partnership will progress with time. One partner may want to cash out in five years and the other may want to hold the properties for thirty years.

It is also a little tougher figuring what the returns will be on rental properties. You know what the profit is after a flip is completed. With rentals, you have equity pay down, tax advantages, appreciation, and cash flow. Some of these returns, such as cash flow, are in the form of cash in your pocket. Others, such as appreciation and equity pay down, are not realized until the home is sold or refinanced. Not only do you have to come up with a percentage of the actual profits (cash flow) that will be split, but also you have to come up with a percentage of the equity that will be split if the properties are sold or if one partner wants to sell out and the other partner wants to keep the properties.

Things to consider when collaborating on rental properties:

Who does the work? Will both partners work to find properties or will one do all the work? How will repairs and maintenance be handled? Who will screen tenants? Will a property manager be used?

How much money will each partner contribute? Will one partner put in all the money and the other do all the work or will it be a mix?

What percentage of the profits will each partner take? It can be very tough figuring the profits on rentals. You will have different amounts of cash flow every month and houses can be depreciated. With depreciation, tax returns will show less profit than you actually make. You also need to have reserves in place for maintenance and vacancies. You have to decide what each partner's role is worth and how profits will be decided.

What percentage of the equity will each partner get? The equity will slowly increase as mortgage payments are made and the property might appreciate as well. If you bought the property below market value, you also increase equity. The equity is not realized until you sell or refinance, but you need to decide what percentage each partner will get if you do sell or refinance.

What happens if one partner wants out? The biggest problem with rental properties and partnerships is ending the relationship. How long do you plan to own the property together? What if one partner needs money and wants out? What if the house does not make as much money as you thought and one partner wants out? Before the partnership begins, you have to figure out how to end the relationship if one partner wants out.

As you can see, it can be very complex handling a partnership with rental properties. It is tough determining the amount of work each person is responsible for, an exit strategy, what percentages each investor gets, and when.

Why does everything need to be in writing with a real estate partnership?

If you decide to enter into a partnership, get everything in writing. I do not care if your partner is your brother or best friend, it should be in writing. There are multiple reasons why everything should be in writing.

People forget things: You would think that a person would never forget the details of a partnership that involves thousands of dollars, but it happens. I wrote an article about private money a while back, and mentioned I pay my sister six percent interest. She read it and was quick to remind me I pay her seven percent! We have everything in writing so there are no mistakes or fall outs from simply forgetting the terms.

Partners need to know roles: If you are doing a flip with a partner and decide to share the work, how much time will each person put in? One partner may have a family emergency or may have to work overtime. How many hours will each person put in and what are the consequences if they do not pull their weight? One of the biggest problems is one partner thinks he does all the work while the other collects the profit without doing anything.

Exit strategies: With rental properties, you have to determine what happens if one partner wants to be bought out or has to sell. How is market value determined, how will costs be split, etc. With a flip, you have to determine what happens if you decide not to flip the house because the market has changed.

Use of professional services: If one partner is a contractor or real estate agent, how will they be paid for their services? Will they get a higher percentage of the profits for their expertise or for the money saved on commissions? Will the contractor or agent be paid as they would any other job?

Rates, terms, payoffs: If you are borrowing money from a partner, all the terms of the loan or agreement need to be in writing. Some agreements are a pure profit split, but others might involve private money lending with interest rates, length of the note, etc.

Decision-making: Who has the final say on how much money to spend, how to repair a house, what properties to buy etc. What happens if the partners do not agree? Decision-making is another big issue that can cause problems if not in writing.

A huge issue with partnerships is when one side either forgets or does not live up to their agreed upon obligations. Having what the obligations are and what happens if those obligations are not met, in writing, will make the partnership much more successful. The partners will have more motivation to work hard, and it will be easier to handle problems when they come up.

Do you need a partner to invest in real estate?

Many people ask me how to structure a partnership when they collaborate on rental properties. One question was, "We have the money and knowledge to buy rentals, but we have the opportunity to partner up with another investor, how do we structure it?"

My answer was, "Why do you need a partner? Why bring someone in to share the profits on a deal when you have the money and know how? You will make much more money on real estate deals when you do not have a partner. The purpose of a partner is to provide something that you cannot or do not want to provide. You give up some of the profits to spend less of your own money, use someone's time or their expertise. If you do not need any of those things, do not give up your profits!"

Do you have anything to offer a partner when investing in real estate?

I also see many people looking for a partner or mentor to help them start investing. They want someone to show them how to buy houses, fix them up, find great deals, and make a ton of money but they have nothing to offer except a willingness to work hard.

I have this partnership proposed to me repeatedly and almost every time there are huge problems on my side of the deal.

- When I ask the person what they can offer me in return, they say determination, hard work, etc., but they list no specific skills. What can you do that will help me become more successful or help the deal be more successful? Are you good with computers? Do you have carpentry skills? Are you an expert marketer? Willingness to learn and work hard is not a skill. Everyone says that they are motivated and will work hard, but words are easy to say. If you want to impress people, be as specific as possible about how you will help them make more money.

- Most successful investors do not have time to train someone the entire process of investing. They also may not want to train someone to compete against him or her! Do not be put off if an investor does not want to mentor someone; it is a very involved process that takes time. Paying for knowledge and experience is also an option and shows you are serious. Most people who want free help and have nothing to offer in return will not even use that help if they get it, and it is a giant waste of time for everyone. Successful people will charge money for their expertise. Nothing is more frustrating to successful people than wasting time. If they know someone has a financial stake to learn, they know that person has a better chance of listening and learning.

- Many aspiring investors looking for a mentor want someone to tell them how to do everything. I have had people come to me asking how I make money by flipping houses. Well, I could write a book on that and still not answer all of your questions (actually, I did write a book on flipping). I point out articles for people to read or point them towards my book and they do not want to take the time to read the articles or pay $6 for a book. They want everything done for them without doing any work. If you want to impress a potential partner or mentor, do your research and learn as much as you possibly can. The more knowledge you have, the better chance you have of impressing someone enough to help you.

If you want to be a partner in a real estate deal, you must have something to offer. You need to bring money, expertise, skills, or pay for the opportunity. There are no shortcuts in becoming a successful real estate investor.

Why did I end my real estate partnership with my father?

I partnered with my father on flips and our real estate team before I bought him out in 2013. The partnership was great to help me get started after I graduated college in 2001. I would not have been able to flip houses right out of college because I had no money and no way to finance a deal. In return for knowledge and money to flip, I gave up most of the profits. For a while, I was even doing the painting, and on one house, most of the repair work. When I did the work myself I did not get a higher percentage, I was paid hourly. Flipping with a partner was great in the beginning, but at the end, I was doing almost all of the work and did not have the final decision on what to buy.

On our real estate team, my father paid the staff, took care of most expenses, and took a big chunk of my commissions. It was nice not having to worry about payroll and everything else, but I also sold most of the houses on the team and I was giving up a lot of profit by having a partner. My father also was tired of running the team and managing all the people.

I had wanted to take over everything for a while, but I was worried about the time it would take to manage it all and what my father would think. I approached him about it and my parents said they were waiting for me to takeover because they were ready to retire! I had my good friend joining the team who could help with the transition, and a good relationship with my portfolio lender so that I could finance the flips. I ended up buying out my parents and taking over the entire business. I love having complete control and keeping the profits!

Partnerships can be a great way to get started if you need help. Partnerships can also be a nightmare if you do not have roles clearly defined and everything in writing. Partnerships evolve and you may have to be flexible as people's priorities in life change. My partnership with my father changed over the years until I ended up buying him out. We had everything in writing when we made changes and that helped things go smoothly.

If you enter a partnership, make sure you take the time to set it up right. If you do not need a partner, it sure is nice having complete control and all the profits.

How to use credit cards to purchase rental property with little money down

Most of us have access to cash, but it is expensive and should be reserved for people looking to do a quick flip. If you have a killer deal that you cannot pass up, you may consider these options, but I do not recommend them unless it is necessary.

The easiest way to get quick cash is with credit cards. You can get a cash advance or pay for repairs using your credit card. If you use a credit card to finance your down payment or repairs and cannot pay it off right away, do not pay the 17 percent interest rate. Try your best to get another card that will allow a balance transfer. Many times, you can transfer all of your balance and pay little to no interest for up to a year. Hopefully, that will give you enough time to pay off the card and not be stuck with a high interest rate eating all your profits. I also suggest using a rewards card for repairs on your investment properties. This is a great way to make a little extra money if you pay it off every month. I have credit cards with a 2 percent cash back program on everything I buy. As long as I pay off the cards every month, I pay no interest on them and get 2 percent cash back. That 2 percent adds up very quickly when you are buying all your materials on credit cards.

How to buy an investment property with no money down using a 401k

Some 401ks allow an investor to take out a loan against the 401k. The loan usually has to be paid back relatively quickly and you will have to pay interest on the loan. You have to be very careful borrowing from a 401k, because the money you borrow is no longer earning interest or growing in your retirement fund. If you lose your job, you also may be required to pay back the loan within 60 days or have to pay a ten percent penalty and income tax on the loan.

You can also borrow against some life insurance policies. They are a great option for buying with less money if you already have the policy. I am not a huge fan of investing in like insurance policies in order to borrow from them at a later date.

How to buy a house with little money down using subject-to loans

Subject-to means you buy a house without paying off the previous owner's mortgage. This is another tricky situation where investors must be very careful. Almost no bank loans are assumable, which means when a house is sold, the loan must be paid off. The bank will most likely have a due-on-sale clause stating that the loans must be paid in full once ownership is transferred. Subject-to is buying a house subject-to an old mortgage and not paying off the loan. There is a chance that the bank will require the loan to be paid off if they find out the home was sold.

Investors buy homes subject-to a mortgage so that they do not have to get a new loan. It may be hard for the investor to qualify for a mortgage or they may be maxed out on being able to get new loans. If you buy a home for $80,000 that has a $75,000 mortgage in place, the investor would only need $5,000 to buy the house instead of the normal 20 percent or more.

When you leave the loan in place, the person who originally borrowed the money, is still responsible for the loan.

How to use a cash-out refinance to get more money for rentals

A cash-out refinance is one of the best tools an investor can use to take money out of their rental properties. When I purchased my first long-term rental, I was able to buy the property from proceeds from a cash-out refinance on my personal residence. I was able to take out $40,000 in equity from my house, just one year after I bought it. I have also refinanced 7 rental properties, which has allowed me to buy even more rentals.

How do increasing values make it easier to do a cash-out refinance on rental properties?

Values are going up across the country and that has created an opportunity for homeowners to do cash-out refinances. Most banks are using stricter guidelines for qualifications and lower loan-to-value ratios than they did five years ago. However, if you purchased your home at a great price or if you have owned it for a while, you still may be able to do a cash-out refinance. Many banks require an 80 percent or lower loan-to-value ratio when refinancing a rental property and they will use an appraisal to determine that value. It is imperative that you have a lot of equity in your property if you want to complete a cash-out refinance with an investment property. If you are refinancing an owner-occupied home, you may be able to refinance up to 95 percent of the value.

What are the risks of a cash-out refinance on a rental property?

A cash-out refinance increases the loan amount on your rental property. For some people who are averse to risk, paying off their home is a great option and they may not want more debt. However, I am not averse to risk and I want to maximize my returns. Debt can be a very bad thing if it is used for the wrong things, but if you use debt to buy cash producing investments that are bought right, it can be a good thing.

In my market, I can get a cash-on-cash return of 15 percent or higher on rental properties, whereas interest rates are less than five percent. It makes more sense to refinance for five percent and use that money to buy properties that will give me over a 15 percent cash-on-cash return. That return does not include possible appreciation, tax benefits, and mortgage pay down.

It is possible that values could go down and a cash-out refinance would reduce the equity in your home. But if you do not need to sell your home, it will not matter how much equity you have in it. If you need to make sure you have a lot of cash flow and are comfortable with a higher payment after the refinance. If refinancing the property creates a negative or break even cash flow situation, you could get yourself in trouble. When I refinance my rentals, I am still getting at least $400 a month in cash flow. I am able to do that because rents have increased since I bought them.

Another problem with taking on more debt, is if you may be decreasing the amount you can qualify for on future homes. If you are close to reaching your maximum debt to income ratio with your lender, a refinance could make it tough to buy new rentals. Make sure you talk to your lender about your debt to income ratios and how the refinance will affect future purchases.

Refinance costs are similar to new loan costs. You may have to pay two to three percent in closing costs, which can add up to a lot of money on higher valued loans. Make sure paying those costs it worth it.

How does a cash-out refinance work on rental property?

I did a cash-out refinance on one of my rentals in 2012, one in 2013, two in 2015, and on three in 2016. On one of my refinances, I was able to pull out about $26,000 with my payment only going up $136 a month. The terms are usually more restrictive and it can be difficult to refinance if you have more than four mortgaged properties with conventional lenders. I was able to do a cash-out refinance with more than four mortgages, because I used a portfolio lender.

When I did a cash-out refinance on my investment property, the max they would loan me was 75 percent of the value of the home.

I purchased rental number two for $92,000 in October 2011. I put about $18,000 into it for repairs. I was able to turn it into a 5-bed, 2-bath and rented it for $1,100 (low because it was rented to my brother-in-law). I had to wait a year to do a cash-out refinance and the current value was determined by an appraisal. The appraisal came in at $140,000, which I thought was low, but I had to go with it. After all the lender fees, interest, and miscellaneous costs of the cash out refinance, I was able to take out over $26,000. My payment went up $136 a month, but I am still able to cash flow every month and I took out more than enough money for a down payment on another rental property. *In 2016, I rent this home for $1,500 a month.*

On the rental properties I refinanced in 2015, I was able to take out almost $50,000 in cash on each property. This was due to buying below market value, making repairs, and appreciation in my area.

The more properties you can buy, the more cash flow builds up and the more wealth you can create. A cash-out refinance can help you purchase more properties and increase your wealth. Make sure you purchase houses below market value, because it will make a future cash-out refinance much easier. Make sure your payments do not increase so much that you are no longer seeing positive cash flow every month.

Which is better, a cash-out refinance or a line of credit?

A cash-out refinance can allow you to take cash out of your home with a long-term mortgage. A home equity line of credit (HELOC) allows a homeowner to take money out with a short-term loan. A home equity line of credit (HELOC) gives you more flexibility on when and how much you can take out, but the line can have shorter terms and higher rates. I have used both a cash-out refinance and a HELOC and I will detail the advantages and disadvantages of each.

A HELOC is a line of credit on a home and is much different from a refinance. When you take out a line of credit, you do not have to use the money right away or ever. You can use as much of the money as you want and pay it back when you like. You can even borrow the money again after you pay back the line.

A HELOC will have closing costs, but many times they will be less than a cash-out refinance. The terms and fees will differ depending on whether you are getting a line on an investment property or a personal residence. The term of the HELOC could be two years, five years, or longer, but not 30 years like a refinance could be.

One of the biggest challenges to buying rentals, is coming up with the down payment. Refinancing my rentals has been one way I have paid for new rentals.

I paid off my first rental property in 2014. I was able to get a HELOC on that property shortly after paying it off. Since this was an investment property, my portfolio lender charges me a one percent origination fee and had an appraisal done to determine the amount of the line of credit.

The appraisal came in at $160,000. My lender allows 75 percent loan-to-value on investment property lines of credit (on a personal residence, they will go up to 90). I was able to get a line for $120,000.

The line of credit has been awesome for my flipping business. With so many fix and flips going, I do not always have the cash available to buy more flips. I use my portfolio lender to finance my flips, but they cannot always close as quickly as I need them to. When I have to close quickly, I use cash and my lines of credit and then refinance the flips with my portfolio lender.

When is a HELOC better than a cash-out refinance?

A HELOC has many advantages over a cash-out refinance. With a HELOC, you do not have to take out the full amount of the loan as you do with a refinance. This gives you the option of taking out the money at some future point if you do not need it now. You can also pay back the money from a HELOC at any time and then take it out again at any time. With a refinance, once you pay back part or the entire loan, you cannot take that money back out of the loan without completing another refinance.

If you have a loan in place on a house and have a lot of equity in the home, you can get a line of credit without paying off the loan. The HELOC can be placed in second position and the first loan can stay in first position. When you refinance a home, you usually have to refinance any loans on the home as well (this makes the loan amount higher and can increase the closing costs).

If you think you may need money in the future for your business or rental properties, but you will not need the money long-term, a HELOC may be perfect. If you need long-term money for financing rental property down payments, then a cash-out refinance may be the better option.

I used money from my cash out refinances to fund the down payments for more rental properties. I knew I did not want to pay back this money any time soon, so a cash-out refinance was perfect for me. If you need long-term money, a cash-out refinance may be the better option than a HELOC. You will be paying interest on the money you take out in a cash-out refinance so it is smart to put it to use right away.

Both a cash-out refinance and HELOC can offer great opportunities to real estate investors. Many times a real estate investor's biggest challenge is finding enough money to fund deals. Both a HELOC and cash out refinance can help to provide funds, which allow investors to buy more properties and make more money.

Conclusion

Buying with little money down can take some work and sacrifice when you first start out. The more rentals you buy below market, and the longer you own those rentals, the easier it gets to buy more. It can take some time to buy your first property, it can take time to buy your second, but when you have multiple properties, your momentum grows and the process gets easier and easier.

8. How to repair and maintain rental properties.

Once you have purchased and financed a rental property you may need to do some work on it. In fact, many of the properties I buy need a lot of work. The more work a property needs, the better deal you can usually get. However, you have to be careful when buying homes that need work, because the deal has to be good enough to compensate for time and money required.

When you buy a rental property that needs work, you want more than the discount that the work will cost you, because it takes time and cash to make repairs. Some lenders will finance repairs on properties, but those lenders are tough to find, especially for an investor. My lender loans me 80 percent of the purchase price of the homes I buy, but they will not loan on any of the repairs. I have to pay cash for any repairs I make, and it takes time to recoup that money unless I refinance the home.

Because it takes cash to make repairs on your properties, you have to be very careful how much you spend on repairs. The cash-on-cash returns that we talked about earlier are greatly affected by the cash you invest. Even though a home may cost more if it needs less work, the cash-on-cash returns may actually be higher on a home that needs less work than a house that is cheaper, but needs more repairs.

Here is an example:

House 1

Purchased for $150,000

Rents for $1,500 a month

Needs $5,000 in repairs

20 percent down

Three percent closing costs

Cash flow is $338 a month*

Cash-on-cash return is 10%

$40,000 is needed

House 2

Purchased for $130,000

Rents for $1,500 a month

Needs $20,000 in repairs

20 percent down

Three percent closing costs

Cash flow is $420 a month*

Cash-on-cash return is 10%

Over $50,000 is needed

(includes property management, maintenance, and vacancies)

As you can see the cash-on-cash return is about the same for both houses, but the cash needed to buy the second house is much more. While you are buying the house for $20,000 less than the first house, you are spending much more of your cash and getting the same return.

I would not like either of these deals very much, because the cash-on-cash return is not 15 percent or higher, but I have very strict buying criteria. If I had to choose between the two, I would pick the first house because it took less of my cash to buy. I would like to see the second house priced at $110,000, and then it would be worth it for me to make the repairs and spend the extra cash.

Whenever you analyze properties, you need to look at the numbers and your personal goals to see if they make sense. Do not buy a house just because it is cheap. If the home needs $50,000 in work and you can buy the equivalent of that house for $50,000 more that does not need work, it does not make any sense to buy the cheap house. Now if you can buy the cheap house for $80,000 less than the fixed up house, it might start to make sense. It might not make sense either to spend that much cash on a rental property no matter how good of a deal it is.

Having said that, I cannot tell you what a good deal is or is not. You have to figure that out. Some people are happy with five percent returns and others want 25 percent returns.

How do you decide what to repair on a rental property?

I spend a lot of money when I repair an investment property and what I do and do not repair is very important. I have 16 long-term rental properties and I fix and flip 10 to 15 homes per year. I have a completely different strategy for repairing investment property depending on whether it is a fix and flip or rental property.

Keeping repair costs as low as possible while still making homes look great is a key to my long-term rental strategy. I tend to make fewer repairs with my long-term rentals than with my fix and flips. I make the rental properties look very nice and make sure they are safe, but I do not do as many repairs as when I am going to sell the home. I do not fix as much on a rental property because renters are not nearly as fussy as buyers are. Most renters do not think of a house they rent as their property and so they are not as concerned with the age of the mechanical systems or the finish details. If something breaks, the tenant knows the property owner will fix it, or at least should fix it. I have found renters to be very nonchalant about light fixtures and paint color, where buyers are very meticulous about these items. In rental property number seven I left brass fixtures in the home as an experiment to see if it would be hard to rent (we usually put in oil rubbed bronze). It rented right away and the renters did not even seem to notice the fixtures.

How I decide what to repair on my fix and flips

In a flip, we always replace the fixtures and make sure to do all the little things because buyers want their new home to be perfect. The buyers will not have a property owner to fix anything, they will have to do the repairs themselves or pay someone if something breaks. A buyer will also most likely hire an inspector to go through the entire house. That inspector will find most things that are wrong with the home, and an inspection that finds many things wrong will often scare off buyers. We try to have as few items mentioned on the inspection as possible. We have an inspection done on our flips before the work is done so that we know everything that has to be fixed. We do another inspection after the home is fixed up to show the buyers that it is in great shape.

What repairs need to be done in both a rental and a flip?

Paint color can make a huge difference in how a house feels. Dark paint can make a house feel small, while white paint can make a home feel stark and boring. Many people love to paint rooms different colors to show their style and personality. The problem is that everyone has a different style and personality. It is impossible to please everyone, so a nice neutral color is the best choice. We use beige paint in all our rentals and flips. If the home has white trim we use Kwal Paint color Sawyer's Fence, for oak trim, we use a color called Millet. Paint colors definitely look different in different houses due to the trim colors and carpet colors. If you are trying out new colors, use paint samples on the wall to see how they look before you paint the entire house.

We sold a flip recently that had brand new paint throughout the entire house. At the closing, the buyers informed me, the first thing they were going to do was repaint almost the entire house. It may seem like a waste when all the new paint is being painted over, but the buyers let me know the paint we picked looked good, it just wasn't what they want. We could have just as easily had buyers that would have kept the paint we used for five years. We still sold the house by choosing a neutral color, if we would have tried to pick trendy colors in multiple rooms, it could have thrown off the feel of the house and scared buyers away.

Just like paint, if you want to sell your house quickly and for a lot of money, other designs should be neutral as well. Carpet Color can range from dark to light, but once again, too dark a color makes a house feel dark and small. If the carpet is too light, people worry about stains and wear and tear showing. We

always put in new carpet or refinish hardwood floors in all of our fix and flips and long-term holds.

For light and plumbing fixtures, the in-style is dark. We have put in brushed bronze fixtures for a few years in all of our properties. Brushed bronze is bronze fixture covered in black paint. After a bit of use the black wears off to show the bronze color, which I think is very cool. My wife recently told me nickel fixtures may be coming back as the "in-style" again. I still prefer the dark fixtures with light paint, because I think it creates a nice contrast. Nickel fixtures are not bad if you want to save a little money, but I would stay away from brass. Brass fixtures really date a home and can take away from the other new features.

The cost to replace all fixtures in a home can add up quickly and can easily cost $700 to $1200 in just materials for basic fixtures from a box store. We usually replace fixtures on all our flips, but if they are in decent shape, we may keep the current fixtures on our rentals.

When you repair investment property, the biggest decision can be how much to update and upgrade. Many of the houses I buy are very dated and that is why I get a great deal on them. The most expensive repair on a home is usually replacing kitchen and baths. I try to avoid replacing kitchens if possible, especially in my rentals. Bathrooms I also like to avoid replacing, because of the price to replace tubs, sinks, toilets and the labor. I do make sure all the mechanicals are working well, because I do not want a plumbing leak destroying all the work I just completed on a home.

On my flips, I tend to replace kitchens more often, because I will be getting that money back right away when I sell the home. On a rental property, a brand new kitchen might help it rent for slightly more, but it will take years to make back that investment. I try my best to save the kitchens in my rental properties and keep costs down. It is tough to know when to replace a kitchen on a flip, but kitchens do make a huge difference in the feel of a home. So many components affect the feel: cabinets, counters, appliances, and layout. One or all of the components can be replaced and be enough to sell the home, but it is tough figuring just how far to go.

We always put stainless steel appliances in our kitchens. They are only a little more expensive and most buyers love them, which helps the home to sell more quickly. We usually replace the counter tops as well. The counters in homes I buy are usually pretty beat up and you can put in nice laminate counters fairly cheap. Depending on the price of the home, we may put in granite counters to spice things up. Nice laminate counters are around $500-$1000 and granite slab around $1,500-$2,500 depending on how many square feet we have to install. For houses under $150,000, we usually use laminate counters and for houses over $150,000, we use granite. What you do would depend on what is common in your market. Replacing cabinets is trickier, because there are so many different types of cabinets in varying condition. Once again, the price of the home will dictate if we try to save cabinets or not. If the cabinets look solid and are in good condition, we may paint them white. I am not a huge fan of white cabinets, but many people love them and most people are okay with them.

I try to save cabinets in my rentals and low range flips. If the cabinets are broken at all, I usually replace the kitchen. We can

replace all the cabinets in a basic kitchen for $3,000 or less from a box store. The box store cabinets are not top of the line, but they offer many styles and work great for us. I am particular to maple cabinets as I think oak has too much grain and makes homes look dated. Cherry is nice too, but can be too dark. The knotty pine look used to bug me, until I bought a house with those cabinets. After a few years, it really grew on me. The problem was that it took a few years for me to like them and when selling a house, you do not have that much time. I think the knotty pine is an acquired taste, and when you repair investment property, you want to appeal to as many people as possible. We always stick to a light to mid color stain and basic maple cabinets.

Additions or large remodel jobs on a fix and flip or rental property

My general rule of thumb is never to put on an addition. In my area, land is not valuable enough to call for an addition and I will almost never get my money back. Remodeling or moving rooms around in an existing structure may make sense in certain circumstances, but I am usually not in favor of moving kitchens, baths, or other major components. It is too expensive to make major changes and usually not worth the cost. In my rental properties I will add a bedroom if it is easy to do because it adds rent and value to the home. Many times, I only have to add a door or a closet in order to add a bedroom. I may have to move a wall or finish a room in the basement to complete a bedroom, but it is usually worth the cost. Many times, I can turn a four-bedroom house into a five-bedroom house for $1,500 or $2,000. If you already have five bedrooms in a single-family home, it is probably not worth it to add a sixth. In my market, there is a big price difference in rent between 2, 3, 4, and 5 bedroom homes. When you get to six or more bedrooms, it does not make nearly as big of a difference, and you are inviting more wear and tear with more people living in a home.

The more expensive the house, the more expensive the repairs will be. This is a key point to remember when you sell a house. The more expensive the house, the nicer buyers will want the home to be. Buyers will want upgraded appliances, kitchens, baths, and everything to be perfect. In the lower price ranges, you can usually get away with houses not being completely upgraded. On our more expensive flips, we usually make less money percentage wise than our lower priced flips, especially if they need many repairs. High-end repairs and upgrades really add up in the pocket book and eat away at profits.

Landscaping can be another tricky repair item and much of what I do depends on the time of the year. I love completing flips in the winter because I do not have to worry if the yard is dead or not. In the summer, a nice green lawn can really make a home look great. We try to make sure our flips have nice yards and great curb appeal. We will sometimes add mulch or other landscaping material to make the home look as good as possible. First impressions make a big impression on buyers.

On my rentals, I make sure every house has a sprinkler system on a timer. I set the sprinklers for the tenants and then do not have to worry about the yard dying. We do various degrees of yard work on our rentals depending on the season and what the tenants want. We make sure the front yard is nice, but many times the tenants do not care about the back yard.

When we repair investment property, we always make sure the mechanicals are working properly. Much of our repair costs go into new hot water heaters, furnaces, and air conditioners. If the units are getting old or show signs of failing on our flips, we replace them. On the rentals, we may wait to replace older units, but we will have them inspected to make sure they are safe. It is best not to wait with hot water heaters as they can rust out and flood a house very easily. I try to keep roofs as long as possible on my rentals, but on our flips, we replace them if they are worn.

Repairing investment property can take a lot of time and money. You want to make sure you are making the right repairs for what you intend to do with the property. I know I did not cover every repair that is needed on a home, but this will give you an idea of the things I do to maximize my investment.

How much will it cost to repair your investment property?

I fix up many houses: my personal residence, my rental properties, and my fix and flips. The most difficult part about fixing up a home is finding a great contractor and estimating how much the repairs will cost. Repair costs will vary based on the quality of products used, how much labor costs in your area, and the contractor you use.

What does it cost to paint a house?

I always paint the house and replace the floor coverings, unless those items had just been completed. The cost of paint and the cost of labor to paint a house has increased a lot the last few years. My costs to paint the interior of a house are about $1.50 to $2.50 a square foot. It costs about $2,500 to paint the interior walls of a 1,500 square foot house beige or gray with white trim.

It costs more to paint the exterior of a house because the paint is more expensive, it needs more prep work, and the weather has to be nice. Painting the exterior of a house can run $3.00 or more a square foot depending on the complexity of the job and the condition of the house. If a home has peeling paint, it will cost much more to scrape and prepare the surface for new paint. If a house has lead based paint, the costs can be much more due to the preparation and clean-up work needed to dispose of the old paint. Your contractor or painter must be certified to remove lead based paint or they can face huge fines from the government. Lead based paint was prohibited after 1978.

How much does it cost to replace flooring?

I usually use carpet for the living areas and vinyl or tile for the kitchens and bathrooms. If a house has hardwood I refinish it, but I do not add or replace hardwood because of the cost. To install hardwood floors costs three times as much as carpet. Replacing the carpet in a 1,500 square foot house costs about $3,000 to $3,500 installed. It costs another $500 to $1,000 for vinyl or tile for the kitchen and baths. These costs are for middle of the road materials that look nice and will last, but do not cost a fortune.

If a house already has hardwood, I do my best to refinish it. Refinishing hardwood is less expensive than installing new carpet. I also like the look of hardwood floors and buyers love them. I can refinish a 1,500 square foot house that is mostly hardwood for about $2,000.

Some people like to use laminate flooring because it looks like hardwood, but is cheaper. I do not like laminate because I think it looks and feels cheap. It also tends to wear very fast if not taken care of, and it cannot be refinished like hardwood can.

How much does it cost to replace fixtures in a house?

Another great update to a house is replacing the light and plumbing fixtures. Brand new lights, door handles, and faucets that all match can transform a home. I like to use antique bronze, but we have also used brushed nickel. Light fixtures are as inexpensive as $10 for basic bedroom and bathroom lights. You can purchase a nice chandelier for less than $150 as well as a nice ceiling fan. Door handles are $20 or less depending on the style and faucets run from $35 to $150. You can replace the lights, door handles, and faucets for an entire house for about $1,200 installed.

How much does it cost to replace the appliances in a house?

Another way to make a house look great is by adding new appliances. We put stainless steel appliances in our houses; I can get a stove for $500 to $600, a dishwasher for $300, and a microwave for $250. I usually do not buy a fridge for my flips. I will buy a fridge for my rentals. I sometimes buy used appliances off Craigslist. Even with dated cabinets, appliances make a huge difference in the look of a kitchen.

How much does it cost to update a house cosmetically?

If you do all the work mentioned above and the rest of the home is in decent shape, it will make a huge difference in the look and feel. I usually do all the repairs I discussed on every fix and flip. With my rentals, I usually do most of those repairs, but if a house is in decent condition, I can get away with less. Here are the total costs for a cosmetic upgrade on a 1,500 square foot house:

New interior paint:	$2,500
New floor coverings:	$4,500
New fixtures:	$1,200
New appliances:	$1,300
Total cost:	**$9,500**

It almost always costs more than you think it will to fix up home, so be prepared to spend more than what you had planned. It is very rare for me ever to spend less than $10,000 on any house that I fix up because there are usually many little things that need repaired as well. Drywall holes, outlet covers, landscaping, and many more things will increase the costs. It is also rare for me not to have more major repairs to complete.

The repairs on my flips and rentals vary from basic cosmetics to massive remodels. Here are other common repairs and the costs that we make on houses.

- **Kitchens**: It is not as expensive as you might thing to replace a kitchen. The materials to replace a basic kitchen including cabinets, counter tops, and sink are $2,500 or less. I can replace a kitchen for well under $5,000 including labor.
- **Baths**: Baths can be gut jobs or a simple vanity replacement. For a full gut job, I can usually get the job done for less than $3,000. I can replace a vanity, toilet, and bath for less than $1,000.
- **Roof**: I have a great roofer who will replace the roof on a 1,500 square foot house for around $6,000.
- **Electrical**: Electric repairs can vary a great deal based on what needs to be done. Minor repairs might be a couple hundred dollars while major rewiring jobs can cost $5,000. It is important to get any electrical concerns checked out to see how serious they are.
- **Plumbing**: Plumbing is similar to electrical. A minor job can be very cheap, but to re-plumb an entire house can cost $5,000 or more.
- **Sewer**: Sewer lines can be very expensive to replace; it can cost $3,000 to $10,000 to replace a line. Luckily, I have never had to replace any.
- **Foundation**: Most foundation repairs are not fun to deal with. There can be many issues such as settling, water leakage, grading issues, or structural problems.

Water problems in the basement or crawl space might be a major foundation issue that could cost $10,000 or more or might be a simple grading issue that some dirt work will fix.

- **Windows:** We end up replacing many windows, because we buy older houses all the time. For basic vinyl windows, I usually pay my contractors about $300 per window for material and install.

- **Doors:** We also replace many interior doors. Six-panel white doors make a home look very nice. Doors are usually $100 to $150 per door installed.

- **Stucco and siding:** I rarely replace the siding on a home, but I have had to on occasion. Currently, I am paying about $8,500 to put brand new stucco on a 1,250 square foot fix and flip. It is less expensive to replace wood siding, but you have to paint it. You can still reside and paint a house for less than stucco in most cases.

- **Drywall/Sheetrock:** With old houses, I see a lot of plaster and bad drywall. An old house looks so much better with brand new drywall than with uneven crumbling plaster. On a recent flip, a drywall specialist charged about $3,000 to do the walls and ceilings in three rooms that totaled about 500 square feet.

- **Furnace/hot water heater:** I had a brand new forced air furnace system installed for about $5,000 this year. To replace just the furnace is about $2,500 and a hot water heater about $800.

How much do I spend on my remodels?

On my most recent fix and flip that is about to be put up for sale, I spent about $18,000 on the remodel. That included interior and exterior paint, new carpet, new doors, new trim, some electrical work, some new drywall, trash out, landscaping work, and many little fixes. On a flip that is about to have the work started, I will spend over $50,000 on the repairs. That house needs new plumbing, new electric, new paint everywhere, siding work, new windows, new doors, new drywall, new baths, new kitchen, new floors, new fixtures, new trim, and more.

I shop at Home Depot and Lowes for most materials including fixtures, doors, windows, door handles, and all the little stuff. I used to buy my appliances at a local store, but they were bought out and raised prices. I buy my appliances at Home Depot now. Home Depot has great discounts if you spend a lot of money on materials. Ask their pro desk about becoming a member and other ways to save money.

Repairing a house does not need to cost $50,000 or $100,000 for basic cosmetic repairs. I see kitchen remodels on television that cost $50,000 and I cannot believe my eyes or ears! Even if you use high-end materials such as granite counters and custom cabinets, you should not spend $50,000 on a kitchen unless it is in a million-dollar home. Repairs can add up quickly on remodels, and I always expect about $5,000 more in costs that I plan to spend due to unknowns. Find a great contractor, make sure that the contractor does their work, and shop around for the best prices to keep your costs down. Remember these costs are what I pay to fix up homes in my area. If you live in an expensive area, your costs may be significantly higher.

How to find a great contractor

One of the most important and difficult parts of investing in real estate is finding a great contractor. Contractors can be hard to find, very expensive, take a long time to finish a job, or even quit on you. Finding a great contractor will make your life easy with detailed bids, great communication, and quality work. It costs a lot of money initially to buy an investment property and it can cost even more to repair it. If you do not have a great contractor, costs can skyrocket due to long timelines and increased repair costs.

I would love to buy only properties that are in perfect shape and can be rented or sold right away. In order to get a great deal, most of the properties I buy need repairs. Usually the more repairs a property needs the more of a discount I can get. Buying homes that need repairs is one way to get a great deal. However, I must have a great contractor to get my rental properties and fix and flips repaired quickly without spending too much money.

Even if I buy homes that need no work at all, at some point things will break. I remodel my rentals before I rent them, but they still need occasional work because they are not new. All homeowners will need a great contractor at some point, unless they are capable of doing all repairs themselves.

What is the easiest way to find a great contractor?

My advice is to ask friends, family, and co-workers for references before you try other sources. A recommendation does not guarantee that the contractor is any good, but it does give you a place to start. Recommendations are usually a better sign of how good a contractor is than advertising. Real estate agents, property managers, or builders may know of a good contractor.

Anyone who owns a home may have used a great contractor at some point, so do not be afraid to ask your friends or family. You will still have to keep on top of that contractor to make sure they are doing what they promised. One of the easiest ways to let a rehab project get out of control is little or no oversight from the property owner when using a new contractor.

Do not rely on just a recommendation

I have tried out many new contractors, because I have so many rehabs going at once. I once received recommendations from my broker and a couple of other agents in my office for a new contractor. The contractor was a builder, seemed to know what he was talking about, and gave great detailed bids. I put him to work on two projects at once that were both sitting and waiting for work to be started. He told me he had a great crew and could handle as much work as I could give him. He ended up finishing one project on budget and mostly on time, but he did not even start the second project for two months!

I had assumed everything was going well since that was what he had told me, but the property was 40 minutes away and I had not physically seen the work start yet. This was completely my fault for not properly overseeing the job and visiting the job site. I was in for a big surprise when I went to visit the property, which I thought was almost done, and no work had been started! I called the contractor and he gave me a story about too many jobs, and his workers getting sick. He had been telling me everything was going great and the work was almost done before I visited the site. Either he had not been overseeing his workers properly or he had lied to me. That job was eventually finished about four months after it was started and three months after it was supposed to be done. I never used that contractor again, not because it took so long to finish the job, but because he had not visited the site for months or he lied to me about the work being done. Even if you get great recommendations you still have to keep track of your contractors.

How can you keep an eye on your contractor?

It is always best to keep an eye on your contractors work and schedule, whether it is the first time you have used them or the twentieth. In my experience, the more communication and oversight you provide on your properties, the better the contractor will do. I have had contractors that I have worked with me on 20 jobs and if I do not keep on them, they slack off. If a contractor does a great job once, it does not mean they will always do a great job.

I had to fire a contractor this year that had worked on many properties for me and had done a great job over and over. On his last projects he stopped visiting his work sites and started telling me jobs were done when they were not. His prices went up and the time he took to finish jobs increased because he was never at the site and did not keep track of his workers.

Here are a few tips on how to make sure your contractor is doing a great job.

- Constant communication
- Visit the property often
- Always get a written bid first
- Get a written estimate for when the work will be finished

- Do not prepay for any work. (This is not always possible. Some contractors require a deposit upfront or material cost. However, never pay for the entire job upfront.)
- Help pick out materials and paint colors

I always talk to a contractor on the phone before I meet them in person. I want to make sure they know what they are talking about and I want to get an idea of how much they charge. A contractor should tell you his hourly rate, how many people he has on his crew, and how long it takes them to do an average job. I also want to know how busy they are and how many other people they are working with.

If I like what I hear on the phone, I set up a meeting at one of my properties. I go over what I want done and have them submit a bid. If you are new to real estate and to finding contractors, always get multiple bids so you know you are not being ripped off. Try to talk to the contractor as much as possible. Ask about his family and what kind of jobs he normally does. In my experience, contractors like to talk a lot, and if you get them to start talking, they may tell you some things that will help you make a decision. One contractor that I interviewed mentioned that he had two recent DUIs including one while he was on the job!

After I meet with a contractor, I ask them to submit a bid. This is another test to see how quickly they get it to me and whether they get back to me. Two contractors I recently talked to never got me a bid, emailed, or called me. It was easy to eliminate them; if they cannot send me a bid, they probably cannot do the job.

The hourly rates for contractors can range from $20 an hour to $100 an hour. If you get a bid that seems outrageous, you may have found one of the expensive contractors. There are really cheap contractors as well, but you sometimes get what you pay for.

How can you find a great contractor through large box stores?

Home Depot offers a rehab program that will actually handle every job on a project, but they are more expensive doing a large job than if you hire a local contractor yourself. I talked to Home Depot to price out their contractor program, and they were very honest and said it would be cheaper for me to use my own contractors. They even mention a few names of contractors who frequent the store often and have been around for years. This was not a recommendation from them in any way, but it gave me a lead on a contractor who I am going to try out.

Another way to meet great contractors is to visit the store early in the morning and see who is buying large amounts of supplies. The people buying materials are probably contractors and they may be looking for more work. You know they currently have at least one job since they are buying materials.

How to find a great contractor online

Many contractors advertise on Craigslist, but it really is hard to know how great they are until they do some work for you. I have hired a handyman and painters through Craigslist when I was desperate. They worked out okay, but it is hard to judge how good a contractor will be until they finish a job. I always ask for references and talk to references about the previous work done by any contractor.

There are many advertisements for contractors on the internet as well. Again, you have to check references thoroughly when using these resources. Yelp gives reviews on contractors if they have done enough work that can help you make a decision.

Home Depot offers contractors anywhere in the country. Even though they are more expensive than a local contractor may be, they offer standard work and stand behind their work. I am aware of a couple of other companies that offer regional or nationwide contracting services as well. These companies may not work with an investor who has only one small job. However, if you can offer them consistent work in one area they may be a great choice.

- Vineyard Services offer contracting services in most states. They have been around for years and do property maintenance on many REO properties.
- Asons offer property preservation and construction.

Angie's List has provided a lot of great information on contractors. It was only $7.99 for the entire year and I have no idea why I waited this long to use it. They list contractors in my area, their area of expertise, and detailed reviews from people who have used them. So far, I have found multiple prospects from Angie's List that I am going to meet at my properties. You can use Angie's List for many other services besides contractors.

Finding a great contractor can be the most difficult part of real estate investing, but it may also be the most important part. It is vitally important you take your time when choosing a contractor, interview multiple contractors, and keep a close eye on any contractor you hire. It usually does not make sense to try to do the work yourself, so hiring the right contractor is extremely important.

How to make sure the contractor you use will do a good job

Once you find a contractor, you have to make sure that they do their job well. No matter how good his references are or how great the contractor says he is, follow these steps to make sure the contractor follows through.

It can be hard to tell the difference between a good or bad contractor until they finsih the job. Contractors can get too busy, take on too big of a job, or not keep track of their workers well. Any of these circumstances can cause a job to take too long to be completed or not to be done correctly. Constant communication, written agreements, and checking on a job often are all keys to making sure your contractor does what he has promised to do.

If you have worked with a contractor on multiple jobs and you know he knows what you want, you may skip walking a job site with him. However, I think it is always a good idea to walk a job with your contractor so they know what needs to be done, even if you have worked with him before. Make sure the contractor is writing things down when you are discussing what needs done. I have had a few contractors who did not write anything down during the walk through and when I came back to the work site, they were doing things I had not asked to be done and had not done things I had asked to be done. Everything should be in writing so there is no confusion. A written bid serves multiple purposes and will save you time and money.

- A written bid makes sure both the contractor and the homeowner know exactly what services and repairs are being done. You do not want any confusion on what was and what was not supposed to be repaired on a home.

- A written bid lists the price that the contractor is charging for specific work. You do not want to be surprised with a massive bill that you did not agree to after the work is completed. A written bid helps keep the contractor honest.

- A written bid may also include a period for when the work will be done. Some investors will add incentives to contractors for getting a job done quickly. The faster they finish, the more the contractor is paid.

Most contractors require bids to be signed by both parties. The written bid not only keeps both parties honest, it reminds every one the scope of work to be done. I have many jobs going at one time, and I tend to forget what was verbally talked about. By having a written bid, there is no confusion on what is to be repaired and how much it will cost.

Keep in constant contact with your contractor

Just because you do not hear from your contractor does not mean things are going great. As discussed previously, I had a job I thought was going well because I never heard a thing from the contractor. I assumed he would have told me if there were any problems or delays. It turned out that he had not even started the job! Call your contractor to get updates on the job and stop by the job site to see how things are progressing. You or someone you trust needs to visit the jobsites at least once a week if not more.

Do not be afraid to ask your contractor if they are on schedule or on budget. Ask your contractor if there are any changes to the bid or if there is any more work to that needs to be done. If there are any changes to the work, make sure the contractor contacts you to approve the changes. Some contractors take it upon themselves to change a job or add on work without asking the homeowner.

Do not pay a contractor for work they have not done

Some contractors want partial payment before they start any work on a job. If you have worked with a contractor before and this is their policy, it may work to pay them some money to get started. In some cases, I pay for materials or a small portion of the job before work is started, but I usually will not pay anything until after some work is done. Many times the contractors are stretched thin from buying materials and they need extra money before the job is done to continue working. Avoid paying large sums of money before any work is done.

If a contractor is not paid, they can place a lien on a home for work they did. It is much easier for a contractor to collect for unpaid work than it is for a homeowner to track down a contractor who takes their money and skips town before any work is done. The contractor should have no problem being paid after a job is done. If the contractor insists on being paid before starting a job, be very careful or find another contractor.

Do a final walkthrough with the contractor to make sure the work has been done properly

A contractor should take pride in his work and be happy to show you what has been repaired. I always do a final walk through to make sure the work has been done correctly. Many times, I must have the contractor go back and fix minor things or fix things we did not notice the first time we looked at the home. Do not be afraid to point out work that you do not think is done correctly. If the contractor is hesitant about fixing it correctly, stand your ground. If the contractor refuses to make repairs or do things correctly, you know not to use them again.

It is very important to do your due diligence to find a great contractor. Once you hire a contractor, make sure they follow through with what they have promised. If you keep in constant contact, get everything in writing, and are clear on the scope of work, you will have much more success.

Should you repair an investment property yourself?

At this point in my career, I use contractors to rehab all my flips and rentals. Many people try to repair a flip or rental property themselves because they think they will save money and it will be fun. In 2006, I decided to rehab a fix and flip myself without using a contractor. I thought I would save money on the labor a contractor would charge. Doing the work myself may have saved me money on the labor, but in the end, I lost money on this deal because of how long it took me to complete the work and because of the opportunities I missed.

I learned a lot repairing a house myself, but I did not have much fun and I did not save any money. The problem with doing the work myself was that I am not a professional contractor and I had to learn how to repair the home. This particular house was about 60 years old, needed paint, carpet, new floors, new doors, new windows, a new kitchen, a wall taken out, and a lot of minor repairs. I may have been qualified to paint the house but that was about it. It was a long process!

Why doing the work myself did not save as much on labor costs as I thought

This home needed a lot of work and although I had done minor repairs on houses before, I had never done anything to this extent. I was sure doing the work myself would save me thousands of dollars. The problem was that it took me six months to finish the work on this house. I had to learn how to do all the work on the job and that took me at least three times as long as it would have taken a professional. It may have saved me a little money on labor, but it cost me more money because it took me so long to make the repairs.

When I fix and flip a house, I use financing for most of the purchase price. I also get insurance on the home, pay utilities, taxes, and have many other costs. All those costs add up very fast, making it important to repair the house fast. The longer it takes to make repairs on a home the fewer profits you will make. When buying rentals, the longer it takes to fix up, the longer you will go without collecting rent.

How much does it cost per day to own a fix and flip?

Let us walk through what it will cost to own a flip. I am lucky that I can finance 75 percent of my purchase price with a 5.25 percent loan, because many times flip loans are much more expensive. Based on this financing, this is how much it costs per day to own a $100,000 purchase with a $75,000 loan:

Interest	$10.79
Insurance:	$4.11 (flip insurance is more expensive)
Taxes:	$2.33 (taxes are very low in Colorado)
Utilities:	$6.25
Total:	$23.28 per day

My costs are cheaper than most fix and flippers, because I have great financing. The cost per day could easily double if you are using hard money.

A 15 percent interest rate is very typical for a hard money loan. An interest rate of 15 percent on our fix and flip example increases financing costs to $30.82 per day. However, with hard money you may be able to finance the entire purchase price or more (one advantage of hard money). If the loan amount is $110,000, the financing costs jump to $45.21 a day for a hard money loan. Now your daily costs are $57.80 a day to own the house.

$23.28 per day equals about $708 a month in costs for me or $1,758 per month with hard money. Owning a fix and flip is costly and for someone who must use hard money it is dangerous to hold a property too long. It takes me about six months to sell a fix and flip once I figure repair time, marketing, getting a contract, and closing.

How much money did it cost me to do the work myself on this flip?

I know it took me at least four months longer than it would have taken a contractor to repair this house. It cost me at least $2,832 in extra carrying costs, which is less than a contractor would have charged me for labor. That actually is not too bad, but the truth is it cost me much more than that.

One of the most important things you can do on a fix and flip is to sell the house quickly. Not only does it save on costs, but also it allows you to use your money to buy more houses and complete more flips. If all your money is tied up in one house for eight months, you may miss an incredible deal because you do not have the ability to buy another flip.

The longer you hold onto a house the better chance the market will change. We are in an appreciating market now, but that could change quickly. I like to sell my flips quickly, because I never know what the future holds.

I did not save all the labor costs because my time is worth something

I may have saved money doing the work myself, but how much time did it cost me? My time is worth something. I was a Realtor when I did the flip. My business suffered greatly because I spent so much time working on the house. I had the worst year of my life as a Realtor, because I did not have time to go after business. Because of this house, I made only about $28,000 in 2006. I did not sell any houses as an agent or buy any more flips while working on this stupid house.

Since I was busy with this house and did not have time to look for new projects, it was the only fix and flip work we were doing at the time. Focusing on this house and not looking for others cost me tens of thousands of dollars.

Another factor I hate to think about is the quality of my work. I am not a professional contractor, yet I was doing jobs a pro should do. I was learning and definitely not doing the high quality work my contractors do. There were some jobs that I had a contractor help with, such as taking out a wall and putting in a header, because I did not want the house to fall down. Other jobs were not done as well as they should have been done because I did them myself.

I hate to think about how much the decision to do the work myself cost me on this house. Not only did it cost me months of my life, it frustrated me, it cost me business as a Realtor, and it cost me business flipping homes. It is hard to put a number on the figure, but I estimate this decision cost me at least $25,000, even though on the surface I may have saved a couple thousand dollars by doing the work myself. The work was not great, and that may have cost me even more money on the sale of the home.

What about doing the work on rental properties

Obviously, this story was about a flip, not a rental property but that same principles apply. You may lose even more money on a rental property, because every day you do not have the rehab complete on a rental, you are losing rent. Not only are you losing rent, but also you still have to pay the financing and carrying costs that I had to pay on my flip. Even though on the surface it looks like a smart move to do the work yourself, you will most likely lose money in the end. We did not even talk about the toll that doing all this work takes on your mental health! When I was doing the work on this flip, I was miserable, I was always working, and it took a toll on my family. I was so happy when I was done with that house!

Should you hire a general contractor to repair your rental or flip?

You have a couple of options when repairing rental properties, flips, or even your personal residence. You can use a general contractor who will do everything and hire all the work to be done or you can hire subcontractors who will each do a specific job. Hiring subcontractors requires more work from the homeowner but can save a lot of money. Using a general contractor can make the process easier, but can also cost a lot more. I have used both options, but I like to use subcontractors for as many jobs as I can for multiple reasons.

When you use a general contractor to do the entire job, they handle almost everything that needs to be done. They figure the entire scope of work, hire subs, schedule, budget, and plan the entire project. It can be very expensive using general contractors, because it takes so much work scheduling and planning everything. The other problem with using general contractors is they can be very slow if they have to do all the repairs on a house. Some contractors may be able to handle huge jobs and get them done on time, but others may struggle the more they have to schedule and plan.

When you use subcontractors to repair a house, you have to hire out certain jobs and schedule the work. The benefit of hiring out specific jobs is that they can be done more quickly and less expensively than a general contractor can. Many times subcontractors will specialize in just one thing such as:

- Electrical
- Plumbing
- Roof
- Foundation
- Sewer
- Landscaping
- Flooring
- HVAC
- Drywall
- Kitchen and baths
- Paint
- Windows

Subcontractors can save money because that is the only job they do and they are really good and fast. A general contractor has to use his own crew or hire out a crew to complete jobs. While a general contracting crew can usually do many jobs, they are not as fast and do not have the expertise of a sub that specializes in one thing. Many general contractors also try to have most of the work done by their crew, which takes a lot of time.

With subcontractors, I can have multiple jobs being done at once, which saves a lot of time. The roof, the plumbing, and the electrical can all be done all at once. Some of the biggest contracting problems I have had were when I gave an entire job to one contractor. The contractors got overwhelmed, took forever, and one quit on me.

Please check state laws regarding making repairs. Some states have stricter guidelines for who must be licensed and how to use subs.

How do we repair rentals and flips?

I have tried many ways to repair my flips and rentals. I have used general contractors, subs, a hired employee to run my projects, and even did the work on a flip myself. I have had some luck with general contractors, but many times, they bite off more than they can chew, over promise, and under deliver. I think most contractors will say they can handle everything and may even believe it, but are not equipped to handle large remodels on their own. I have had good luck using subs for parts of jobs and then contractors for the majority of the work. Here is an example:

Subcontractor jobs:
- Electrical
- Plumbing
- Roof
- Landscaping
- HVAC
- Contractor jobs:
- Replace doors
- Replace windows
- Paint
- Kitchen
- Baths

- Fixtures

While the contractor is working on his jobs, the subcontractors can be working on their jobs. In cases like this, I do not use a general contractor, because I do not need someone to schedule and hire everyone. I do the scheduling and hiring or have someone on my team do it.

This last year I hired a full-time employee to handle the hiring, scheduling, and project management on my rehabs. I thought this would be a great way to give myself more time and possibly start a new business in the future (contracting for other people). However, this venture has not gone as well as I hoped, and we are bringing the management back in-house for my team to handle. My new plan is to hire as many subs out as I can. Here are the benefits:

- I should be able to get jobs done faster, because I will not have to wait for a contractor to have time to complete a big job. I will have a list of subs and can use the ones that are able to get work done the fastest.
- I will be able to save money, because subs are usually cheaper due to the reasons we have already discussed.
- I will not be relying on one contractor to get things right. If a subcontractor messes up, they will only mess up part of the rehab and other work can still be done. If the contractor messes up, it can screw up the entire project.

I will still use some contractors and still look for great new contractors to repair my houses. Maybe someday I will find that magical contractor who is affordable, has a huge crew, and is honest and fast. When I am doing ten flips at once, it is tough to find contractors that can handle that much volume without falling behind.

Is it smart to start to use subcontractors right away?

The more experience you have, the easier it will be to find subcontractors and hire out jobs. If you have no contacts and must find all new subs from scratch, it can be a bit daunting. It might not hurt to try to find a general contractor and then slowly start looking for subs. If you are just starting out, try not to take on huge remodel projects that require an awesome contractor or many subs. As your business matures and you gain more experience you will meet good subs and contractors. Make sure you keep track of their names and contact information!

9. How to manage your rental properties.

Owning rental properties is a great investment, but they have to be managed well to make money. Some people think of rental properties as a passive income source, but if you manage properties yourself, they are not truly passive. A property owner must take the time and work to screen tenants, check on the houses, take care of your property, and make sure your tenants pay on time.

Many property owners start out managing properties themselves to save money. However, you need to make sure you are cut out to be a self-manager. You must be tough on your tenants, have systems in place, account for all expenses, and be quick to fix any problems that come up. Most people, including me, are not good property managers! I am not tough on my tenants, I am not always quick to jump on problems, and I believe sob stories. I managed my properties until I had seven, and then I switched over the management to my team.

When I turned the management over to my team, things became so much easier and I made more money! Even though I had to pay my team to manage the properties they were better at choosing tenants, better at keeping on them to pay rent, and were quicker to fix problems. I actually made more money by not managing my properties myself and it removed a lot of stress from my life. Do not get stressed out thinking about how hard it will be to manage your properties. Remember that you can always hire a property manager, and they will most likely do a better job and will not cost that much.

Should you manage your rental properties yourself?

My rental properties are all single-family properties and easier to manage than multifamily rentals, but it still takes time. Not only does it take time, but also you have to pay attention to details and be firm with tenants in order to manage rental properties successfully. If you are not hands-on and tough on your tenants, you will have problems.

What is involved in managing rental properties?

There are many tasks associated with managing a rental property. However, most tasks occur when first renting a property. Once you rent the home, there is much less work involved.

- **Determine what to repair before you rent the property.** I want to control what is repaired whether I am the one managing the rental or I have a property manager. A property manager may help you with repairs before you rent a property, but they also may only help with maintenance and repairs after a home is rented. Even before you buy a rental property, you should have a good idea of what is going to be repaired and how much it is going to cost. Out-of-state rental property owners may have to depend on someone else to manage the rental property repair process.

- **Determine how much rent to charge.** I also like to have control of this whether I am managing a house or using a property manager. A property manager wants to get houses rented fast, because they collect money based on rent. They may not try to get top dollar, although some might. An agent on my team recently sold a home to an investor who used a property manager. We had told the investor the home would rent for $1,500, before they bought it. The property manager they hired said they would rent it for $1,200! We urged the investor to rent it for more and they ended up asking for $1,600 a month. They rented it at $1,600 in two days and they were very happy they did not blindly take that property manager's advice.

- **Rent the home.** Renting a home is the hardest part of management, at least it should be. If you take time to screen and select the best tenants, you will make more money and save many future headaches. You have to advertise the property, show the home, check references, check credit, create a lease, and collect money. Do not pick a tenant because they are the only ones that will pay what you are asking. Do not choose the first tenant that wants the house because you are tired of showing it. Pick the best tenant and if you have doubts about a tenant, do not convince yourself it will work out just so you can start collecting rent. Property managers should have strict guidelines regarding to whom they rent homes.

- **Collect rent.** When you rent a home, make sure your tenants pay on time and charge late fees if they do not. If you let late rent slide, the tenants will think it is okay and they will keep paying late. If they have no consequences, they will pay later and later and may stop paying completely. You have to be strict no matter who is late and what their story is. If tenants get too far behind do not be afraid to start the eviction process. Starting the eviction process usually gets your tenants attention and they start paying rent. A property manager will collect rent and have no problem charging late fees.

- **Evict a tenant**. It is never fun to evict anyone and I try to avoid it; an eviction is just asking your tenant to trash a house. I have yet to go through a full eviction, but I have had mutually agreed upon move outs. If I can have a tenant move out on good terms, they are more likely to take care of the home and possibly pay me what is owed. I would rather lose a tenant who is not paying rent or is constantly behind and rent the home to a tenant who will pay me. A property manager will handle rent collections and evictions.

- **Check on your houses**. Just because you have a tenant who always pays on time and never causes a problem, does not mean they are taking care of your property. I always write in the lease that I have the right to inspect the property with proper notice. I use this time to make sure the home is well maintained; I change furnace filters, check smoke detectors, and make sure no other repairs are needed. Some of the biggest problems come from property owners who rent a house and then never check on it. A tenant may be in a house for years and absolutely destroy it, but the property owner never knows because they never checked on it. It is possible to destroy a house quickly, but the worst damage usually occurs over years. Some renters always pay on time so that the property owner will not come to see the house. They may be trashing the property or doing something illegal such as selling or making drugs. Property managers should check on your houses, but you never know if they are.

- **Maintaining a house**. I have contractors inspect all my properties before I rent them, but I still have maintenance issues. Things break when you own a rental and you have to repair them. I am not interested in being a slumlord that does not make repairs. I always plan for vacancies and maintenance when I figure my cash flow so that when costs come up it does not hurt my bottom line. I always fix water issues, roof issues, electrical issues, or any problem. You want your house to be safe and well maintained. If you cannot afford to maintain your rental properties, you should not buy them. Problems will happen at all hours of the day and night and if you are managing your rentals, you will have to take those calls. A property manager will handle maintenance issues and should check with the owner of the property on any non-emergency issues before work is done.

- **Accounting and taxes**. When you manage your own properties you have to keep track of expenses, rents, profit, loss, etc. A good property manager will give you a year-end report that has all your profit, losses, and accounting and tax information. I always send all my information to an accountant to make sure the expenses and taxes are calculated correctly. It is not easy to calculate taxes on rental properties because you can depreciate the structure, which is an awesome tax advantage.

How much does a property manager charge?

There is a lot involved in managing rental properties, but not every rental will have issues that require a lot of management. I have had rental houses that have never had a problem; the tenants maintained them well and always paid on time. I have had other rentals where the tenants are always having problems and paid late or stop paying completely. I had one tenant who had a heart attack and could not work anymore. We came up with a mutually agreed upon plan where he would move out and try to pay me for back rent owed. He never paid, but I rented the house right away for more than he was supposed to pay and it worked out okay.

Many people find it is worth using a property manager, especially if they cannot handle being tough on tenants. As the owner of the house, the tenant and you both know you make all the decisions. This can make it hard to be tough on the tenants when they cause problems or get behind on rent. Property managers can be tough, because they answer to the owner. If they don't do their job, they could get fired.

Property managers cut into your profits, but save you time. Property management fees usually range from eight to twelve percent of the monthly rent. Some property managers also charge a leasing fee, which could be one half or one month's rent. In my area, I can find property managers who charge eight percent of the monthly rents with no leasing fees. I have thought about starting a property management company, but with fees that low it is hard to make much money.

How much time does it take to manage rental properties?

There are many tasks associated with managing rentals, but it does not take a lot of time for one property. The most time-consuming part of managing properties is getting them rented. If you only have one rental property, it should take just a few hours a month managing it. Many of those hours come from renting the home and much fewer hours from collecting rent and dealing with maintenance and other issues.

Managing two or three rental properties is not too difficult either. Once you have four or more rental properties, it can take a significant amount of time to manage them. If you do not have the time to manage them, get help. When you do not take the time to screen tenants or check on your properties you can have serious problems.

Is it easier to manage single-family homes?

All of my rental properties are single-family homes. I like single-family homes for a number of reasons. They are easier to manage because people are more likely to treat them as their own home. Most people do not want to live in an apartment their entire life; they eventually want a house with a yard and a place they can call home. Many people eventually want to buy a house, but some would rather rent. Because people are more likely to call a single-family rental their home, they stay longer. My parents have had the same renter in one of their single-family homes for 14 years. Many renters take care of single-family homes better and even do some repairs themselves. On most single-family rentals, the tenants pay all utilities, which is less hassle when managing a rental property.

If you want to manage your own rentals, create systems to help you. Create a system to check your houses, to make sure rent is on time, and to make sure accounting information is logged every month. It was not difficult for me to manage my rental properties, but I began to let things slide at the end and that is when problems occur. If the tenants do not think you are paying attention, they will be more likely to try to take advantage of the situation. If you are looking to buy rental properties and do not think you can handle managing them, make sure to account for the cost of a property manager when figuring your cash flow.

In my experience, it is well worth hiring a property manager for the peace of mind and reduction of stress. I will talk much more about finding property managers later on. For now, let us focus on how to self-manage properties.

How to rent out your property

There are many ways to rent a home and I will break down exactly how I advertise and pick a tenant as well as how I write a lease. I will also go over how I decide market rent, another very important piece of investing in long-term rentals.

You should determine market rent long before you are ready to rent a house; it is one of the first things to do as a real estate investor.

Why is it difficult to determine how much a home will rent for?

Because I am a real estate agent, I am able to pull up sold comparable properties on our MLS system to help determine market value for a home. I can see what sold, for how much, and most of the details of the transaction. However, in my area, MLS is not used very often for rental properties. I have to come up with a different way to determine market rent.

With rental properties, there is no way to pull up comparable properties that show how much a home is actually rented for. In Colorado and many other states, home sales are public record, but what a home rents for is not. The only way to determine market rent is to look at active listings for rentals or to talk to experts in your area. The most commonly used place to advertise rentals in my area is Craigslist or Zillow Postlets.

Craigslist is a great way to determine rent in my area, because most rental properties are advertised on Craigslist.

Before I buy a home or put a home up for rent, I check Craigslist to see what is for rent in an area. Rental listings give me an idea of what market rents are, but they are not always reliable. I have no way of knowing whether the asking prices for rent are indicative of what the home will eventually rent for. Checking Craigslist daily to see if the homes that were previously listed for rent are still listed is one way to track whether homes are renting. There is a good chance that any home that has been rented will be removed from Craigslist. Make a list of homes that are similar to your rental and save the ad, especially the contact information. If you check back and that listing has been removed, call or email the listing to see if they rented the home.

You can also search the Internet to find market rent. Some property management companies may not list their homes in Craigslist, but they may use their own website or another rental website to advertise. You can use those listings much like Craigslist to determine market rents. You may also find other rental websites in your area that list rental properties for rent. Each market advertises rental properties differently.

A property manager is a great resource for an investor. A property manager can determine rental rates in many ways and help investors figure rental rates. You can use their rental listings as a guideline for rental rates as was just discussed. You can probably trust a property managers rent listings more than an individual who may or may not know for how much to rent a house. You have to be careful with property managers that charge too little rent, so they can rent homes faster. Make sure you check with multiple sources to determine rents.

You can also ask a property manager directly what they think market rents are. If you are an investor looking to buy rental properties, a property manager should be happy to help you determine rental rates. If they help you out as an investor, you may use them as a property manager at some point.

Some real estate agents are experts on investment properties and some have no idea. It is important to find an investor-friendly real estate agent to help you find rental properties. It helps if the real estate agent can also help you determine rents a well, but not necessary. I would listen to what your real estate agent tells you and compare that to the other information you are able to gather. In areas of the country where they are a vital part of the rental market, real estate agents can be a huge help in determining market rents.

How to price a rental property

I have tried a couple of different methods of pricing my rentals.

- Price at the top of the market and try to find a renter who will pay a premium.
- Price a little below market and take my pick of great renters.

My experience has been better with taking my pick of great renters. Even though the rent is lower, I usually have less worry about late rent and excessive wear and tear. Whenever I price a rental high, I am waiting for a decent to mediocre candidate to send an application in, instead of picking the best tenant from many applications.

Once I have a decent idea of the market rent, I place an ad on Craigslist and Zillow, put a For Rent sign in the yard, and post it on Facebook. Be sure you research what the most prominent way to advertise in your area is.

When I show rentals, I try to have an open house where every prospective tenant shows up at the same time. This saves me or my management team time and gives the tenants a sense of scarcity and urgency to get us an application if they want to rent the home.

I use a rental application that I found online and altered slightly. I originally did not charge an application fee or run a credit check, but I do now. I charge $50 for an application fee and credit check. Potential tenants have had no problem paying the application fee and it helps make sure all tenants submitting an application are serious.

A great way to judge a tenant is by talking to them as much as possible and looking at their application. I want to see an application that is filled out as thoroughly as possible with multiple references. If potential renters have barely filled out the application, they are not taking the process seriously or they are trying to hide something.

When I talk to a potential renter, I want to learn as much about their previous living situation as possible. I ask about pets, employment, and who will be living in the property. The longer you talk to a tenant the more you can learn about them. When you first talk to a tenant on the phone, take notes so you remember what they said. Then when you meet them in person ask them some of the same questions to make sure they give you the same answers. It is a very bad sign if someone is lying to you.

I always call references for all applicants to whom I am considering renting. I want to talk to the reference for the applicant's previous residence and their current employer. I want to know if they paid rent on time, took care of the residence, or were high maintenance. By high maintenance, I mean calling in every week for minor issues, causing plumbing problems because their children like to flush toys down the toilet, or any number of other items. I want to see if they have pets and if that information matches up with what they are telling me on their application.

I ask their employer how long they have worked for them. I want to know if they are a good worker and how solid their position is. I will also ask how much money they make to see if it lines up with what the applicant is telling me.

Should you allow pets in your rental property?

I prefer not to rent to tenants with pets, but in some cases, I allow some pets. I have a dog that I love and there is no way I would give up that dog, so I understand why tenants want to have pets. It is tricky allowing pets, because they can destroy a house, but also add revenue to a rental property.

If a pet is trained well or the pet lives outside, there is a great chance that pet will never harm a home. If a pet is not trained well or is an older pet, they can do a lot of damage to a house. The biggest risk with pets doing damage to a home is urination inside the house. If you have had the pleasure of being in a home that has pet damage, you know it is not pretty and smells horrible. The smell can be overwhelming, especially from cats.

Pets can destroy carpet, hard wood floors, sub floors, and even drywall. In some cases, pets will try to chew through doors and trim or destroy grass in the backyard. If you are going to allow pets, you have to do your due diligence on the pet and weigh the risk of damage versus the reward of more money.

Why would any property owner allow pets in their rental property?

People with pets still need a place to live and many times they will pay more to rent a house than non-pet owners will. Pet owners may pay more in monthly rent or pay a higher security deposit. I have rented my homes to tenants with pets, but I have always charged a higher deposit or monthly pet fee. That higher rent or deposit can make the risk of allowing pets worth it if you check out the pet first.

I have never allowed a cat in my rental properties, because cat smell is so much worse than dog smell and much harder to get out. I have smelled houses with cats from 50 feet away with the doors closed. If you have the pleasure of entering a house like that, the smell sticks with you once you leave the home; it is not fun.

In my experience the larger the pet, the better the chance they will do damage. A large dog is stronger and can do more damage than a smaller dog. A large dog also urinates more and leaves bigger messes. If I do allow a dog in a home, it will be a small dog and I definitely charge more.

Many cities have ordinances against aggressive dogs such as pit bulls. Cities declaring it illegal to own a pit bull should tell a property owner something about how wise it is to allow pit bulls in their rental. If an aggressive breed hurts someone and a property owner knowingly rented a home with an aggressive breed dog, that property owner could be held liable. This is another great reason to stick with smaller, less aggressive breeds.

The more dogs and cats, the better the chance damage will be done to a house. The more pets there are the better the chances that the owners are not cleaning up or paying attention to their pets. The pets will be more likely to play aggressively with each other and cause damage as well. The fewer pets, if any, a tenant has, the better off you will be when you rent a home.

How do you know if a pet will do damage to a rental property?

Just as you ask tenants for references, you can also ask for pet references. The best way to see how well a pet will behave is to check with previous property owners to see if the tenants had pets and if the pets did any damage. If the tenants cannot provide a pet reference, then it can be very hard to see how the pets behave unless the tenants are willing to show you their current home. It is not a bad idea to see how well the tenants take care of their current residence if they will allow you to see it.

I usually adjust rent or the deposit increase based on the individual situation. The more pets, the better chance for damage and the more I charge a tenant. For a small dog that I think has very little chance of doing damage, I may charge $250 more in deposit and $25 to $50 more per month. For multiple dogs, I may charge a $500 deposit and $50 a month more. All things being equal, I would rather have a tenant without any pets at all.

In my lease, I have clauses that the tenants must adhere to or they can be fined. In the lease, it says that if any pet is found on the property without permission from the property owner, the tenant can be charged $750 per occurrence. That is a hefty fine and I hope it makes my tenants think twice about having pets that are not allowed. This clause does not protect against every potential problem, and I think it is also wise to set up routine inspections on your rental properties to change furnace filters and light bulbs to see if there are any signs of pets. I have a sixth sense for pets, because I am allergic to them, especially cats.

I try to avoid tenants with pets, but I don't avoid them at all costs. The biggest factor I look for when renting a home is how qualified is the tenant. If I have a choice between two equally qualified tenants and one does not have pets, I would obviously prefer the tenants without the pets. If I have one tenant with pets, who I think is much more qualified than a tenant who does not have pets, I may go with the more qualified tenant even though they have a pet. Often times a pet will behave good or bad depending on how well they are trained and how well their owner takes care of them.

Should you allow smoking in rental properties?

I do not allow smoking in my rental properties at any time. If anyone is caught smoking or breaking any of the other rules, the lease states that I can fine them $750 per occurrence.

How to write a lease after you rent a property

I am lucky that my sister is a property manager. I was able to combine her lease with one I found online and customize it for myself. Everything needs to be in writing including rent, term, late fees, date rent is due, and things the tenant can and cannot do. I include a few things that cannot be done.

- No painting without written approval
- Do not hang curtain rods without written approval
- No smoking on the property
- No pets on the property
- Only people on the lease and their children may live in the home
- No overnight visitors for over three consecutive nights
- No illegal activities on the property

If any of these rules are broken, the lease states that I can fine the tenants $750 per occurrence. If there are any exceptions to these policies, such as pets, I put them in writing in additional provisions in the lease.

I have a section that states what utilities the tenants pay. In my case, the tenants pay all utilities.

I have a section that says if the tenants break their lease early, they owe the remainder of the rent due for the entire lease. If I can rent the home again, I cannot charge the previous tenants for rent as well, but I will charge a one-month rent lease-break fee.

I have many other items in the lease, but I am not an attorney and I highly suggest you have an attorney look over any lease you create.

Lead based paint disclosure in rental properties

I have to provide a lead based paint pamphlet explaining the dangers of lead based paint with any house built prior to 1978. I have a lead based paint disclosure signed by the tenants as well.

Deposit on rental properties

I charge one month's rent for the deposit and it must be paid with the first month's rent before the tenants move in. The only time I split up the rent and deposit is if the tenants want to reserve the home before they move in. They can pay the deposit first and then pay rent when they move in.

Carbon monoxide detectors and smoke detectors in rental properties

Each state has different laws regarding carbon monoxide detectors and smoke alarms. No matter what your state law is, I would put them in. In Colorado, we have to have carbon monoxide detectors within 15 feet of every bedroom. They are very cheap for the protection they offer and you can plug them straight into an outlet.

Colorado enacted this law after a family of five died in a short-term rental property from carbon monoxide poisoning. The furnace had a cracked heat exchange and the leaking gas killed them while they were sleeping.

How to find a property manager

Investing in real estate is supposed to create passive income, but if you are managing your rental properties, they are not that passive. To create a truly passive income you need to hire a great property manager who can take care of the renting, repairs, accounting, and everything else that comes along with rental properties. After reading what it takes to manage properties yourself, you can see the value a property manager provides. However, you cannot hire just any property manager you find. You need to make sure you hire the right manager who will do a great job.

My real estate team manages my properties for me. I pay them eight percent of the gross rents and they take care of the renting, managing, and hassles that come with rentals. It leaves me free to concentrate on buying new properties, which is much more fun for me.

My experience with property managers

I helped my sister start her property management company when I was in high school in 1996. I was not a full-time employee, but I helped show houses while she was going to school about an hour away. Her property management company focused on college rentals, because those were her primary investments. She started investing in college rentals at a very young age and has seven college rental properties. That may not seem like many properties, but they all have multiple units (about 20 units) and a lot of cash flow. She managed 120 houses at the peak of her property management company, but scaled down to handle just her own rentals in 2011. She has a doctorate in physics, and decided she would prefer to concentrate on teaching and physics projects rather than on property management.

I saw how a good property manager operated when I worked with my sister, but I have seen how bad property managers do business as well. There is a property management company in my town that is horrible. I can usually spot their houses because the lawns are dead, the roofs are bad, and the homes need paint. I also have dealt with many of their property owners and have seen them rent houses 30 percent below market rents. You need to take your time hiring a property management company and make sure they will take care of your properties.

How much does a property manager charge?

Typically, a property management company charges between eight and twelve percent of the gross rents received and some companies charge leasing fees on top of that. A typical leasing fee can run as much as one-month's rent. If you are paying ten percent of gross rents and one month's rent for a leasing fee, it can eat into profits very quickly. I think most investors should be able to find a decent property management company that does not charge that leasing fee. You do not want to hire a property management company based on their cost, it is better to pay a little more if you know they will take care of your properties.

The first step is finding potential property management companies. By performing a simple web search, you should be able to find the largest property management companies, but also many smaller companies may not show up in web searches. My real estate office, which has about 30 agents, has three property managers and none of them advertises except by word of mouth. My suggestion is to always ask your contacts in the area who they know. Ask a Realtor, title company, investor, or anyone else in the area who they recommend.

Do these things first before you interview a property manager

Property managers will promise great service, but how will you know until you actually hire them and see how they do? Here are some tips to help you find a great management company.

- Check to see how many vacant properties a property management company has listed before you call them. They should have a website or directory that lists the properties they have for rent. When you call the property management company later on, ask them how many total units they manage. You can then calculate the vacancy rate for that particular company. Check the vacancy rates in your area and see how close the company's vacancy rates are to the regions vacancy rates. My sister knows of a few companies in our area that have 10 to 20 percent vacancy rates while our regional vacancy rate is less than two percent. Red flag!

- Call the property management company as a potential renter on a house they have listed for rent. According to my sister, you will most likely reach someone's voice mail. See how long it takes them to call you back, how knowledgeable they are, and how soon they could show the property. When asking questions about the home, ask simple questions that the manager should know. Ask how old the home is, how many square feet it has, how many parking spaces, what type of heating. This will give you a great idea of their knowledge and service level. My sister said people would be very surprised by how many companies do not call back potential renters.

- Drive by properties a property management company has for rent and see how well they are maintained. As an investor, you will be depending on the property management company to maintain or make sure the tenants are maintaining the property. If there is a dead lawn in front of every house, that is not a good sign.

- Check the Better Business Bureau to see if a management company is a member or has had many complaints filed against them. This suggestion can be deceiving, because almost every company that does a lot of business is liable to make a couple of people mad. Some people just like to complain, no matter how fairly or unfairly they are treated. The BBB gives companies that have complaints against them a chance to respond and give their side of the story. If a property management company cares, they should at least be responding to complaints to explain how they saw the situation. A company with an abnormally large number of complaints against them may be a bad sign.

Eventually you will need to interview property managers. There are many questions to ask the property manager and they will have their own sales pitch to give you as well. Here are some questions to ask a property manager once you have narrowed down a few good candidates.

- How many properties/units do you manage?
- What is your specialty? College rental, single-family, multifamily, commercial?
- How long have you been in business?

- Ask if they are a member in good standing with the BBB. You should have already checked on this, but you can see how their answers compare with your research.

- How many people work for you? This will give you an idea of how much they can handle.

- Do they have a real estate license? Many states, including Colorado, require property managers to have a license.

- What do you charge and are there fees for leasing?

- Do you have any monetary agreements or affiliations with the contractors you use? Most states require property managers to disclose any kickbacks they receive from contractors. Many property managers use contractors as an extra source of income, by either marking up prices or having ownership.

- Do you own rental properties yourself, what kind, how many do you own? If a property management company manages 100 units and owns 85 of them, whose properties do you think they are going to try to rent first?

- What type of insurance do you carry? A property manager should have E & O insurance if licensed and general liability insurance at a minimum. The last thing you want is someone getting hurt on one of your properties and suing you, because the property manager who screwed up has no insurance and no money.

Do not be surprised if many of the companies you call are not taking new clients. It takes a lot of work to manage properties and many companies do not add new clients. I know my sister would not add new clients for years unless she knew them personally.

10. What are the different exit strategies with rental properties?

When I buy my rental properties, I plan to keep them as long as I can. I have no exit strategy and no short-term or long-term goal to cash out. What I want is long-term cash flow. I figure if I buy enough rentals to provide the cash flow that I need every month, I can retire at that point in my life. I doubt I will every retire, because I love what I do, but it would be awesome to have the security of knowing I will have as much money as I need for the rest of my life, every month for as long as I live. However, not everyone has the same plan or goals that I do. Some people may want to cash out and sell their rentals at some point. There are many things to consider when selling or planning to sell. There are many costs when you sell a house and there can be some huge tax liabilities as well.

How much does it cost to sell a house?

Selling a house can be a fantastic experience if you bought the home below market value, accounted for all the costs, and make a nice profit. Selling a house can also be a disappointing experience if you are forced to sell at a bad time, miscalculated the costs involved, and lose money. There are many costs involved in selling a house and knowing those costs before you buy will make the experience much more enjoyable. You will most likely have to pay a real estate agent, title insurance, recording fees, closing fees, and possibly much more when you sell a house.

The costs can vary greatly when you sell a house depending on real estate commissions, closing fees, closing costs, title insurance, and more. Seven to ten percent of the selling price is a rough estimate for the cost of selling a house with a real estate agent. This figure can be quite shocking to many sellers, but if you want to get top dollar for your house, it costs money. I am in Colorado where we have no transfer tax, attorneys are rarely involved, and minimal title insurance costs. In states like Maryland the costs to sell could be thousands more, because of their transfer tax and other costs. Make sure you research the costs to sell in your state, before you buy.

By far the biggest cost when selling a house is the cost to pay real estate agents. There is no set commission, but HUD pays six percent commission with three percent to the selling agent and three percent to the listing agent. I will use HUD's commission structure as an example, but all real estate commissions are negotiable.

I believe paying a real estate agent to sell your house is a necessary cost. The agent knows the market and is an expert in selling houses. If you do not use an agent you could underprice or overprice your home, which could easily cost you the amount of money or more that an agent charges. An agent also knows the contract process and selling process in your state. Trying to figure out pricing, contracts, marketing, showings, negotiations, inspections on your own could be a nightmare. An agent can help with all of this and make the process easier while getting you the most money for your house at the same time.

In most states, it is customary for the seller to pay for title insurance. Title insurance is a guarantee to the buyer that a home has clear title when they buy. The title insurance makes sure all loans are paid off and all liens, judgments, and title defects are taken care of. It is always smart to get title insurance when you buy a home. In Colorado, title insurance costs between $600 and $1,200 depending in the price of the home. This cost can vary by state as some states have different laws regarding title insurance.

Many other fees are involved when you sell a home. The closing company will charge a fee to handle the closing, which can range from $200 to $800 (usually on the lower end). In some states, you must use an attorney to close on a house. Typically, in Colorado, the closing fee is split between the buyer and seller, but that can be negotiated as well.

There are also recording fees for the deed, recording fees for any mortgages that have to be released, wiring fees for loan pay-offs, and many banks charge to provide pay-off figures. These fees can range from $50 to $500 depending on the amount of loans and pay-offs there are.

In most cases, when you sell a house, you pay the taxes and utilities up to the day you close. In Colorado, we have property taxes, but usually no transfer taxes or local taxes that have to be paid. Even though your mortgage company may be paying your property taxes through an escrow account, there may be taxes owed at closing. These taxes have to be paid at closing before the house is sold and if the escrow account holds extra money, it will be returned to the seller after closing.

The same can happen on water bills in my area. The water account balance has to be brought down to zero before a house can close. The title company will typically escrow a small amount for the water bill so they can pay the final water after closing and any money not used will be returned to the seller.

Taxes and the water escrow can vary greatly depending on the cost of a home. Colorado property taxes are low, about .05 percent of the sales price in my county. A water escrow may be $100.

When you live in a neighborhood with an HOA, you usually have to pay a monthly fee. Many costs besides the monthly fee come with an HOA, as well as different payment structures. I just sold a house for sellers that had an HOA, but had no monthly HOA payments. The HOA charged .05 percent of the sales price of every home sold in the neighborhood; the fee was split between buyer and seller. The sellers were unaware of this policy and were quite surprised at closing.

Most HOAs do not work this way, but many charge transfer fees or fees for a status letter. These fees can be $20 to $150 or more. The purchase contract determines who pays for these fees.

What are the total direct costs when you sell a house?

Costs discussed up to this point are direct costs when you sell a house. On a $200,000 house, the costs may be as follows:

Real estate agent commissions	$12,000
Title insurance	$1,000
HOA transfer fees	$150
Recording fees, pay-off fees	$150
Water escrow	$100
Prorated taxes	$750
Closing fee	$200
Total	**$14,350**

Many people are surprised at how high the mortgage pay-off is on a house they are selling. The pay-off on a mortgage is figured to the day of the sale just as the taxes are. When you receive your statement in the mail for your mortgage, the principal amount listed is calculated just after you made a payment on the loan. The interest increases every day after that principal amount was calculated by the bank. An $180,000 loan balance at five percent interest will accrue about $25 a day in interest. If you decide not to pay your last mortgage payment because you are closing on the fifth of the month, there may be 30 days of interest accrued on the loan that must be paid when you sell the house. That adds up to $750 dollars and can be a shock to sellers who expected their payoff to be the same amount as their last mortgage statement principal balance.

In some instances, buyers may need the seller to pay closing costs for them in order to get a loan. Closing costs are common and can range from two to four percent, and many times the buyers do not have the cash to pay these costs. It is very common for the seller to pay three percent of the closing costs for the buyer. In some cases, the price of the home is increased to account for the closing costs and in other cases, it is not. Closing costs are negotiable just as the price of a home is. Sellers should be aware that many buyers with owner-occupied financing might ask for closing costs, which will decrease the seller's bottom line.

It costs a lot of money to sell a house but remember the person you bought the house from paid those costs when they sold it to you. When you add in real estate commissions, money to repair the home, closing costs and fees it can be a significant amount. If you are planning to use the proceeds from the sale toward the purchase of another house, make sure you figure the correct amounts so you are not shocked when you get your figures for closing! If you are buying a house to flip, or plan to sell a rental in a few years, make sure you account for selling costs.

Why you should always use a real estate agent to sell a house

Real estate agents are expensive and many sellers think selling a house themselves is a great way to save money. Sellers may save a commission by selling a house themselves, but trying to sell a house without an agent may actually cost them more than the commission they saved. I see people claim to save thousands on selling their home and they sold it in one day without an agent. There is a reason they sold it in one day, they left a lot of money on the table! A great real estate agent could have more than made up for the commission they charged by pricing a house right and working in the best interests of the seller.

Real estate agents are experts in marketing, educated in the sales process, and know how to value a home. Agents are not paid just for the time they spend selling your house. They are paid for all the licensing courses and continuing education they must take, for their experiencing marketing homes, and for getting the most money possible for a seller.

You may not save as much as you think when you sell a house yourself

When you try to sell a home yourself, it may appear you can save 5, 6 or even 7 percent of the sales price by not paying a commission (all commissions are negotiable). However, most buyers work with real estate agents when they are looking for a house (the seller pays for the buyer's agent so it makes sense that they use one). If you are not going to pay a commission to the real estate agent representing the buyer, you have eliminated most of the buyers in your market. Eliminating most buyers will definitely decrease your selling price and cost you money. If you do agree to pay a cooperating broker, you are only saving half of a commission. On top of only saving half of a commission, the buyer is represented by a real estate agent and you are not. Who will have the upper hand in negotiations and the selling process? The buyer's agent will have the best interest of the buyer in mind, not yours.

If you underprice or overprice a home, it can cost you thousands of dollars. The best opportunity to sell a home is when it first comes on the market, especially in a seller's market such as the one we have now. There are buyers waiting for the perfect home to come up for sale, and it is vital that a home is priced right from the beginning.

FSBOs (for sale by owner) accounted for nine percent of home sales in 2012. The typical FSBO home sold for $174,900 compared to $215,000 for agent-assisted home sales. This figure is now $208,000 for an FSBO and $234,000 for an agent assisted sale in 2014. The reason for sale by owners sell for so much less money, is most sellers do not know what they are doing.

Why will overpricing a home cost the seller money?

If a home comes up for sale and is overpriced, a buyer may not even look at it. An overpriced home may sit on the market for weeks or even months until the price is reduced. When buyers see that a home has been on the market for an extended period, they start to wonder what is wrong with it. Even if the price is dropped to the right value after a few weeks, the home still may not sell for what it would have sold if it had been valued correctly to begin with. Houses become stigmatized the longer they sit on the market. For an investor or homeowner that no longer lives in the home, a stigmatized listing is very bad. Every month a home sits vacant costs the seller money and if there is a loan on the house, it can cost the seller thousands of dollars a month. If the seller had priced the home correctly to begin with, they would have sold the home quickly and saved thousands of dollars.

How will underpricing a home cost a seller money?

Underpricing a home can cost just as much money as overpricing a home. When you underprice a home you will most likely sell it very quickly, but there is a good chance you will sell it for less money than it is worth. It is true that underpricing a home can stir up a lot of activity and produce multiple offers. You may even get offers above list price, but the problem with a low asking price is it attracts buyers who want a great deal (like me). Many times, a multiple offer situation will actually scare away some buyers. Some buyers do not want to get into a bidding war and will not make an offer on a house that has multiple offers.

If you underprice a home and get an offer over asking price, the chances are you could have gotten an even higher offer had you priced the home correctly. Most buyers will base their offer on the list price and not on what the home is actually worth. I hear all the time from buyers that they offered $10,000 over asking price and still did not get the home! They are basing their offer on the list price assuming the seller is asking fair market value. They are not basing their offer on what the home may actually be worth. Another downside to an offer that is well above asking price is that it may give an appraiser a reason to come in at a low value. If an appraisal comes in low, it could cost the seller even more money! By pricing the home right to begin with, you will usually sell the home for the most money.

If you end up with a buyer who is getting a loan, they will most likely need an appraisal done on the home. The bank will loan money to the buyer based on that appraisal and if the appraisal comes in low, there is a good chance the buyer will need to reduce the price of the home. We see appraisals come in low all the time with rising home prices and there is a way to deal with appraisers. A real estate agent knows how to be proactive to help the appraiser and knows how to challenge an appraisal if it comes in low.

Why is valuing a house difficult without a real estate agent?

Valuing a property is the most important aspect of selling a house. Without MLS access, it is very hard to get information on recently sold properties. Recently sold properties are the most important piece of information needed to value a home. People have access to active listings through websites like Zillow, but only licensed agents have access to MLS, which lists sold homes. Active listings can give an idea of house values, but you have no idea if houses are overpriced or for what price they will actually sell.

Every house is different, because every house has different features and locations. A real estate agent is an expert at determining value based on these characteristics. It can take years to understand local markets and those markets can change extremely fast. It is tough for an agent to determine value correctly; it is much more difficult for someone who is not an agent.

Many people use Zillow values since Zillow provides a Zestimate for house values. Zillow was off by as much as 40 percent on one of my properties! You should never value a home based solely on a Zestimate.

There is an art to marketing and pricing a home correctly. You cannot just stick a home on the MLS and wait for offers to come in. A real estate agent knows how to take the best pictures, do virtual tours, create the best brochures, what websites to use, which magazines and newspapers to advertise in, and much more. Real estate agents also know many people. Many times an agent will have buyers waiting for a house just like yours.

Why a seller should not use a low fee service to enter a home in the MLS?

Many companies offer a low fee MLS service; pay a couple hundred dollars and get your home entered into the MLS. There are many problems with using this type of service.

- The service may never see your home and may enter incorrect information and no pictures
- The seller still has to take calls and set up showings with many of these services
- You have to pay the buyer's agent and pay for the MLS listing so are you really saving much money?
- You still have all the disadvantages of not having an agent represent you while the buyer is represented.

- You get no help with contracts, negotiations, inspections, appraisals, etc.

In Colorado, the state contract is 17 pages long not including the four addendums and disclosures that must be completed as well. California contracts are much longer. A real estate agent knows exactly what to look for in a state contract, what is customary for the seller to pay, and what is customary for the buyer to pay. In Colorado, it is customary for the seller to pay for title insurance with many other costs to be split by the buyer and the seller. If you do not have an agent to guide you on what is normal for a seller to pay and what is not, you could easily pay many more costs than you should.

A real estate agent knows the market and they know people in the business. They can help a seller find a title company with the lowest fees and best service. They can help the seller find the best contractor if repairs are needed before listing or after an inspection.

It is almost always better to use a real estate agent to sell a home instead of selling it yourself. A real estate agent will make you more money by pricing right, marketing right, negotiating right, and working for you. The money they make you will more than make up for the commissions they charge. I know many investors who have their real estate license and they still use another real estate agent to sell their house for them. Those investors know that another agent has the time needed and the market expertise to sell the house. Before you try to sell a house on your own, consider whether it is worth the time it will take to understand the process and if you will actually save any money.

How does a 1031 exchange work?

Rental properties have many great benefits including favorable tax benefits with the IRS. Not only can you depreciate rental properties to save on taxes, but also a 1031 exchange allows you to sell rental properties and defer the taxes on any profit you make or recaptured depreciation. A 1031 exchange has many rules and regulations and you have to make sure you complete the exchange correctly to avoid a large tax bill from the IRS. *I am not an accountant or an attorney; please consult your attorney or accountant for any tax or legal advice.*

A 1031 exchange is a real estate transaction that involves two like properties, one being sold and one being bought within a certain period. There are many restrictions on a 1031 exchange and the IRS is not perfectly clear when describing the restrictions. Some basic principles are that the properties must be held at least a year, must be used for business, the replacement property must be identified in 45 days and bought in 180 days. If all of these requirements and a few others are met, a rental property can be sold without paying any taxes on the profit or recaptured depreciation.

When you sell a rental property, you have to pay taxes on any profit you make. You also may have to pay recaptured depreciation on a rental property. The IRS allows you to depreciate a rental property because the structure has a limited life span and decreases in value every year. You can deduct that depreciated amount from your taxes every year, which is a huge advantage to owning rental properties. However, if you sell a property for more than the depreciated amount, it shows that the structure did not decrease in value and you will have to pay back those taxes you saved.

If you have owned a rental property for several years, the recaptured depreciation can add up to thousands and thousands of dollars. Luckily, the 1031 exchange allows you to move the profit and recaptured depreciation into another similar property without paying taxes.

What properties can be used in a 1031 exchange?

The IRS has determined that many forms of real estate can be used for a 1031 exchange. Any property used for a business, which includes a store, manufacturing facility, or office building. Investment property, including rentals, can also be used for a 1031 exchange. It has even been determined that water rights and mineral rights qualify for a 1031 exchange.

These cannot be used for a 1031 exchange:

- Stock in trade or other property held primarily for sale
- Stocks, bonds, or notes
- Other securities or evidences of indebtedness or interest
- Interests in a partnership
- Certificates of trust or beneficial interests
- Choses in action (a right to something, such as payment of a debt or damages for injury, that can be recovered in a lawsuit)

Can you use fix and flips for a 1031 exchange?

The IRS has determined fix and flips cannot be used for a 1031 exchange unless you meet certain guidelines. The IRS does not want real estate investors who fix and flip constantly to be able to use a 1031 exchange to defer taxes. If you only fix and flip occasionally and meet the guidelines you may be able to use a 1031 exchange.

- The flip must be rented out for at least one year after it is repaired.
- The home cannot be sold until after it has been rented at least one year and should not be listed before being rented for a year.

The problem with this strategy is that the IRS does not say you have to hold a flip one year to do an exchange. The IRS simply says a flip needs to be held for an acceptable amount of time and it is up to the accountant and investor to determine if their transaction qualifies. Some people have determined that to be a year, but if the IRS thinks you are a professional house flipper trying to cheat them out of money, you still may get in trouble.

How do you complete a 1031 exchange?

When completing a 1031 exchange, a qualified intermediary must be used by the investor to oversee the transaction. The IRS does not tell you who can be an intermediary, only that these people cannot be one:

- The TP's attorney
- The TP's CPA
- The TP's real estate agent
- Any relative of the TP
- Any employee of the TP
- Any business associate of the TP

The intermediary holds the funds after one property is sold in the 1031 exchange and uses that money to buy the new replacement property. When doing a 1031 exchange, the owner must identify the property he is exchanging and declare it before the sale. Once the subject property is sold, the investor has 45 days to identify a new property to exchange with the old property. Once the new property is identified, the investor has 180 days to close on the new property.

In order to avoid paying taxes in a 1031 exchange, the investor must use all the cash from the sale of one property to buy the new property and the new property must cost at least as much as the sales price of the old property. If the investor does not use all the cash from the sale of his old property or if buys a less expensive property, he may have to pay taxes on the unused cash or price difference in the properties.

In a 1031 exchange, the investor must take title to the new property in the same name as he owned the property being replaced.

You cannot use a 1031 exchange to sell property to someone you are related to.

You can sell one property and buy multiple new properties in an exchange.

What is a Reverse 1031 exchange?

Most investors will sell a property they own and then purchase a replacement property. It is possible to buy the replacement property and then sell your original property. This can be a difficult maneuver because the investor will not have the cash from the sale of his original property to buy the new property.

It may make sense for an investor who is building a replacement property to do an exchange. Since it may take more than 180 days to build and buy a property, an investor might do a reverse exchange for large companies, exchanging manufacturing facilities, or other unique buildings that must be built to spec and are not available on the market.

Can you refinance a property after doing a 1031 exchange?

One way to get the cash out of a rental property you exchange into, is to refinance the replacement property. You may have $100,000 in cash proceeds from a rental property you are exchanging. That money can be used to buy a replacement property in a 1031 exchange, but that is a lot of money to have locked up. If you refinance the property after buying it, you can take out some of that cash without paying taxes on it. The government does not consider money from a refinance profit.

It is also possible to complete a 1031 exchange into a personal residence and then eliminate the taxes altogether. Exchange a property into a house that you would like to live in at some point. The replacement house must be rented for at least one year after the exchange is completed. Once that year is up, move into the replacement house and live there for at least two years. Since you are living in the home for at least two out of five years as a personal residence when you sell the house your profit could be tax-free! *There are some restrictions to this; please talk to your accountant! I have heard that the tax law has been modified to change this rule so that you may be liable for some taxes using this strategy.*

There are many intricacies and details in the IRS tax code that must be adhered to when completing a 1031 exchange. Investors will run into more types of 1031 exchanges and many more situations. Talk to an accountant or attorney to make sure you are following all the guidelines.

Should you pay off your mortgages early?

Many financial experts recommend people pay off their homes as quickly as possible to reduce debt, but I do not always agree with this strategy. Debt is not a bad thing if you use debt to invest and make more money than the debt costs you. Debt can allow investors and businesses to create greater returns on their investments than paying all cash.

We already talked about how leveraging your money to buy rental properties gives you higher returns than paying cash. Rental properties also generate much better returns than most consumer debt including car loans. I feel as long as my returns on my investments are greater than the debt used to fund those investments, it is good debt. I am a very aggressive investor and this strategy may not work well for everyone.

Should you pay off the mortgage on your personal residence?

Most people are able to get a very low interest rate and put little money down on their personal residence. Interest rates are below five percent on an owner-occupied, 30-year, fixed-rate loan. This is cheap money! If you can find an investment that gives you a better return than a five percent interest rate, it may make sense to invest that money and not pay your mortgage off early.

It does not make any sense to pay off my house quickly when I have such a low rate locked in for 30 years and I am making so much money on my rental properties. I pay the absolute minimum payment I can on my personal home mortgage and save that money to buy more rental properties. If you have nowhere else to put your money besides a CD or bank account that pays less than one percent interest, it would make sense to pay off your mortgage quickly. If you are willing to work a little harder and find an investment with a better return than your mortgage, stop paying extra towards your house payments, and invest that money!

Should you pay off car loans early or invest the extra money?

The experts will also tell you how horrible it is to have a car loan. Their reasoning is that debt on any item that will depreciate is bad, but I completely disagree with this as well. I look at it as a numbers game, why would I care what my debt is secured against as long as the debt allows me to buy more rental properties? The rental properties give a higher rate of return than the auto loan interest rate. I have my current car loans locked in for six years at less than three percent interest. I do not pay one cent extra on them, because I want as much cash as possible available to buy more rental properties. I am not advocating purchasing the most expensive car you can, because you still want to save as much as possible to invest with. If you have the cash available to buy a car, why not finance the car instead and invest that cash in something else?

What about the security of paying off my mortgage early

Do not get me wrong, I am not condoning racking up debt to go on vacation or buy furniture. A lot of debt can be very, very destructive if you have no assets providing you cash flow or a return on that debt. People will still ask, "What happens if I lose my job and I have all this debt I cannot pay off?" I think you are going to be better off with cash producing properties than if you had paid off your primary house.

Let us assume you have a $200,000 house that you have an $180,000 mortgage on. If you put all of your extra cash into the mortgage to pay it off early, you will eliminate your mortgage payment, and save about $900 in principal and interest every month. We will assume you paid about $150,000 extra into your mortgage to pay it off early. I could buy five rental properties with that cash, which would cash flow at least $500 a month each. I am making $2,500 a month off those rentals, a lot more than the $900 I would be saving on my mortgage.

Not only I am making more money each month with rentals, I also see an immediate return on my investment. If you accelerate your mortgage pay off, you will not see that $900 savings until the mortgage is completely paid off. With rental properties, I start seeing immediate cash flow as soon as I rent the first property.

If you are choosing the accelerated mortgage payoff route and lose your income before your house is paid off, you still have the same mortgage payment to make. The only way to get that money back that you invested in your home is to sell your house or refinance. You may not be able to refinance with no income and your only option may be to sell. If you lose your job and you have rental properties, you still have income from the rentals. You could sell a rental property to get immediate cash, and refinancing a property would be much easier because you are still showing some income from the rentals.

On the surface, it may seem like paying off your mortgage faster will offer more security, but there is actually a better chance of making it through rough times if you have rental properties producing income. I know I would rather sell off a rental property in bad times than my personal house.

One of InvestFourMore's readers recently paid off her mortgage, decided to retire early and focus her time on investing in real estate. It was a lot of hard work saving and diverting her money towards her mortgage and it felt great when it was finally paid off. Now that she is actively investing in real estate, she wanted to tap into the huge amount of equity in her house. Since she has no job and very little income at this point, she cannot find a bank to refinance her house. Even though she did what the experts told her to do and worked hard to pay off her mortgage, she cannot access that money unless she sells her home. This is another reason to think twice before you start sinking all of your extra money into your principal home. If she had bought more rental properties with that money instead of paying off her mortgage, the bank may have been willing to loan to her because of all the rental income coming in.

Investing your money in real estate, instead of paying off your debt will leave you thousands and thousands of dollars ahead. Just because the experts tell you to do it, does not mean it makes sense to pay off a mortgage early. Think about where you are putting your money and what kind of returns you are getting.

Should you pay off your mortgages early on rental properties?

I used to use my cash flow from all my rentals to pay off the mortgage on my first rental. This is often called the snowball method and is a great way to pay off debt. The snowball method involves taking cash flow from all my rentals and paying down one mortgage at a time. When one mortgage is paid off, I apply the cash flow from all my properties to another mortgage and so on. Using this strategy, I paid off my first rental property about three years after I bought it. It was awesome to pay off a house, but for some people it may make more sense to save the cash flow from rental properties and not pay off their mortgages early.

If you are just starting to buy rental properties or your cash is very tight, it may make sense to save your cash flow instead of paying off properties. There are many factors that you must consider when deciding whether to pay off loans or save the cash flow. How much cash you have, what your goals are, how long you want to invest, interest rates, and returns all play a role.

Why I previously used the snowball method to pay off my rental properties

The snowball method uses the cash flow from all your rental properties to pay off one house at time. I was using the snowball method when I first started investing, because I wanted to pay off my loans before they had a chance to adjust to a higher rate. But I realized I would be ahead to buy as many rentals as I can, without paying any off. I am okay with a higher interest rate if my ARM adjusts, because I can handle the higher payments and I make much more money buying new rentals than I do paying off debt.

Another reason I used the snowball method is I do not know if my portfolio lender will always finance as many rental properties as I want. It is very difficult to get more than ten loans with a conventional lender and the fewer mortgages I have, the more properties I could buy if my portfolio lender changes their policies. In fact, it has gotten tougher to get loans with my portfolio lender, once I hit 2.5 million dollars in loans with that lender.

Even though I changed my strategy to not pay off rentals early, I am still glad I did it. One key to being a successful real estate investor is to have cash available for purchases or repairs. Having a paid off property allowed me to get a line of credit from a bank. I can use that money when I need it and pay it back when I do not need it. Banks like to loan to investors who have debt-free properties and are happy to give a line of credit on those properties. The more properties an investor has paid off, the more stable they look to banks.

If you are in a situation where you need more money to buy rental properties, the snowball method might not be the right strategy. The snowball method works best when you have multiple properties, have a lot of cash flow coming in, and are not aggressively buying new properties. If you cannot save enough money to buy multiple rentals, it may be smarter to save your cash flow, instead of paying off the mortgage.

Why shouldn't you pay off 30-year fixed rate loans?

If you are buying your first rental properties, there is a good chance you will be able to get a 30-year fixed mortgage. You will not have to worry about interest rates rising in the future because the interest rate is locked in for 30 years. You can use that money to buy more properties.

If you are just beginning to invest in rental properties, you may not be concerned about financing more than ten rentals. Most likely, you are focused on buying one, two, or three properties. After you buy multiple properties and decide that you like having rental properties, you can think about a larger portfolio. If you only have a few rental properties, it could be too early to decide whether paying off mortgages is the right move. I like to error on the side of caution and have plenty of cash available. If you are not sure whether paying off loans is right for you, don't pay them off. Hold the cash, because you can always pay down debt later, but you cannot get money back from the bank after you pay down loans.

The biggest issue most people run into when buying rental properties is having enough cash for down payments. It can take a long time to save enough money for your first rental property. It will be easier to buy another rental property if you save your cash flow for future down payments. You will also need to have extra cash for emergencies and expenses on your rental properties. It is not wise to use all of your money to buy a rental property. You should always reserve some extra cash to make it through the tough times.

If you are just starting out investing in rental properties, there is no rush to pay off your mortgage early. It can be a good strategy to save your cash flow to buy more properties. If money is tight, you may need that money for repairs or vacancies on your rentals. That extra money can help you buy properties sooner and increase your cash flow. You may decide you do not like investing in rental properties, and you only want one rental or want to get out of it all together. If you do decide to use the snowball method later on, it will be easy to make a large payment toward your mortgage with that saved up money.

11. How to buy rentals in an expensive market.

Housing prices have increased in many areas of the county over the last few years. In my market, prices have increased 50 to 100 percent in the last five years. It has been much more difficult for me to buy rental properties, but I have found good deals even in an appreciating market. The key is always getting a great deal and making sure you can still cash flow in that market. It might not make sense to buy rentals in some areas.

With housing prices rising, it gets more difficult to cash flow on properties. Rents usually do not rise as high as housing prices. I bought homes from $80,000 to $120,000 in 2010 to 2013. Now I cannot find any decent houses for less than $150,000. I have to face the reality that if I want to keep buying rental properties in my market I will have to pay more money for them or find different ways to buy them. Even when finding great deals, it is still tough to cash flow.

When I first started out, it was easy to find houses that would produce 20 percent cash-on-cash return. Now I am lucky to find anything that will return 15 percent cash-on-cash. I have gone from buying $80,000 to $100,000 homes, to buying $120,000 to $160,000 homes. Although rents have increased, they have not gone up nearly as much as housing prices have.

How to buy rentals when housing prices are high

Sometimes I go months without seeing a good deal in my market, especially for a rental (it is actually easier for me to find flips). If I cannot find cash flowing rental properties in my area, I do not buy just to buy. I think it is a bad idea to buy hoping for appreciation while losing money every month.

I know I can still get great deals in my area. I have multiple flips going and I purchased five rentals in 2015. Many markets are harder to cash flow in than my market and many people are not in the business as I am. If you cannot dedicate the amount of time that I do to finding great deals or if prices are even higher compared to rents in your area, you may have to look in another state. You could also look into buying rental properties in a slightly larger geographical area. I have looked in areas within a 45-mile radius, but my town seems to have the best rent-to-value ratios.

When prices get higher, you have to look at the numbers. Are you making enough money to justify the risk versus the reward? Are you buying for cash flow and not appreciation? Are you getting a great deal? If you can satisfy all of these requirements, it may make sense to keep buying even as prices increase. If you get to a point where you cannot cash flow, it might be time to reevaluate your strategy.

Should you sell your rentals when prices increase?

Colorado has had one of the highest appreciating markets in the country and it is expected to keep going up. An incredibly hot real estate market is great for some, but it creates many questions for investors. My properties keep going up in value, which has been great for my net worth, but it makes it harder to cash flow. With prices increasing so much, I wonder if the market can sustain high prices. Would it be smart to sell my properties and reinvest the money?

How much has the Colorado real estate market increased?

Five years ago, the median house price in my area was around $120,000. In 2016, the median price was $260,000 and prices continue to rise. Zillow has shown that Colorado has had the highest appreciating market in the country for the last 13 months. Many investors predict Colorado prices will continue to rise. Colorado has one of the fastest growing populations in the country and not enough houses for everyone.

In Northern Colorado, our economy has had a huge boost from oil and gas, and many had predicted that our market would slow down with lower oil prices, but it has not. I cannot predict whether our market will keep increasing, stay the same, or go down, but my gut tells me it will stay strong for the immediate future. The thought has crossed my mind to sell my proprieties and use the cash to buy more properties either in my area or in a different market.

How have rent to value ranges changed in Colorado?

When I bought houses from $80,000 to $120,000, and made $5,000 to $15,000 in repairs, I would rent them for $1,100 to $1,300 a month. Now I can buy houses for $150,000, make $10,000 to $20,000 in repairs, and rent them for $1,500 to $1,600 month. At those numbers I would be finding amazing deals, not just buying whatever is available. Prices have increased much more than rents have, which makes it harder to make money as an investor. Both of these price points assume I am getting a great deal on the house. I would have to work hard to find a $150,000 house that would rent for $1,500 or $1,600 even if it needs work.

With prices increasing so much, there is also the risk that prices or rents could drop. I do not think prices will drop anytime soon, but when prices increase that much it makes me a little nervous. I would be fine with my current rentals if prices dropped, but if I stretched my criteria to buy more rentals at even higher prices, I might be asking for trouble.

How much have my rental houses increased in value?

I bought my first rental property in December 2010. I made money through appreciation and I increased the value of my properties when I first bought them by buying them below market. Here is a list of my rentals showing the approximate amount I spent on repairs and how much they are currently worth.

Rental Property	Price Paid	Repairs Made	Value in 2016	Value at Purchase
12/2010	$97,000	$2,000	$215,000	$130,000
10/2011	$94,000	$15,000	$210,000	$140,000
11/2011	$92,000	$14,000	$205,000	$135,000
01/2012	$109,000	$14,000	$225,000	$150,000
12/2012	$88,000	$18,000	$200,000	$130,000
03/2013	$115,000	$15,000	$205,000	$150,000
07/2013	$113,000	$9,000	$220,000	$140,000
11/2013	$97,500	$15,000	$195,000	$140,000
03/2014	$133,000	$4,000	$185,000	$155,000
02/2014	$100,000	$3,500	$165,000	$125,000
07/2014	$109,000	$16,000	$190,000	$145,000
03/2015	$133,000	$15,000	$205,000	$185,000
06/2015	$120,000	$1,000	$185,000	$140,000

07/2015	$134,000	$15,000	$195,000	$175,000
08/2015	$45,000	$0	$45,000	$45,000
09/2015	$92,000	$5,000	$155,000	$135,000
Totals	$1,671,500	$161,500	$3,000,000	$2,220,000

If you subtract the purchase price and repair cost from what my houses are worth now, I have gained $1,167,000. That is a lot of money to gain from buying properties over the last five or six years. That number does not quite tell the whole story, if I were to decide to cash out my rentals.

How much money would I make if I sold my rental properties?

If I sold my rentals, I would not get to keep the entire sale price. I would have to pay selling costs and taxes on the profit I made. The nice part about rental properties is that you only pay long-term capital gains tax when you sell them if you own them long enough (long-term capital gains is less than ordinary income.) However, I would also have to pay taxes on any depreciation I recapture when I sell the houses.

If I sell the houses I would have to pay another agent to represent the buyer, but I could list them myself. There would be closing costs, and I would want to market the properties as vacant to get the most money from them since they are single-family homes. I would have to wait until the leases are up, put the home up for sale after the tenants moved out, and make any repairs at that time as well. To account for selling costs, vacancies, and repairs I will assume it will take eight percent of the selling price.

- 8 percent of the selling price $240,000
- Profit $927,000
- 20% of profit for capital gains tax $185,400

- Estimated depreciation recapture $100,000
- **Total profit after taxes** **$641,600**

I have refinanced seven properties over the last four years, which has given me much more money to invest. Refinancing also increased the amount of money I owe on some of my properties. I also paid off my first rental property, which reduced how much I owe. Right now, I owe the bank $1,383,000 on my 16 rental properties. If I subtract the amount I owe on my properties from what I bought them for, I owe $285,000 less. I would actually get back about $926,600 in cash after paying taxes.

That is a great deal of cash to get back from my rental properties, but that does not mean it is worth selling them all.

How much money do my rental properties make me now?

At the time I completed all of these calculations, my rentals were cash flowing about $8,000 a month or $96,000 a year. Including repairs and down payments, I have spent about $495,000 buying my houses. That does not include any carrying costs or closing costs, but many times I have the seller pay closing costs and as a real estate agent, I also make a commission. I am going to assume the closing costs and commissions cancel each other out. I also refinanced seven of my properties, which gave me about $320,000 in cash back. Overall, I have spent about $175,000 of my cash to buy my rentals. The $96,000 a year I cash flow is about a 55 percent return on the money.

55 percent is an awesome return on my investment, but I need to look at the cash I would have available, not the cash I already invested, in order to make a decision about selling.

$96,000 a year divided by the $926,000 in cash I could take out of the rentals would equal about a ten percent return. I know I can make more than ten percent buying new properties below market value, fixing them up, and renting them. However, is it worth all the hassle to sell my houses and is it wise to do in our market?

How many houses could I buy with $926,000?

If I sold all my properties and bought new properties, I could buy many more than 16 properties. Historically it has cost me about $32,000 to buy a house, fix it up, and rent it (assuming 20 percent down). In theory, I could buy 28 houses with that money. The problem with that theory is houses are more expensive and it is much harder to find great deals than it was three years ago. I would probably have to spend $40,000 to $50,000 a house now, which would mean I could buy only 18 houses in my market.

If I sold out, I would have a hard time finding 18 houses that would be great deals at the same time. I would also have a hard time finding properties in this market that would cash flow as well as mine do. There is the risk of the market declining and I would be stuck with 18 houses with much higher loan amounts than I have now.

What if I were to cash out my rental properties and buy in another market?

In 2015, I bought a turnkey rental with my self-directed IRA. I have thought about investing in other areas of the country where I may be able to buy below market value, repair, and rent the properties.

Here are the issues I have with buying out-of-state:

- I would need time to research and visit an area, in addition to finding a good agent, contractor, and property manager.
- I am not a Realtor in another state and would not be paid a commission.
- I would not know the area as well; the farther away I am, the less I would be able keep track of my properties.
- I would have to find new financing, as my portfolio lender will not loan in most states.

With all these negatives, I have previously thought it was not worth it to buy out of state. However, with our market continuing to increase it is harder and harder to find great rentals. I am seriously thinking about buying more rentals in another state.

If I bought out of state, I could use the cash I have now to invest or I could exchange properties. A 1031 exchange can be used to sell my properties and buy new proprieties tax-free. This would save me $200,000 in taxes, which would let me buy five more houses. Again, I would run into the problem of finding enough great deals to replace my current houses, and I would have to find them quickly with a 1031 exchange. If I were to sell out, I think using a 1031 exchange would be the best way to reinvest my money, but I do not think it is worth all the hassle and risk.

I suppose I could sell out and use the money to buy a couple of exotic cars, but that would not be the wisest decision! I also would have a hard time reaching my goal of purchasing 100 rental proprieties.

I considered selling my rentals because our market is going so crazy. However, if I sold my rentals and bought new properties in the same area I would have higher loans and more risk if our market declined. It is not worth selling all of my properties to buy in a different location, but it might be worth starting to invest in a new location. It might make sense to sell some of my properties and use that money to buy more in a new location.

Do housing prices indicate another housing bubble?

One reason I am worried about buying new rentals is prices are so high in our area. The real estate market is improving in almost every part of the country. In some areas, prices are at or above the peak that we saw in the mid-2000s, possibly indicating another housing bubble. In my market, prices have gone up 50 to 100 percent, if not more, in the last five years. Even though the price increase is great for those who already own homes, it makes it difficult for those looking for a new home. Buyers have to compete with multiple offers and they are forced into bidding wars for any chance of finding a new home.

For investors such as me, rising prices make it very difficult to find good deals on homes that will cash flow as rentals. There is also concern that the market could drop again in a few years and we could see another housing crisis. As an investor, I have made the decision to keep buying rentals, but only if they continue to meet my guidelines and criteria. I cannot be swept up in the market frenzy and buy houses for too much money, because they are the only homes available. One of the biggest mistakes investors make is paying too much for properties that cash flow too little. I can pay a little more now than I could last year because rents have gone up with the prices, but it is going to take a lot more work to find deals even if I do pay more. Despite rising prices, I am still confident that I can reach my goal of purchasing 100 rental properties by January 2023.

The price increases have been good and bad for me. I have been able to refinance multiple properties and use that cash to buy more rentals. I had planned to refinance those properties originally, but the price increases have allowed me to take out more money than I had anticipated. I have also seen increased rents due to increasing prices and low inventory of houses for sale and for rent. My most recent properties have all rented for more than I expected when I bought them.

Due to lack of inventory and increasing prices, I have not seen any deals on MLS in the last few months that are even close to my buying criteria.

What is causing the high real estate prices and possible housing bubble?

In my market, lack of inventory is definitely causing our price increase. There are many homebuyers looking for houses and very few houses for sale. Sellers are realizing that they have the advantage and are raising their asking prices. There are so few houses available on the market that buyers are forced to pay more if they want a house. Most of the United States is seeing a lack of inventory right now mostly due to low foreclosure numbers. We went from an extremely high number of foreclosures to a very low number in a short amount of time.

In other areas of the country, we are seeing many factors that contribute to price increases. Hedge funds have become massive buyers of investment properties and in many urban areas such as Atlanta, Phoenix, Las Vegas, and Chicago they are buying up thousands of homes. Naturally, that kind of buying is going to drive up prices and decrease inventory. We have not seen much hedge fund buying here, but we are not in a major metro area either, I have heard that the funds are starting to move into the Denver area.

Why is there so little housing inventory?

A few years ago, we saw record numbers of foreclosures on the market, which caused a huge decrease in prices. That decrease virtually stopped new construction dead and the market has had to rely on existing homes to fill demand. Most sellers could not afford to sell their homes, so buyers depended heavily on foreclosures. The foreclosures slowly started to decrease after 2008, but many of us in the real estate industry kept hearing about a tsunami of foreclosures that would be coming on the market soon. From 2010 to 2012, we kept hearing next quarter the flood gates will open and the inventory will increase substantially. The inventory never came; in fact, it has decreased! I think that threat of the oncoming foreclosure tsunami stopped many builders from beginning to build sooner.

The price increases have allowed homebuilders to start building again. In my county, there are 42 builders with new construction homes listed in MLS. A couple of years ago, there may have been one or two builders with new houses on the market. However, almost all the new construction in my market is priced above $300,000 and our average price is much lower. The new construction is adding inventory to the higher price ranges but it is not going to solve the problem of the lack of inventory in that middle and lower price range. I have talked to builders in the area and they would love to build lower prices homes, but they all agree it is not possible due to city and county fees on utilities, land, and other new construction costs. The other problem is lenders are scared to lend to builders for large projects. If builders can only build a handful of houses at a time, they will build high-end homes that make them more money per house.

I believe we need an increase in inventory to meet buyer demand in my area. There are enough buyers to absorb that inventory without a market pull back. You have to remember that every market is different and what is happening in Colorado may not be happening where you are. However, I have talked to many investors across the country and they all seem to have the same trends in their market.

I do not think we are in a housing bubble, because the increase in prices is based on supply and demand, not loose lending guidelines. In the 2000s, the housing frenzy was caused because anyone with a heartbeat could get a loan. People were buying houses they could not afford, assuming that prices would always go up. Just because prices are going up, does not mean they will not drop down to where they were before.

Even though we may not be in a housing bubble, that does not mean it is smart to buy rentals in really hot markets, especially if you cannot cash flow with them.

How to buy rental properties in another market

Since prices are high in my area and there is little cash flow, I am considering buying in other states. There are a couple of options for real estate investors when buying out-of-state. You can buy turnkey properties that are already repaired, rented, and managed or you can buy properties that are below market, get them repaired yourself, and find a property manager. Buying turnkey properties involve much less hassle and work, but the returns are not as good. When you find the great deals yourself and find a contractor and property manager, the returns are usually much greater.

One of the most important factors when investing in real estate is buying properties below market value. If you can buy a home 20 percent below market value, you have built-in equity and it is much easier to cash flow. One of the disadvantages of investing in turnkey properties is that they have been purchased by investors, repaired, rented, and property management is already in place. These features are great, but they come at a price. They are not going to be priced well below market value.

Is it worth investing in rental properties in another market?

In the past, I have not seriously considered investing in another market, because I was able to get good returns in Colorado. However, I bought a turnkey rental in Ohio with my IRA in 2015 as an experiment to see how it would work to invest in a turnkey. If I were to invest out-of-state again I would buy houses below market, repair the property, and find a property manager myself. The main reason I have not seriously considered buying out of the area is because it would take a lot of work and I already have a lot going on. If the deals were just slightly better in other states than what I could get here, I would not invest somewhere else.

Here are some advantages of investing locally:
- I have my real estate license in Colorado, which can only be used in Colorado, that saves me a lot of money when investing

- I have many contractor, lender, and investor contacts in the area.
- I know my market very well, which is very important when investing.
- I can have my team manage my rentals and I can keep a close eye on them as well.

It is a huge advantage to invest locally, but if I am not making money on local rental properties, it does not make sense to keep buying here. I know there are other markets throughout the country that have much better rent-to-value ratios.

How do you start looking for rental property locations?

I have a huge advantage when researching locations for rental properties. I run InvestFourMore, which gives me access to thousands of people investing all over the country. I talk to many investors for my podcasts, in my coaching programs, and people who email me. I have a long list of areas across the country with much better cash flow than Colorado. Florida, upstate New York, the Midwest, Milwaukee, and many other places have much better rent-to-price ratios.

There are steps you can take to narrow down your search criteria when looking for a new place to invest.

- Before you start looking out of your own state, increase the geographical area in which you search for rentals. It would be more appealing to have to drive only a couple of hours to find a good location to invest in, rather than looking three states away. You would probably be more familiar with the area as well.

- If you cannot find a close geographical location, start looking in areas with which you are familiar. Did you grow up somewhere different from where you live now? Do you have friends or family in a different area of the country? The more familiar you are with an area, the easier it will be to learn the market and find good deals. If you have family or friends in an area, they can help you learn a market and keep an eye on your properties.
- If you cannot find a suitable location where you know someone, where would you like to spend time researching a market? I think you have to visit any area you want to invest in and it helps if you have a little fun while you do it (beach, mountains, etc.).
- Check out publications for the best rental property locations. Many sites will show you the best rent-to-value ratios. Do not blindly accept the lists of the best places to invest. Many of these lists ignore things like cash flow, taxes, and other factors that make a good rental property. The lists only focus on economic factors, which may not be an indication of good rental property ratios.

How do you know if an area will be good for rental properties?

Once you have found a few places to research you need to know if you can make money in those areas. You also need to know if the economy is stable. Some areas may have great numbers, but a decreasing population and a shaky economy.

- Is the population increasing or decreasing? A rising population is a good thing and is a major factor for economic growth.

- Have housing prices been increasing or decreasing? It is not the end of the world if housing prices are decreasing. It might mean opportunity. If housing prices are decreasing and population are decreasing, the area may be in trouble. If housing prices are increasing sharply it may be hard to get a good deal that cash flows.

- What risks are there in an area? Is the area susceptible to floods, natural disasters, economic downturns, or wild swings in housing prices? These risks can be overcome, but make sure you know what you are getting into. Houses close to the ocean or in flood plains will have very expensive insurance.

- What are the property taxes? In Colorado, we have low property taxes. Some of my properties have taxes less than $500 a year. Other states have taxes ten times that or more! What may look like an awesome cash flowing property quickly becomes a bad deal once you factor in the high taxes.

There are other factors to consider when deciding where to invest such as crime rates, vacancies, and price points. To truly learn about an area, you need to visit, talk to agents and property managers, and if possible, other investors in the area.

How do you overcome the disadvantages of investing out-of-state?

I mentioned the advantages of investing locally here. So how do I overcome these advantages when investing in another area?

- I can get a real estate license in another state. It may take some time and I might have to pass another test, but I can do it. I would have to find a broker to hang my license with, but I could find a low-cost broker to do that.

- I know many people across the country that have contacts that could help me. I also know how to find a portfolio lender and I believe I could find one in any market.

- I could learn a new market. It would take time and effort, but I could do it. I could also use my contacts to help me learn markets faster.

- I would have to take the time to find a great property manager. However, I do not have to rely on them to watch my properties for me. I could hire a third party to take pictures of my properties, make sure they are rented, and even value properties for me (BPOs).

- I have a huge advantage when investing out of my area, because of the people I have met and know. However, many investors on this site and on other sites are happy to share their knowledge. I also share many of my contacts and resources with people in my coaching programs.

How to find a team for out-of-state investing

It will be virtually impossible to buy, repair, and manage homes from another state by yourself. It will save you money in the end to use local professionals who know the market. You will need a great team to handle buying and renting a long-distance property for you.

- **Real estate agents:** A great real estate agent can help you find great deals and help you find the rest of your team. A key to getting great deals is being able to act quickly. You have to be able to trust your real estate agent enough to make an offer for you sight unseen. Investors do not have time to fly out to see a good deal or plan a trip and hope that a good deal pops up while they are in town. I sometimes have to wait months to find a great deal and if I waited three days or a week to make an offer, that deal would be gone.

- **Property managers:** You have to have a property manager who will look out for your rental and rent it for you. A bad property manager can cost thousands and thousands of dollars. A good property manager will make you thousands and thousands of dollars. A great Realtor should be able to help you find a good property manager as well as this book.
- **Contractors:** This is probably the trickiest part of building your team. Contractors can be great or horrible and can change from great to horrible very quickly. We are constantly hiring new contractors. You have to be able to depend on your team to help you find a great contractor. Realtors and property managers should know local contractors to whom they can refer you. You should not have to pay in advance for work done. Always keep in constant touch with your contractors. Always get a written bid from any contractor before they start any work.

There are many different areas across the country with great cash flow to invest in. If you do not happen to live in one of those places, it does not mean you cannot invest in real estate. It may take more work to invest out-of-state, but it is not impossible. I think it will be fun exploring new markets and finding new places to invest. If you have questions about investing out of your area or questions about what areas are good, you can always send me an email at mark@investfourmore.com.

How to invest in turn-key rental properties

Turn-key rentals are fully repaired, rented, and managed by a property manager. Buying a turn-key property allows a long-distance investor to buy a property that cash flows with minimal work.

Some consider a turn-key property to be a house that is remodeled and needs no repairs, but it may not be rented. I consider turn-key to mean the home needs no repairs, has a tenant in place, and has property management in place. Make sure you have the same definition of turnkey properties as whomever you are talking with does! If you are investing out-of-state for a turn-key property, make sure it is already rented and has property management in place.

Here are a few advantages of buying turn-key rentals:

- **Easy to find:** You can buy a turn-key property very quickly from a turnkey provider who has many properties available for purchase. Turn-key companies can have a large inventory of turn-keys because the properties are providing cash flow and making them money while they own the properties.
- **Less work than a normal rental:** Turn-key properties are already rented, managed, and repaired. You do not have to find contractors, property managers, or real estate

agents. You should still perform due diligence on the company and their team.

- **Provide cash flow from day one:** The first day you buy a turn-key, it will have a tenant in place paying rent. You do not have to worry how long the repairs will take or how long it will take to get a tenant.
- **Provide a great return:** Most turn-key rentals provide returns from 10 to 15 percent. That return begins right away and takes little work to maintain, because a property manager takes care of the house for you.
- **Provide diversification:** Buying turn-key rentals in different markets of the country gives you diversification.
- **Can be bought for cash:** Many foreign investors have trouble buying properties because they cannot get financing. Turn-key rentals can be as cheap as $30,000 making it easier to buy with cash.
- **You can invest your retirement savings:** You can invest a self-directed IRA or 401k into turn-key rentals. You can do this with regular rentals as well, but it may be easier with turn-key properties because the price points are lower.

How can you find turn-key rental properties?

There are many turn-key rental property providers throughout the United States. Some companies are local to specific markets such as Memphis, Ohio, Missouri, Florida, Texas, Chicago, and Wisconsin while other companies have properties all over the country. The properties vary in price, rents, financing options, and returns, but good turn-key properties will cash flow. Even with cash flow, I would advise investors to spend time researching the property manager and the area that they want to invest in before buying any turn-key property.

A Google search for turn-key rentals will give many results for property managers and houses for sale that are not rented. I have spent a lot of time researching turn-key companies and have met with turnkey companies in person. You are welcome to email me at mark@investfourmore.com about the turn-key company I used.

Every turnkey property is different and every location for turn-key properties is different. I have seen turnkey rentals that are repaired, rented, and managed range from $35,000 to $150,000. I do not usually see turn-key properties in higher price ranges, because it is much harder to cash flow on a higher priced than a lower priced rental property. The lower priced turn-key rental properties usually provide better cash flow and may be a good option for foreign investors who have a hard time getting a loan on properties in the United States.

I usually do not buy rental properties that are turn-key ready, because it is hard to get a great deal on them. It is the same reason I rarely buy properties that are fully repaired. Rental property number nine, is the closest thing I have purchase to a fully repaired property. It needed a bit of paint, but that was about it. In a perfect world I would love for all the rentals I buy to be repaired and rented before I buy them, which is one advantage of turn-keys.

When I buy my rentals, they usually need work and I get a discount for the money and time I have to put into repairing the homes. In fact, it is less helpful to buy a home that needs repairs than purchasing a home fixed up, unless you can get a great deal. It is harder to have built in equity on a turn-key rental, but you do not have to spend time repairing the home, renting it, or finding a property manager.

When would investing in a long-distance, turn-key property be a good idea?

I have had many people reach out to me about investing in rental properties, but they do not know how to start because their market is too expensive. When starter homes are $300,000 or more in an area, it is almost impossible to cash flow on a rental property unless you pay cash. When you pay cash, your return is not nearly as good as if you can get a loan (as long as the property cash flows). Rents are almost never high enough on a $300,000 home to cash flow no matter where you live (unless you are buying multifamily).

The down payments on a $300,000 property are going to be at least $60,000 unless you use a technique to buy with less money down. Then you have to add closing costs, reserves, repairs and other costs associated with buying a rental property. I can buy two or three rental properties in my market, where someone in a more expensive area could only buy one rental property that may not cash flow at all.

What are the possible downfalls to investing in turn-key properties?

Just because a home is rented, repaired, and managed by a property manager does not mean you may not run into problems. You must do your homework and make sure the person or company you are buying the property from follows through on their promises. There can be problems with renters, property managers, maintenance, and repairs.

Here are some proactive things you can do to prevent a disaster with a turn-key property.

- Always get references for any company with which you are going to do business. Ask the company for references from current customers and search online for any reviews of that particular company.
- Always check the value on the properties you are looking to buy. Find a local Realtor that can tell you what a home is worth in the area. Even if a home cash flows great, you should shy away from houses that are priced 10 or 20 percent above market value.
- Always check out the property manager that is managing your rental property
- Check the history and record of accomplishment of a company. Check the BBB, see how long they have been in business, and ask how many deals they have done.
- Ask for the details on any home you want to buy. How old is the furnace, hot water heater, wiring, plumbing, etc. You want to make sure the major components are good and the company did not put lipstick on a pig to cover up faults. Don't be afraid to hire your own inspector to check out the property.
- How realistic are the company's projections and estimates for cash flow? Even with a turn-key property, you may still have some maintenance and vacancies, unless the turnkey company guarantees those. Some turn-key companies will not list any expenses for vacancies or maintenance, which is a huge red flag to me.

Turn-key rental properties are a great way to invest for cash flow when cash flow is hard to find in your market. Turn-key rental properties are also a way to invest in rental properties without having to repair a house, rent a house, or find a property manager. However, it is hard to get a great deal on turnkey rentals, because the turn-key provider wants compensation for all the work they do.

Can foreigners invest in United States real estate?

There are no restrictions on foreigners (including Canadians) buying real estate in the United States. However, that does not mean it is easy for foreigners to invest in property in the U.S. I have had many inquiries on my blog from foreigners wondering how they can invest in the U.S. housing market, because their market is very hard in which to invest.

There are many things a foreigner needs to consider such as financing, U.S. taxes, taxes in their home country, and the cost to buy a home in the United States. Just because it is possible for foreigners to buy a home in the United States, does not mean it will be worthwhile. They really have to do their homework. I love investing in the United States, because I live here and the U.S. has one of the best markets in which to invest.

Why is the United States one of the best places in the world to invest in real estate?

I have talked to many foreign investors through coaching, comments on the blog, and on my podcast. The United States has a unique system for buying real estate. In most areas of the world, you cannot get a 30-year mortgage. A 25-year mortgage is about the maximum term you can get, but that is not available everywhere either. Many parts of the country also have great rent-to-value ratios. It is common to get $1,000 rent per month on a $100,000 house. Some markets are different from others, but those numbers are almost impossible to find when you look at other parts of the world such as England, Australia, Canada, and many other countries. With the United States real estate system, it is also safe and easy to buy a home. Many countries have much different systems to buy houses that are not as clear-cut as the U.S. Because the United States has such an incredible housing market with incredible lending options, many investors look here to buy.

There is no law that foreigners cannot buy houses in the United States or get a loan. That does not mean it is easy to get a loan or find a lender that will loan to a foreigner. Most of the information I have found on this subject is in regards to Canadian policies since Canadian citizens are the most common foreigners trying to buy real estate in the U.S. Most U.S. banks do not want to loan money to a foreigner who has never paid taxes in the U.S., has no permanent address in the U.S., and no ties to the country. There is obviously going to be a lot more risk to lenders when they loan to a foreigner who lives outside the country. It is also difficult for a Canadian or any other foreigner to get a loan in their home country on a property in another country. Most lenders do not want to loan outside their home country or may not even be able to, depending on the laws and regulations of that country.

The good news is that it is possible for a foreigner to get a loan on a property in the U.S. There are banks that will loan to Canadians who can prove income and work history, much like a U.S. citizen would have to do. The problem may be finding a bank that will do it. I found a bank that specializes in helping Canadians get loans for U.S. real estate. RBC bank claims they are the best at hooking up Canadians with U.S. lenders to facilitate financing. I personally have no experience with them and have no connection to them. Many local lenders will also loan to foreigners.

What does a loan cost in the U.S. for Canadian citizens?

The loan process in Canada is much different from the U.S. In the U.S., the cost to get a loan includes an origination fee, appraisal fee, flood certifications, recording fees, closing fees, prepaid interest, and insurance. These can easily reach two to three percent of the mortgage amount for a U.S. citizen, but the costs may be higher for a Canadian citizen due to the increased work and risk the bank is taking on. The interest rates and closing costs will most likely be higher as well.

Rental properties have great tax advantages for U.S. citizens, but taxes are the tricky part for any foreigner buying property in the United States. The U.S. requires foreigners to pay taxes in the U.S. on real estate gains. Foreigners may be required to pay taxes in their home country as well. The United States and Canada have an agreement that meets some of these concerns regarding income taxes for Canadian citizens. I would talk to a tax professional in both countries before buying any property, as I am not an accountant or offering legal advice.

You have to include the cost of travel in any investment you make, unless you never plan to see the property. One thing Canadians need to consider is that their health insurance may not cover them when they travel to the U.S. You must also factor in airfare, hotel costs, and other travel costs when looking at property in the US.

Can you get a great deal on U.S. houses from Canada?

I think the biggest issue for any foreign investor is being able to act quickly to get a great deal. I get great deals on my rentals because I can act very quickly on deals that come up in my area. To get a great deal there may not be time for a foreigner to see the home personally unless they are already in the country and if you are in the country, a great deal may not pop up while you are here. It can take me months to find a great deal in which I want to invest. The best option may be to find a real estate agent you can trust to find a great deal for you.

Because of the unique housing market in the U.S., it may be worth it for many foreign investors to buy houses here. It will not be easy to do and it is hard for me to say whether it is worth all the trouble for foreigners to invest in the United States. One thing I have learned is that it takes work, research, and trust to become investors who successfully invest outside their own country.

For those looking to buy out of state, it can be a daunting process. If you would like more information on the process I did a webinar on the subject, you can find on my YouTube Channel: https://www.youtube.com/watch?v=CmRHSJkG59w

12. Success may not be as far away as you think.

You may have seen many references to my plan to purchase 100 rentals in this book. I made that plan back in 2013 as a public goal. I made it public to help motivate myself and keep me accountable. I am behind on that goal, but I still have confidence I can reach it. You can read that goal and my updates at: https://investfourmore.com/2013/05/01/my-plan-to-purchase-100-rental-properties-by-january-of-2023/

Another public goal I made was to purchase a Lamborghini, which I did in 2014. Buying a Lamborghini has been a goal of mine since I was a little kid. Thanks to my real estate business, I was able to buy one in May 2014 that was delivered to me a month later on Father's Day. I was not planning to buy one so soon, but circumstances lined up and I could not pass this car up. My real estate business took off, the blog has taken off, and this car was the perfect color as well as a great deal.

One of the most important keys to wealth is saving money. Saving money gives you options that allow you to make much more money, such as investing in rental properties and buying fix and flips. Saving money also allows you to be more flexible with your career or even start a business. If you never save any money, it is very hard to get ahead in life no matter what you do. I would never have bought a car like this if I was not in a very good financial position and it was not extremely important to me.

I also do not believe in being cheap and skimping out on the things that make you happy. I have worked very hard to be in the position I am in now, and I believe people need to do things that make them happy. Not everything that makes us happy takes money, but some things do. Do not refuse or be afraid to spend money on things that truly make you happy when you have saved enough money to afford them.

Many people will question the wisdom of buying a $100,000 car, but I think it was a great decision. Wanting this car motivated me every day and allowed to me to improve my business, take chances, and be more successful. I am a car nut and buying a car like this may not motivate others as it has me. Pick something that you really want and use it to motivate you and push you further.

How making goals helped me buy a Lamborghini

I also believe that making big goals which motivate you will make you more successful. Making big goals that are exciting and easily visualized, such as buying a Lamborghini, can really motivate you. Some might say making goals such as providing for your family or retiring early are more important, but how easy is it to picture providing for your family or retiring early? Obviously, these are important big picture goals, but these goals are very vague and it is difficult to picture them. Saying I want a 1999 blue Lamborghini Diablo is specific and easy to picture!

I have had many bigger and small goals including my plan to purchase 100 rental properties. Goals have helped me tremendously in making more money, buying more investments, saving money, and improving my personal life. I am less stressed now than I have ever been and I spend more time with my family than I ever have.

Why was this car important to me?

I have loved exotic cars since I was a young child. I had many car books, hot wheels, and model cars that I always played with. I loved Ferraris, Lamborghinis, Maseratis, Aston Martins, and many other makes of cars. Over the years, Lamborghinis grew on me more and more. They are extremely rare, very fast, unique, and outrageous automobiles.

I have always wanted a Lamborghini and I believed I would have one when I was a kid. Then after college, I entered the real world. Everyone tells you to do your job, make a decent living, save for retirement, and you will be happy. It was hammered into my head not to want expensive cars or houses because chances were, I would never have those things. After a few years of taking the traditional route, I decided I wanted more.

I decided in my late twenties I could have an exotic car and I could do it in the next decade or two. I started setting goals, making plans, and planning my future. I became a REO agent (real estate agent who sells bank foreclosures), my real estate career took off, and I started being able to save a lot of money. I began investing in rental properties and doing more fix and flips. I started InvestFourMore.com and took over the real estate business from my father.

Suddenly I was reaching goals more quickly than I ever thought possible. I had to constantly change and create new goals, because I was reaching things so quickly.

On a side note, I believe in very aggressive goals, because they will push you harder than easy goals will. If you achieve all your goals quickly then you may not be motivated to keep working hard. If you do not reach your goals, it is not a big deal because you will be better off having chased that huge goal than not having goals or reaching an easy goal.

After all of this change and success, I decided to set a huge goal to buy a Diablo in 2014.

Why did I want to buy a Lamborghini Diablo?

When I was a child, my dream car was a Lamborghini Countach. The Countach was an outrageous, rear engine V-12, sports car that was introduced in the early 1970s. The Countach was like nothing else on the road in the 70s, 80s, or even now.

I did a lot of research on the Countach and found it was very small, not easy to drive, not very reliable, and more of a show car than a driving car. I like to drive my cars, not look at them in the garage. At a conference in Dallas at the end of 2013, I stopped at Lamborghini of Dallas because they had a Diablo. I had wanted to sit in a Diablo or Countach to see how small they were.

Lamborghini Countach versus a Diablo

The Diablo was an awesome car and I liked it much more than the newer Lamborghini Models: the Gallardo and Murcielago. The Aventador is the newest model; a 700 horsepower work of art, but they cost $450,000 to $550,000. The best part about the Diablo was I fit! Although my shoe would not fit between the brake pedal and sidewall to touch the gas pedal, I had plenty of legroom and headroom. I figured I could figure out the pedal problem later.

After seeing the Diablo and learning about the Countach, my new goal was to buy a Diablo. The Diablo is still a rear engine V-12 with outrageous styling, 530 horsepower, and the first production car to go 200 MPH (unless you count the Ferrari F40 which is more of a race car). They built a little over 2,000 Diablos from 1991 to 2001. The Diablos are much rarer than the newer model Lamborghinis and in my opinion better looking and more exotic.

You have to do a lot of homework before buying a car like this. I found a local dealership that will work on the Diablo as well as Lamborghini of Denver, which is about 45 miles from me. The car needs an oil change every 7,500 miles, which is about $750 (some Ferraris require engine out oil changes which are much more expensive). The cars need a major service every 15,000 miles that costs about $2,500 to $3,000. These costs are from the local shop, not Lamborghini of Denver, which is more expensive.

Insurance for the car through my regular insurance company was only $800 a year! There are some other items that break such as the clutch ($5,000 +) and parts wear out on a 15 to 25-year-old car. Before I bought this car, I had everything repaired that was close to needing done (door struts, suspensions work, etc)

My Lamborghini Diablo (boy it feels good saying that) is a 1999 VT Alpine edition with a five speed manual transmission. They made twelve Alpine Edition Diablos. They have upgraded stereos as well as more carbon fiber than the regular Diablo. The Alpine edition is rare, but does not add much value since there are no performance upgrades.

The car is finished in Monterey Blue with snow corn white interior. I love this color and that is one reason I bought this car. I wanted a blue Diablo with a light or white interior. The interior is not actually white, but more of a tan color. There are no numbers on how many Diablos are Monterey Blue, but from what I have read I would guess fewer than twenty.

The year is also important, because Audi bought Lamborghini in 1998 and from that point forward, they became much more reliable cars. Lamborghini was actually owned by Chrysler in the late 1980s when the Diablo was developed. In 1999 and 2001 (they did not make any in 2000), the Diablos became more reliable, more refined, and more comfortable. I knew I wanted a 1999 or 2001 Diablo, which also had a new interior that was much more modern than the earlier cars.

The car is a VT, which stands for vicious traction and means it is all wheel drive. Most people do not realize most Lamborghinis are all wheel drive, although some are made with rear wheel drive to make them lighter and faster. The car has a five speed manual transmission, the only option. Now Lamborghinis are more likely to have an E gear (automatic transmission with paddle shifter) than a true manual transmission with a clutch. Now Lamborghini or Ferrari do not even offer manual transmission cars.

My particular Diablo had 21,000 miles, looked to be in great shape, and was for sale at Cats Exotics in Washington State, one of the best dealerships for Diablos and exotic cars in the country.

The owner is an exotic car lover who started a dealership. I had a pre-purchase inspection done and found a few items in need of repair. The rear bushings, a door strut, and spark were replaced ($50 each) as part of the deal before I had the car shipped to me. The inspection showed the compression in the engine was good and the rest of the car looked to be in great shape.

I was not planning to buy a Diablo this soon; I thought I might be able to buy one at the end of 2014. In the beginning of 2014 I saw this car was for sale for months and I noticed it was scheduled to go to auction. If it went to auction, I would not have a chance to inspect the car and I would be charged a five percent buyer's premium on top of my bid. There was no guarantee my bid would hit the reserve, and I had to pay $100 just to register at the auction (Mecum). I knew my best chance to buy the car was to buy it from the dealer before the auction. I knew if someone else bought this car, my chances of finding a similar car this color or any blue color would be very small.

It may seem a little crazy but I bought this car without seeing it in person. In fact, I had never driven a Diablo before I bought this car. I put my trust in a dealership with an awesome reputation and a mechanic who had worked for Ferrari and Lamborghini.

How much was the Lamborghini Diablo?

The car was listed for $134,900 on the dealer's website. I knew since it was going to auction that the dealer would be motivated. He agreed sell it for $125,000 since it was going to auction. I tried to negotiate further, but there was no budging. After thinking about the car for weeks, I decided to move forward with the purchase. The inspection revealed a few items that were worn, but did not need to be replaced right away. As part of the deal, I had the worn items fixed or replaced and purchased the car for $126,000.

I actually bought the car in early May, but had to wait for a door strut to come from Italy and have the mechanic fix it before the car was shipped. Shipping took another ten days and the car arrived on Father's Day!

I mentioned the Countach was a dream of mine but one reason the Diablo worked out better was the cost of a Countach. The Countach has seen its value increase 300 percent in the last four years. I believe the Diablo is at its low value now and will start to increase as well. Not that I bought the car as an investment, but it will be nice to see it go up in value instead of down as most cars do. The car was about $300,000 new in 1999! (One and a half years later the Diablo is worth about $200,000)

How did real estate help me buy the Diablo?

My real estate career has been great to me as soon as I started setting goals and planning my future. I did not do so well in the beginning when I thought everything would come to me, and I would not have to work hard to make a lot of money. With real estate, I was able to start small, build up my business, hire assistants, and then start hiring agents. I now have a team of ten people. The real estate team does great, although I am constantly trying to increase production. Rental properties were a huge factor in my decision to buy this car. At the time, I made over $50,000 a year in cash flow from my rental properties. I knew that cash flow was constant and I could afford the car.

My future plans for the Diablo

You have to see this car in person to appreciate it. It is lower and wider than almost any car you will ever see. I own a 1986 Porsche 928, which is very wide and low; the Diablo is eight inches shorter and wider than the 928. Every day that I drive it, there are people taking pictures of it in parking lots, on the road, and one woman stopped in the middle of traffic at a green light to take a picture of it! I have to watch out for people swerving and not paying attention while they take their pictures.

The car obviously attracts a lot of attention and I am working on ways to use that to my advantage. I have a flyer that I put on the dash while it is parked with information on our team and myself. I am also looking into license plate frames with our team phone number on it and a few other options. I will not wrap the car with advertisements, but every time I stop anywhere, multiple people come to talk to me. Every good real estate agent looks for reasons to talk to as many people as they can and with the Diablo, everyone comes to me. I have a feeling the car will more than pay for itself.

New goals for the future now that I have the Diablo.

My wife and kids absolutely love the car. Every time I drive it, my five-year old twins come running out of the house to watch me drive away laughing hysterically (the car is very loud). My wife asked me what I am going to do now that I achieved this goal, how will I motivate myself? I showed her my phone, which already has a picture of a 1970 Lamborghini

Miura on the home screen. I had a picture of a Blue Lamborghini Diablo on my home screen for months before I bought the Diablo. The Miura is the most beautiful car ever built in my opinion and about eight times as expensive as the Diablo. That will give me something to shoot for! I still love the looks of the Countach as well.

Do not be afraid to have big goals or want nice things. Those goals and things will help motivate you to make more money, be happier, and even be a better person. Visualizing every day how awesome it would be to drive my Lamborghini Diablo helped me be more successful and make more money. If you want to see the car, please check out InvestFourMore.com.

It may seem completely out of place for me to spend so much time talking about a car in a rental property book. I wanted to tell that story so that you could see my passion for cars and how that passion helped motivate me in my real estate career. You do not need to have a passion for cars, but everyone has a passion for something. Something they love to do or would love to have. I am not talking about buying the newest SUV, because the neighbors just bought one, but something you personally love without outside influence. Too many people hide their passions because they are worried what others will think or they want to fit in with society norms. Find your passion and use it to your advantage. Set goals for how your investing or career will help you achieve your passions in life and remind yourself of them constantly!

I hope you have enjoyed this book and that you have found many tips, techniques, and methods to buy rental properties. Not just to buy them retail, but to get great deals and a lot of cash flow with them as well. Rentals have been awesome to me and has given me many choices. It has given me time, and it has allowed me to pursue what I love in life.

One of the things I love to do is help others succeed. I have many articles on my website and many resources for those of you looking for more help. I have coaching programs as well. These are not the $30,000 plus coaching programs that many real estate gurus promote and then have someone else you have never heard of teach them. I created these affordable programs that I teach and interact in. Many of the programs include coaching calls with me personally. I love helping people solve problems, analyze deals and get started investing in real estate. However, I am not a hand holder and I won't do any of the work for you. I am still an active investor and only have time for those who are super motivated and hard workers. My goal is to teach others how to analyze deals and build their own business so that they don't have to rely on anyone else. Please check out my blog, InvestFourMore.com, for more information or send me an email to Mark@InvestFourMore.com. Yes, that is my personal email as well. I answer my emails, not a minion that I hired (I have five-year-old twins and I am very familiar with minions!).

I wish you personal and financial success! -Mark

13. What is the next step?

When I work with people as a coach, my goal is to **help them make as much money as they possibly can with real estate.** Different people have different goals and like doing different things. I help some investors buy more rentals, I help other learn to flip, and I even help people become successful real estate agents. Two of the real estate agents on my team made over $100,000 in their first year! Those results won't happen for everyone, but there is a lot of money to be made in real estate.

This book talks about how rental properties can be an awesome investment and business. I am a current investor and Realtor working in today's market (at least at the time of the writing of this book in 2016). If you want to get involved in real estate I would love to help you learn the ins and outs. It is not as easy as they make it look on television.

If you invest the right way, rental properties and flips can change your life. They changed my life, by giving me a better way to invest, a better way to make money, a better way to retire. I am 37 years old now and am in a better position to retire right now than most people will ever be. I am by no means done!

There is a lot going on at my blog Investfourmore.com. I have a podcast, a forum, the blog, eBooks, paperback books, coaching programs and many videos. I encourage you to sign up for my email list, if you have not already done so. The emails I send you, will help you navigate through the site, give you the most valuable resources and help you decide how much or little you want to be involved with real estate.

- You can sign up for my email list here: https://investfourmore.com/real-estate-investor-email-subscription/
- If you are interested in becoming an agent, I have a separate email list with more resources here: https://investfourmore.com/real-estate-agent-email-subscription/
- If you want to become a real estate agent, I just came out with How to Make it Big as a Real Estate Agent, which is a 200 + page book on how I sold over 200 houses in one year and how I created my team. I am still an agent, but rarely talk with sellers or buyers, my team does it all. http://www.amazon.com/How-Make-Real-Estate-Agent/dp/153366160X/ref=asap_bc?ie=UTF8
- If you want to learn about how mindset and attitude can determine your success check out my book How to Change your Mindset to Achieve Huge Success: https://www.amazon.com/Change-Your-Mindset-Achieve-Success-ebook/dp/B01HT1470G/ref=asap_bc?ie=UTF8
- I have a fix and flip video training course here that has over 3 hours of video and more resources for learning how to successfully flip houses. https://shop.investfourmore.com/product/fix-and-flip-video-training-course/
- I have a quick start video training program that shows exactly how I get awesome deals. Including videos of me touring potential deals and how I search the MLS. You can find my coaching products on my blog here: https://investfourmore.com/resources/

I have made my books and coaching products as affordable as possible. I know people who are starting out in a new business, do not have a lot of extra money. For those of you who know you need a little extra push and accountability, I created more in depth training courses. These come with conference calls and email training with me personally. The Complete Blueprint for Successful Real Estate Investing is a rental property program that I created and comes with personal coaching from me as well as audio CD's/MP3s, videos, a huge how to guide and much more. If you are interested send me an email and I may have a special coupon for those that read this book all the way through! Mark@investfourmore.com.

I hope you enjoyed the book and if you want connect we me on social media check out the links below:

- Facebook
- LinkedIn
- Twitter
- Instagram
- Google +

About Mark Ferguson

I created Invest Four More to help people become real estate investors either as rental property owners, flippers, wholesalers, real estate agents, and even note owners. You may see pictures of me with my Lamborghini. It is a 1999 Lamborghini Diablo, which I bought in 2014. I had dreamed of owning a Lamborghini since I was a kid, and one of my public goals I wrote about was buying one in 2014. It was an awesome experience making that goal, being held accountable by my readers, and then accomplishing it. I even make sure I buy my cars below market value. I bought this car for $126,000 and it is worth about double that two years later.

The car is not a flashy marketing ploy, but a reward for hard work and to signify that we really can have what we want, if we out our mind to it.

How did I get started?

I have been a licensed Realtor since 2001. My father has been a Realtor since 1978 and I was surrounded by real estate in my youth. I remember sleeping under my dad's desk when I was three while he worked tirelessly in the office. Surprisingly, or maybe not, I never wanted anything to do with real estate. I graduated from the University of Colorado with a degree in business finance in 2001. I could not find a job that was appealing to me so I reluctantly decided to work with my father part-time in real estate. Fifteen years later I am sure glad I got into the real estate business!

Even though I had help getting started in real estate, I did not find success until I was in the business five years. I tried to follow my father's path, which did not mesh well with me. I found my own path as a REO agent and my career took off. Many people think I had a huge advantage working with my father, and he was a great help, but I think that I actually would have been more successful sooner if I had been working on my own and forced to find my own path.

Now I run a real estate team of 10, who sells 100 to 200 homes each year. I fix and flip 10-15 homes a year and I own 16 long-term rentals. I love real estate and investing because of the money you can make and the freedom running your own business brings. I also love big goals and one of those goals is my plan to purchase 100 rental properties by January 2023.

I started Invest Four More in March 2013 and the primary objective was to provide information on investing in long-term rentals. I was not a writer at any time in my life, until I started this blog. In fact, I had not written anything besides a basic letter since college. Readers who have been with me from the beginning may remember how tough it was to read my first articles with all the typos and poor grammar (I know it is still not perfect!). My goal has always been to provide incredible information, not to provide perfect articles with perfect grammar.

The name "InvestFourMore" is a play on words indicating that it is possible to finance more than four properties. The blog provides articles on financing, finding, buying, rehabbing and renting rental properties. The blog also discusses mortgage pay down strategies, fix and flips, advice for real estate agents and many other real estate related topics.

I live in Greeley Colorado, which is about 50 miles North of Denver. I married my beautiful wife Jeni in 2008 and we have twins who turned five in June of 2016. Jeni was a Realtor when we met in 2005, but has since put her license on ice while she takes care of the twins. Jeni loves to sew and makes children's dresses under the label Kaiya Papaya.

Outside of work I love to travel, play golf and work/play with my cars.

Acknowledgements

I could not be where I am at without a lot of help from many people. I tried to go at it alone when I first started in the real estate business. I thought I was smart and could figure it out, without anyone else telling me how to do things. I let my ego make some very bad decisions for me. Here are a few people I have to thank.

My Dad Jim Ferguson, who has been an entrepreneur most of his life. He taught me a lot about flipping houses and being a real estate agent. He was very patient with me, when I was not patient with myself.

My wife Jeni, who has been incredibly supportive through the good times and the bad. The year I met her, I made $28,000 (2006). Things were not easy in the beginning and it was a struggle for me to break out of the grind and find my way in real estate. She was there for me when I started to find success and was working 80 or more hours a week to get everything done. She put up with me working on vacations and never really taking time off in the beginning. Luckily, I was able to create a business where we can now take real vacations without me working, where I rarely work more than 40 hours a week (if that), and we have a wonderful family. Most importantly she supported my car addiction!

Justin Gesso is my team manager and keeps our team together. He works with our agents, helps with the blog, helps with my coaching programs, helps with my books and keeps me sane. Thank you Justin!

Nikki True has been my assistant for 6 years. She was the person who helped me stop working 80 hours a week and take control of my life. She has always been extremely proactive, has an incredible work ethic, and been willing to work on any project. She is now helping me with my flipping business and doing an amazing job.

John Pfalzgraff has been our team's contract manager for many years. He is the reason I can make offers while I am still viewing a home. He keeps tabs on all the details that I hate thinking about. He is integral to our real estate agents success and mine.

Jack Canfield coaching was a program I took a few years ago. It gave me the confidence to buy my father's business, take the blog to new levels, hire more staff, and take more chances. Not only that, but I gained more freedom, reduced stress, and am a happier person because of it. My personal coach John Beaman is still someone I talk to on a monthly basis.

Josh Elledge with Upend PR has helped me be featured on numerous major media sites like Washington Post, Yahoo, Zillow, The Street, Forbes and many more.

Made in the USA
San Bernardino, CA
19 October 2016